i Francesco e famiglia di Vittorio e famiglia
pasolina e famiglia e saluta caramente
stra moglia susta commare nonsa ancora
none Americo di lostesso conla famiglia
ro figlio allaltra lettera tefo conoscere
llo basta

io Ma vostra madre di mantiamo
La Santa Benedizione per sempre tanto
doi como puro vostra moglia e puro
inotti e famiglia sempre Benedetti
l vostro Affmo padre Vincenzo Sannuzzi

Caro figlio oricevuto la vostra libre
conla precura adoputo antare a Roma
bratta e precura bene caro figlio caro
di

Adio pronta risposta e Buone
notizie

Copyright @2025 by Annette Januzzi Wick

Three Arch Press supports the right to free expression and the value of copyright. Copyrights allow writers and artists to create works that enrich all. If you would like permission to use material from this book (other than for reviews), please contact the author directly at amjwick@gmail.com.

Three Arch Press
Cincinnati, OH 45202

Three Arch Press books may be purchased in bulk for businesses, educational, or promotional use. For more information, please contact the author or local bookseller. The press also supports speaking engagements for its authors on subject matters related to published books.

Photographs courtesy of the author, Romain Mayambi, various relatives and other community resources.

Cover design and inside: Anna Perotti
bythebookdesign.com
Editor: Christine McKnight

ISBN 978-0-9774856-4-2
LCCN 2025920429

10 9 8 7 6 5 4 3 2 1

Printed in the USA

SOMETHING ITALIAN

*From Distant Shores to Family Tables,
The Recipes That Held Us Together*

Annette Januzzi Wick

For Ettore Anselmo Iannuzzi and Vinzenzella Jean Giuliani

CONTENTS

Preface ... 9

Giuliani Family Chart ... 14
Scurti Family Chart ... 16
Iannuzzi-Mazzà Family Chart ... 18

Part I
From Distant Shores to Family Tables ... 21
I'M FROM HERE ... 22
    From Abruzzo ... 28
    From Calabria ... 38
    From Pennsylvania ... 55

COMING TO LORAIN ... 64
    Industry ... 66
    Italian American Mutual Aid Societies and Other Cultural Outlets ... 68
    An Italian's Two Religions: Faith and Food ... 71

BECOMING ITALIAN ... 75
    Layers of Ancestors ... 75
    A Reverse Migration ... 104

Part II
The Recipes That Held Us Together ... 117
THE FIRST RECIPES ... 118
    Grandma DeLuca's Cannoli ... 125
    Aunt Mary DeLuca's Biscotti ... 126
    Grandma Mazzà's Fried Twists ... 127
    Bow Ties (*Chiacchiere*) ... 128
    Pecan Nut Cups (*Bocconotti*) ... 129

BASEMENT KITCHENS & COOKIE ALTARS ... 130
    Italian Rolled Cookies ... 137
    Caviciuni ... 138
    Bones of the Dead Cookies (*Ossi dei Morti*) ... 140
    Totos ... 141
    Nut Horns ... 142
    Lemon Cookies (*Agnetti*) ... 143
    Nut Rolls ... 144

CAKES AND PIES IN HARVEST-GOLD LIGHT ... 146
    Italian Love Cake ... 151
    Maple Pecan Chiffon Cake ... 152
    Swiss Chocolate Squares ... 153
    Old Fashioned Raisin Pie ... 154
    Pistachio Cheesecake ... 155

FROM THE GARDEN WITH LOVE ... 156
    Basic Tomato Sauce ... 163
    Pizza Dough ... 164
    Zucchini Squares ... 165

Zucchini Casserole with Cottage Cheese and Monterey Jack Cheese	166
Eggplant Parmesan	167
Marinated Eggplant	168
Stuffed Cabbage	169

SUPPERS OF SUBSTANCE — 170

Braciola	175
Chicken Piccata	176
Chicken Paprikas and Dumplings	177
Chicken Cacciatore	178
Veal Scallopini with Mushrooms and Peppers	179
Zucchini and Italian Sausage Skillet Supper	180
Vegetable Lasagna (*Lasagna Primavera*)	181
Rice Croquettes (*Arancini*)	182

BLISSFUL WEDDING SOUP — 183

Meatballs for Wedding Soup and Sauce	188
Cheese Croutons (*Crostini di Formaggio*)	189
Chicken Broth (*Brodo di Pollo*)	190
Wedding Soup	191
Chestnut Dressing	192

SOUPS FOR SALVATION — 193

Escarole and Orzo Soup with Turkey Parmesan Meatballs	198
Cheese Tortellini Soup with Cannellini, Kielbasa, and Kale	199
Cioppino	200
Caramelized Onion and Portobello Mushroom Soup with Goat Cheese Croutons	201
Minestrone	202

EASTER DAY TRIUMPHS — 203

Hot Cross Buns	208
Leg of Lamb, Italian Style	209
Lamb Kabobs (*Arrosticini*)	210
Classic Tiramisu	211

CHRISTMAS MADE BY RAVIOLI PRESS — 212

Breaded Calamari	217
Ravioli with Ricotta and Meat Fillings	218
Grandma DeLuca's Gnocchi	220

CARRYING ABRUZZO AND CALABRIA HOME — 221

Lentil Soup (*Zuppa di Lenticchie*)	227
Gnocchetti Stew (*Stufato con Gnocchetti*)	228
Ricotta Gnocchetti	228
Chestnut Puree (*Purea di Castagne*)	229
Pizzelle	230
Viola's Crostata	231
Celli Ripieni (or Celli Pieni)	232
Fried Dough (*Crespelle*)	233

Afterword	234
Endnotes	238
Acknowledgements	240
About the Author	243

A Note

Like my mother's recipes handed down from on high, the anecdotes of my grandparents and great-grandparents, of my parents, sisters, brother, and me, are *tipici* of many Italian American families, regardless of what region in Italy the family originated from or where they settled in the US. Centuries of stories about Italian food and peoples were influenced by a variety of external invading powers and internal geographical and social conflicts—not to mention the personal ones. Inextricably intertwined, these stories were always changing, always missing one ingredient.

When the hands that shaped us are no longer here, we shape what's handed down to the next generations and share it with those who gather at the family table.

These are my stories to pass down. Much of the information has been gleaned from birth records, handwritten recipes, travelogues, and personal exchanges, while the narratives are rooted in what was true to me at the time.

"Cooking came to me as though it had been there all along, waiting to be expressed; it came as words come to a child when it is time for her to speak."
— Marcella Hazan, *Amarcord: Marcella Remembers*

"To make something well is to give yourself to it, to seek wholeness, to follow spirit. To learn to make something well can take your whole life. It's worth it."
— Ursula K. Le Guin, *Steering the Craft*

"Cooking demands attention, patience, and, above all, a respect for the gifts of the earth. It is a form of worship, a way of giving thanks."
— Judith Jones

A tavola non s' invecchia.
(At the table, one never grows old.)
—Italian proverb

Raffaela Scurti, ca 1920   Vincenzo Giuliani, circa 1920

PREFACE

What is it like to gaze into the chestnut-colored eyes of someone you recognize only through photographs and hope to find, in the richness of their land, a grounding that has yet to exist on yours?

These questions have endured, ever present, beating at my subconscious erratically like heart palpitations, since my parents' death.

A year after my mother died, my father already deceased, I was hit by a car while on a morning walk. The impact from the 3,500-pound metal monster finally pushed me to see inside my sadness. As I recovered during a global pandemic, my diary entries contained multitudes of stories of unexplored grief, family ties, and kitchen tables.

I wrote about fennel. How the vegetable reminded me of my father, his pronunciation of the Italian word *finocch*, dropping the last vowel.

Throughout summer, my niece and I worked to scan my mother's handwritten recipes into the computer. I cooked and cried and cooked again. Italian language classes presented themselves to me. Sitting in those initial lessons, first in-person then over Zoom, I realized the participants surrounding me possessed a greater knowledge of what they were there to pursue.

I don't mean knowledge of the language, but of *why* they should learn.

My *why* was gone. I would have to build my case from the ground up.

No recipe went untouched; no census record was immune from my chase. I unearthed birth certificates and made calls to Catholic dioceses to seek documents from churches no longer standing. What I found would open the doors my parents had presumably closed when their Italian families became American. In conversation with the Italian mother of a friend, she called those who left Italy for America *selfless*. And over time, I came to the same view.

Two years flew by. At each step, I felt like an imposter, given that I had yet to step foot on the actual soil of my ancestors. With the pandemic subsiding, plans took shape for three trips abroad over the seasons that would beckon me into my sixth decade of life: to Abruzzo, the region of my mother's family; to Calabria, the region of my father's family; and an eventual combination of both that would push my competence and comfort to the edge long enough for me to stand still in my roots.

In 2022, a few weeks prior to embarking on a journey to Abruzzo, I woke one Sunday morning. My husband, Mark, had left earlier for call at the hospital. The gloomy day served as the best excuse to sit with laptop and pen and force open a path that would widen my view of the world—and myself.

Combing through social media, I discovered a Facebook page for *Spoltore Notizie*, the news site of my mother's family hometown in Italy. I clicked on its website link. My eyes scanned the entries. Surely, someone reading in Spoltore would/could/might recognize a name. Using my rudimentary knowledge of Italian, I asked the editor if they might publish my request to find that reader prior to my arrival in town that very month.

"*Buon giorno! Ho trovato Spoltore Notizie attraverso Facebook.*

PREFACE

Vengo a Spoltore dal 18 al 21 settembre per visitare il borgo. I miei nonni erano di Spoltore. Se ne andarono nel 1928 con mia madre nel grembo materno. Ho i nomi di altri parenti. Mi piacerebbe trovare qualcuno che è legato a me."

"Good day. I found your news site on Facebook. I come to Spoltore September 18-21 to visit the town. My grandparents were from Spoltore. They left in 1928 with my mother in her mother's womb. I have the names of other relatives. I would like to find someone who is related to me."

From there, I listed the surnames of relatives I had obtained through my own research, from my mother's papers and recitations, and with the help of a local genealogist.

The journal editor wrote back in Italian. I greedily translated: "Our hope is that through this article of ours you can find, during your stay in Spoltore, what you are looking for: that is, your origins, the history of your family and your relatives from Spoltore."

My hope indeed. I would be duly rewarded for my persistence; the mark of many a desperate writer. The next morning, my inbox was flooded with replies from Viola Guiliani, Luigina Dottore, and Antonio Dottore, three siblings who were second cousins once removed. They were the great-grandchildren of my grandmother's sister. All three lived in or near Spoltore. We planned to meet and hug. Somehow communicate. Soon the anticipation of what was yet to come filled my days.

Entering the territory of family is like entering into a conversation with a fine wine. You want to know the makers: the people who have crafted you and your family, raised you up from your roots, bottled you. You want to know their practices and processes, the terrain over which their feet traveled for many years to form you, carry you. You desire to feel the same bows of sun and the rain, to soak in. And you want to understand what's inside, underneath, and between the layers of the terra, the land. You want your eyes, fingers, and toes to see and touch everything. Whatever they cannot sense, your nose, ears, and tongue will.

Another two years passed. Two family weddings. A grandchild on her way. A relentless chase to publish my work.

Still stalking the ghosts of Abruzzo, I tracked down permissions for a photograph of the *Società Abruzzesi, September, 1934,* discovered on Facebook.

My grandmother had been a founder of the *Società Femminile Abruzzese*. My eyes darting back and forth across the black and white image caught the broad nape of a woman, a neckline, a downward-pointing cowlick I knew. How many times had I washed my mother's hair, combed it, run my hands along those same shoulders to rub them as she aged and noticed a similar neckline? While that image was not of my mother, I swear it was my grandmother. Seated only feet away were two young children, a girl and boy, about ages seven and five. The ages my mother and my uncle would have been in 1934.

With my mother's family story somewhat reconstructed, I began to anticipate the trip to Calabria planned for the end of the summer. I used social media to post on a *Comune di San Donato di Ninea, Calabria* page using the names and dates of my father's ancestors, which I had procured through an agency based in Calabria. The following morning, messages from Concetta Macrini, another second cousin once removed, lit up my notifications. She and I emailed and used WhatsApp for over a year. Concetta only communicated in Italian. Weeks before our departure came her generous offer for my husband and I to stay with her family in San Donato di Ninea.

There, the talk would flow like a river about us, around us, over us, and sometimes through us. Hours spent together over lunches and dinners and coffees stretched long. The only family member who spoke a reliable English was Concetta's teen-aged daughter, often away at school, but the language never mattered. Only the bottle of life that had been opened for us. Our time would age well.

Why go back to the home of one's ancestor? For legitimacy, for curiosity, for the food and wine and cheese…. And to learn, *how hard was it really, to leave?*

To understand the burdens stored inside of those who left, and the unbridled joys of those who stayed. Those families in Abruzzo and Calabria seemed intact, emotionally and mentally, carrying an air of confidence and contentedness that matched the brisk mountain air and sea breezes. They were still bound to the land that understood them, and the land bound to them.

When we are uncertain if our lives have meaning or will outlast our bodies, we make art, we cook, we preserve photos and journals, to inhabit memories that won't dissolve. We push at the boundaries of our living bodies to find what's inside that was borne by those now dead across the seas. We eat from the land—the pigs, the goats, the chickens, the chestnuts, the famed Calabrian chili peppers, the *arrosticini* (a type of lamb skewers), the pecorino (both a cheese and a wine), calamari, the *pizzelle* (cookies), the olive oil—at the same table as family who grew those products, who harvested and served them, knowing or sensing that someday one of us might return to correct the root shock experienced by immigrants and replant ourselves. Somehow this propagates a transference of existence, a growth for the next Iannuzzi or Mazzà or Scurti or Giuliani in our line, and the next.

GIULIANI FAMILY CHART

◇◇◇◇◇◇◇◇◇ = Marriage

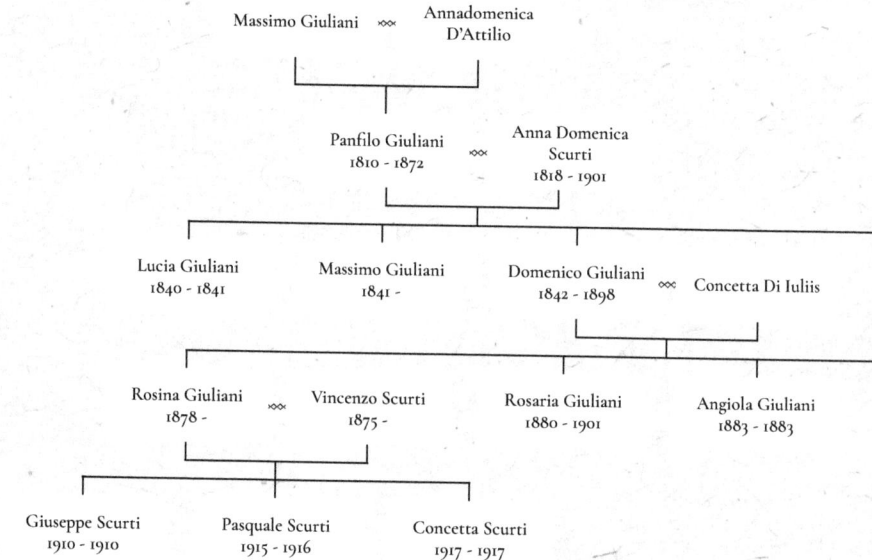

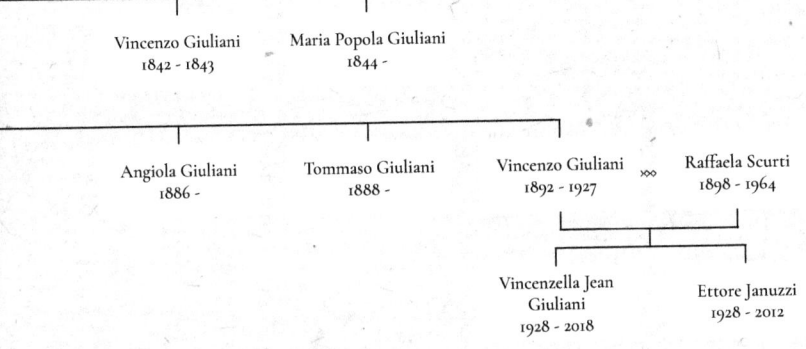

SCURTI FAMILY CHART

∞∞∞∞∞∞ = Marriage

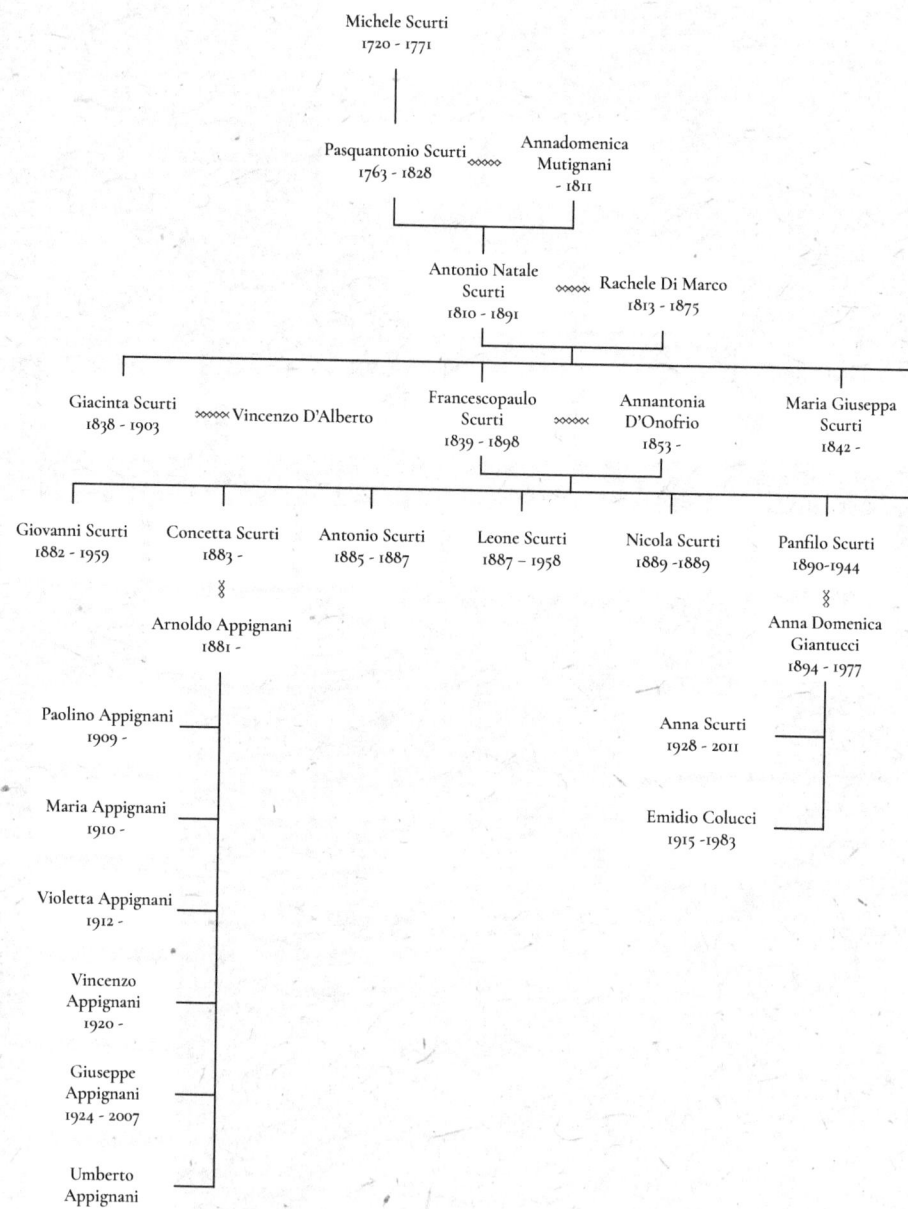

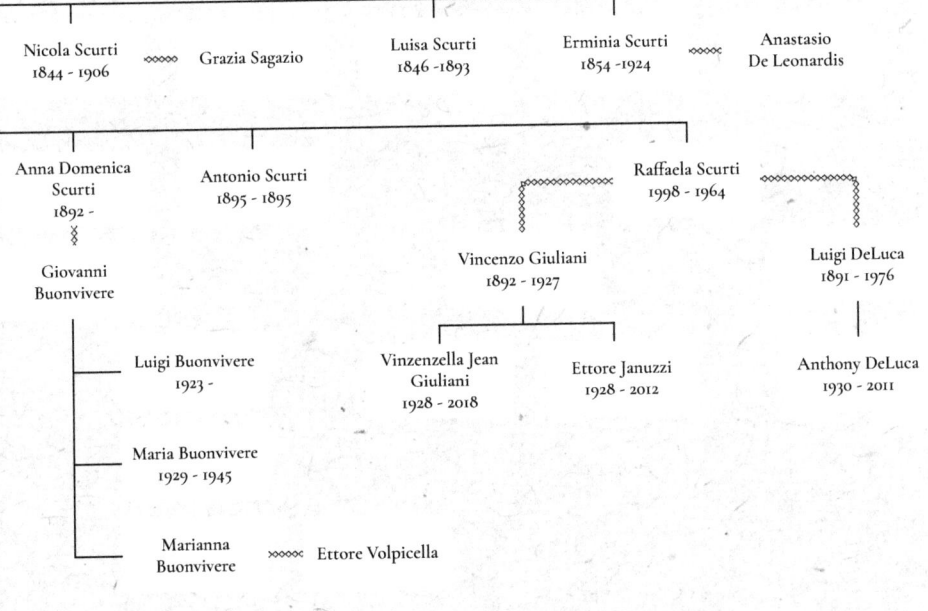

IANNUZZI-MAZZÀ FAMILY CHART

◇◇◇◇◇◇◇◇ = Marriage

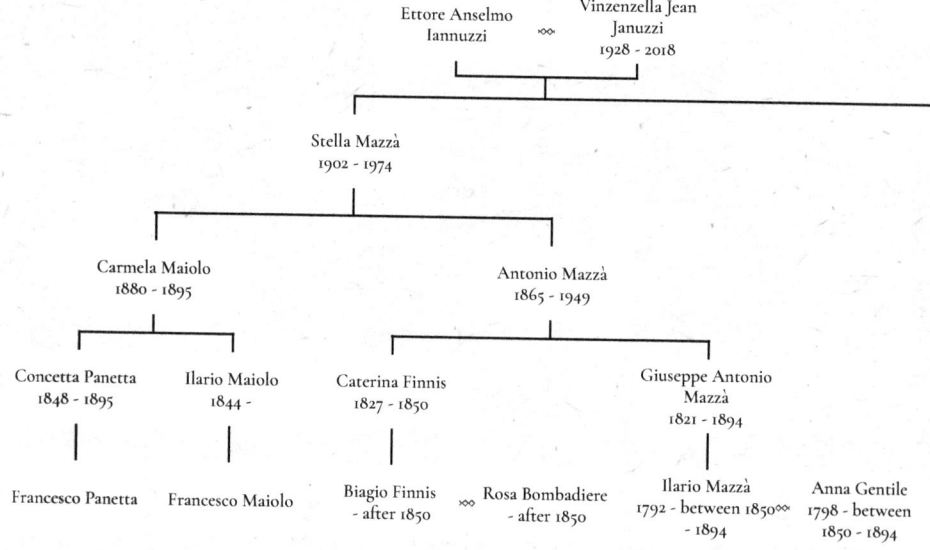

Ettore Anselmo Iannuzzi ◇◇ Vinzenzella Jean Januzzi 1928 - 2018

Stella Mazzà 1902 - 1974

Carmela Maiolo 1880 - 1895

Antonio Mazzà 1865 - 1949

Concetta Panetta 1848 - 1895

Ilario Maiolo 1844 -

Caterina Finnis 1827 - 1850

Giuseppe Antonio Mazzà 1821 - 1894

Francesco Panetta

Francesco Maiolo

Biagio Finnis - after 1850 ◇◇ Rosa Bombadiere - after 1850

Ilario Mazzà 1792 - between 1850 ◇◇ - 1894

Anna Gentile 1798 - between 1850 - 1894

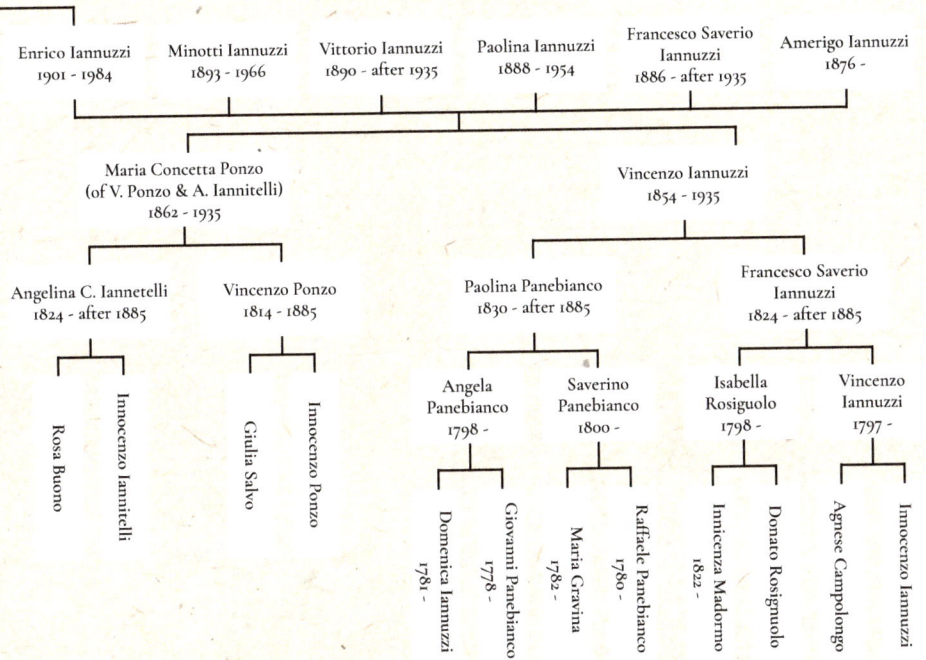

S Donato ninea li 3 novembre 1925
carissimo figlio subito risponto alla vostra
lettera molto ci siamo consolati nel sentir
che state bene conta vostra cara moglie e
minotti e famiglia noi puro tutti fina oggi
ci la passiamo bene solo la vostra matre non è
lo bene gua vita si sta facento una cura n
e una cura troppo lunga caro figlio e stav
la mia disgrazia questa malattia di vost
madre sono sette mese manneia quell
de pette tutto santo di ciolo basta car
mo figlio aspettamo i vostri ritratti g
per giorno fatecci sapere il nome della s
moglia che abiamo piacere caro figlio c
lete odere 100 anni sempre contente e s
tesi bene voi caro figlio e la nostra nori
caro figlio volete sapere di a merico si
adese si trova si trova a buenes aires a
lo lettera giorno per giorno il vostro fr
lo Francesco parte conta famiglia il g
10 di dicembre per Buenes aires a se
lo stutto vittorio ancora sta basta

Part I

From Distant Shores to Family Tables

I'M FROM HERE

In the 1990s, while dining at an Italian restaurant on a northeastern Ohio winter night, a waiter asked for my order.

"Gnocch," I said, dropping off the soft Italian *i* sound, instead ending with a harsh *k*. The server—not Italian—corrected me. My new boyfriend and I, both of us in our late twenties, laughed while steam poured forth in the form of breath. "In my family, it's gnocch," I said, emphasizing the long, throaty *k* consonant again.

It's taken me thirty-five years, two husbands, and a first-grader's command of the Italian language to understand why that episode lodged itself deep inside my culinary soul.

Throughout the late 1800s and early 1900s, my ancestors had fled Italy for America.

In their new land, my great-uncle lost an eye in an explosion on a railroad line. Another great uncle was pressured by finances and attracted by fine cars to join the mafia. Great-grandparents on my father's side moved every year, keeping within a twenty-five-mile radius, whenever a new seam of coal opened for mining. One grandmother lost her childhood love yet discovered her strength in activism and serving others. One grandfather lost his life in an outbreak of encephalitis lethargica. The other grandfather and grandmother worked long hours to grow a chain of shoe stores, but the female head of the household, who would receive little credit, would have to claim her strength through philanthropy toward her in-laws left behind. My grandfather's brother lost two children to sicknesses as they immigrated to Argentina. Aunts and cousins lost a father who would renounce his family overseas. Another uncle rose early seven days a week to proof bread at his family bakery.

Did they really choose to leave their way of existence for such things? Or was it chosen for them? Surely, they didn't depart only for their descendants to argue—a full century later—with a waiter over minutiae of a language they didn't know.

At the time of my ancestors' exits from the regions of Abruzzo and Calabria, sandstone-flecked churches in small-town Italy shone in the sun but no longer provided shelter from parishioners' griefs. What lingered were mutual aid societies that would attempt to soothe their ills, the same clubs that would be replicated in the New World. Before they left, pastoral greens stretched out like fresh-made beds of grass, yet forests gave back no sustenance, having been plundered for lumber by barons and kings or beset by disease. Bright blue seas only mentally quenched their thirst in the fields, and beckoned them to cross their fingers and the waters.

Meanwhile, General Giuseppe Garibaldi's 1861 reunification strategy for Italy unleashed political and economic forces that overlooked plenty of southern Italian citizens. Dirt lodged itself in the stopped gears of their rusted farming implements, pasted together their longing tongues and parched lips when wine stores dried up, and clogged the pores of their skin darkened by despair. Northern Italians were the first of the migrants to cross the seas, primarily wanted for their artisan skills.

Those considered southern, like my Abruzzese and Calabrese ancestors, would come later, bringing with them their unskilled but profoundly hardworking ways.

My *bisnonni* (great-grandparents) in Calabria struggled to find good labor in Caulonia, and then nearby Placanica, with its distant view of the Ionian Sea and aptly described by Edward Lear as "built as a marvel for the passer-by." Verdant communities of oak, chestnut, pine, and fir there were pillaged. Two hundred and fifty kilometers to the north, another set of bisnonni lived in San Donato di Ninea, also in Calabria, where in the nearby mountains one could view the Ionian and the Tyrrhenian seas simultaneously. Yet hills in the vicinity were pocked by former mines and a family was forced to break from the rhythms of town for seasonal work. Five hundred kilometers to the northeast, a third set of bisnonni roamed in Spoltore, in the region of Abruzzo, along castle ramparts built to protect from the ancient Saracen mariners. Cyclical migration for work required constant movement. The home fires of family connections and food traditions were always in a smoldering state.

Assessing the impoverished conditions that grew out of their own plowed fields and rutted streets, they asked, what could be worse?

If a crinkled letter from abroad turned up in Spoltore, written by a relative who had found a short-lived bounty of work, or sly advertisements from America printed in local publications were posted near their doorstep in San Donato to turn their gaze east toward the Atlantic and steel mills and coal mines, they might be tempted to journey overseas. Water was water. They would carry with them their traditions of family, fortitude, and food. Did it matter what direction they faced, over what body of sea? Roughly four million Italians asked this same question. They took drastic measures to resolve the famine-like conditions and feudal systems that divided their families and resorted to quarters on steamships, many of them headed to the United States.

The reach of my family's foundations encompassed those two regions of Italy. Our bodies of influence spanned three provinces: Pescara (formerly in Terramo), Cosenza, and Reggio Calabria. They extended from the calf of the boot along the interior of the foot's top toward the place where the sole begins to bow. My ancestors' migration paths traversed through New York, Maryland, Pennsylvania, and Ohio, and converged upon Lorain, a smaller northeastern Ohio town, where dozens of other ethnicities—or "racial stocks" as they were referred to in the 1930s—made a place for themselves. For how long had *home* been stationary, before it suddenly became a verb? A movement to redefine the word.

Within a wisdom rooted in so much upheaval, within cultural and culinary traditions separate and the same, lies the cumulative and confusing nature of being Italian American. A hallmark of being Italian is that regionality is everything—and sometimes, nothing at all.

Had my mother's family remained in Spoltore, language barriers would have existed between the Abruzzese on her side—where an Upper Southern Italo-Romance language was spoken—and my father's family from the mounts of Calabria, where San Donatese resided in the Consenza province. There the influence of Norman and Greek conquerors lent itself toward a dialect that split the northern and southern half of the region. The dialects were further split between two provinces, the other being the southernmost on the peninsula, Reggio Calabria. Relatives in Lorain could gather from the same Calabrian homeland, possibly unable to understand what other Calabrese said. And their children would know no Italian language at all. Well, maybe a swear word or two rubbed off on them.

There was a singular geographical vein, however, that did affix one Italian to the other. In a country where forty percent of the topography is mountainous, the Apennines Mountains form a spine, adjoining a large majority of the Italian peninsula until they run right in through the granite mountains of Calabria. These ranges tied together could also be claimed as one soil for Italians, whose sweat carried on the winds from one rise over to the next, linking the hardworking people as one.

That same flow of earth allows most Italians their charms. My husband says I can walk into any room, no matter where I am, and find the person who is *something* Italian. There is no secret handshake, no scent of *aglio e olio* wafting in the air or *lievito: pane degli angeli* sprinkled around the room; there is simply a desire to find familiarity in every face and space they encounter. This manner of being in the world is rooted in the home country's many invasions over the years by Visigoths and Saracens, Normans and Greeks, Spanish and Hapsburgs. It's reflected in a geography that runs from alpine to near-tropical climes. Italians are content in most of the world, having been driven off their lands to press toward the far reaches of Australia, the United States, Argentina, or even Scotland. They have understood victory and defeat; they have been the conqueror and the conquered. They fear no strangers. Have you ever met an Italian that did?

Italianness is expressed, too, in a certain *la mancanza*: a missing. A longing for the people they once loved and the places that no longer exist. A regret for or mourning of what was left behind, whether by compulsion or demand.

And always a hunger for the kind of food that would soothe that ache.

Italians open doors to guests, invite them in. We seat them at our table, and instruct them that *this is Italian something, this is Italian something else*, as if putting *Italian* in front of or behind anything makes it so. It does. Whatever the repast or time of day, the food has been imbued with a certain kind of *italianità*, our essence of being us.

The history of Italian and Italian American cooking is not a singular account of *la cucina d'Italia*—because that doesn't exist. However, the big-heartedness and endeavoring for nourishment that arises out of even the dimmest and tiniest of kitchens has been explored by writers and palates throughout history, from the greatest to the most commonplace. From Apicus, said to have been a Roman lover of gourmet food in the first century AD, who claimed, "Anyone who would know something worthwhile about the private and public lives of the ancients should be well-acquainted with their table"[1]; to the Mediterranean cookbook author Claudia Roden, who wrote, "Part of the pleasure of researching food was meeting people, sharing a moment of their lives, and discovering their worlds"[2]; to me, an ordinary essayist cataloguing my mother's propensities in cooking, my father's desire for the outdoors, and our family's peculiarities in judging ourselves and each other through what was consumed; this *something Italian* captivates us all.

What Italians do all have in common is the family table.

Round, square, oval; a shared Formica counter or a pebbled curb. Covered in tatted embroidery or a plastic cloth, that table is where the day's news is laid out like a four-course meal. Its where adolescent stomachs are pushed to their outer gastronomical limits and teenaged hearts are healed. It's where conversations about living wills and how to die cannot be avoided, despite the stereotypical inclinations to sweep it all beneath. It's where families speak only Italian to an American cousin doing her best to translate her gratitude. Where arguments of politics, religion, and general braggadocio conclude with no conclusion, and the professing of love is on repeat with every dish served.

But the table is hardly where a feast cooked by any Italian begins.

To unearth those origins, one must start with the impulses of the ancestors, *antinati* (loosely meaning "before our birth"). Our lineage is a womb, and we are forever feeling around for its cavity's borders.

Mine has been created through a burrowing together of grandparents, parents, aunts and uncles who weren't always blood relatives, and now cousins—third or fourth generation, once removed on the chart, it doesn't matter. That line is twined with husbands, here and gone. Twisted around stepfamilies and in-laws. My own son, the children from my second husband's first marriage, my nieces and nephews, and the offspring of my relatives back in Italy are nestled in with whoever I have called my own.

For my mother, V. Jean Giuliani, her origin story of paternal loss became one of stepfamily gains. Her narrative included incessant sermonizing from her mother that "you American now," while the entire household clung to their Italian social club belongings. My father, Ettore Anselmo Iannuzzi, changed to Januzzi, drove in the stakes to claim his family's home country. With Italian spoken in broken whispers or loud cackles around him, he preached the mantra, *family is everything*.

Certainly, there were questions to be asked of any immigrant and their progeny, such as who defines *family*? But both sets of my grandparents were deceased by the time I turned eighteen, both grandmothers before I turned nine. This left a gaping hole in our Italian American family's cultural knowledge, one my imagination longed to fill after my parents' deaths.

Did my grand- and great-grandparents find what they had hoped for in America? How did they succeed among other ethnicities, and among their own kind? Did their blending of regional cultures find compatibility with a way of life that suited them? Did love or money win? Or was our culinary ethos victorious over all? In the Italian language, there are many words for *to leave*. For example, *uscire*, to exit from, or go out somewhere like a club; *partire*, to depart from, say, Rome; and *lasciare*, to leave, as in breaking away, permanently, as in *hanno lasciato i loro cari e la loro terra natia*. They broke away from their loved ones and their homeland. What happened to those who were left behind?

For centuries, the individual states of Italy had been pushed around by competing factions. When Garibaldi emboldened peasants to fight in *il risorgimento* to reclaim their cultural touchstones, did he realize how that movement would do more to tear families apart than reunite them? Did he know, hundreds of years later, many of us would single out the threads of family and food that had frayed, and strengthen them to become *something Italian* again?

From Abruzzo

My mother's full name was Vinzenzella Jean Giuliani Januzzi, though I wouldn't find the documented spelling of the first name until locating her birth certificate upon her death. With a round face, soft brunette hair, long legs, a petite frame, and bright, brown eyes that softened to hazel when she aged, she was often heard chanting, through reddish-bronze Loreal lipstick–swathed lips, an intonation of her parents' homeland: "Spoltore, near Pescara, in Abruzzi." Abruzzo (changed from Abruzzi in 1963) is a rather easy two-hour drive now east from Rome. Its major provincial port, Pescara, sits along the Adriatic Sea. The town of Spoltore, with a 2023 population estimate of 19,000, is situated seven miles inland above Pescara. Its borders have developed like a sea creature, with tentacles reaching toward a cemetery, a soccer stadium, a former convent, an airport, and the town of Chieti in the distance. The province of Pescara is known as the birthplace of Gabriele D'Annunzio, the famed poet, politician, and leading writer of his time, who helped inform the concept of fascism.

There is a contemporary ski-to-sea consciousness underlying the surrounding region, given two-thirds of the area is mountainous. Nicknamed the "green lung of Italy," Abruzzo is host to three national parks. Along with its brushed denim–blue Adriatic coastline, the Parco Nazionale d'Abruzzo, Lazio e Molise, home of the endangered Marsican brown bear, Parco Nazionale della Maiella, and Parco Nazionale di Gran Sasso e Monti della Laga are the region's main attractions.

Looking west from Spoltore, the fortress-like stoney outcropping of the Gran Sasso is perceptible, about an hour's drive away. In Italy, these peaks are called *massifs* (compact groups of mountains). The Gran Sasso d'Italia boasts of the highest peak in the Apennine range and the second-highest mountain in Italy outside the Alps—the Corno Grande. It's also the land of the Campo Imperatore (Emperor's Field), a high basin-shaped alpine meadow. From Castello di Spoltore, one looks out to the east for ships at sea. And to the south, La Bella Addormentata, the rocky outline of a sleeping beauty in the range, lies in repose along the Grand Maiella. According to legend, Maja (Maiella), a nymph of Pleiades and daughter of Atlas and Pleione, ran away to the Gran Sasso after her son, Hermes, was wounded in battle. He died alone, while she sought after remedial herbs. Gran Maiella boasts seven different peaks of over 8,500 feet within its boundaries. To the east of Spoltore lie the famous fields of saffron around L'Aquila.

In the nearby province of Chieti sits the famed Villa Santa Maria, founded in the 16th century and known as the "Home of Italian Chefs." At what was considered the first professional culinary school in Italy, the Caracciolos, aristocrats of Naples, once hosted banquets to inspire young chefs. Every October 13th, the municipality marked the *Sagra dei Cuochi* (festival of cooks) to honor their institution.

The *comune* (township) of Spoltore historically was considered a cereal- and grain-making area. Spelt grain was a driver in the economy, hence the name Spoltore. Sheep are also a focal point, raised for their milk and their mutton. The region is known for its preservation and public education efforts around sheep farming and the ancient practice of *transhumanza*, or the seasonal movement of livestock. During my grandparents' time there, sheep were herded between specific summer and winter pastures up and down the peninsula. Poor residents were steered too by the feudal land systems, stepping in the hoofprints of sheep for work.

Lamb is served at many trattorias in Abruzzo as *spiedini* (skewers). But seafood is the main draw for anyone residing close to the coast, including calamari, scallops, cod, and plenty of other fish. At a local Spoltorese restaurant, Bella Addormentata, where we dined with family members, the owner proudly focused on seafood and the mountains in homage to local traditions: truffles spilling over ravioli, a lone scallop plated in a buttery sauce topped by caviar, and a singular, airy fish chip served on a local stone.

There's also a strong history of baking here—what other ethnicity can compare when it comes to holiday or special occasion baking? In Abruzzo, you'll find pizzelle, also known as *ferratelle*, (snow-flaked shaped cookies), made in a cast-iron press, and *crostate di frutta* (fruit crostatas) at every turn. *Zafferano* (saffron) is collected in the pastures of Navelli, and *elicriso* (helichrysum Italicum, the sun and gold plant), known as Italian curry, is used often for tea, seasonings, and in oils and balms. The regional pasta is typically shaped into *chittara*, pressed through a device that looks like guitar strings. One local proprietor turned me on to *orzo pupo*, a caffeine-free barley beverage served warm that eventually I discovered throughout the rest of Italy. Abruzzo's regional alcoholic beverages, not readily available in the US, consist of juicy, cherry-flavored *ratafia* (drunk when a contract has been ratified), *genziana* (made from the gentian root used in other *amari* or bitters), *cerasuolo* (a wine whose cherry color comes from very brief skin contact with the deeply pigmented skins of the Montepulciano grape), and, around Spoltore, two predominant white wines: Pecorino and Trebbiano. And one cannot forget the area's most well-known wine, Montepulciano d'Abruzzo, not to be confused with the Montepulciano wine from the town in Tuscany.

In Italy, a *festa* is organized around a religious occasion. A *sagra* is one celebrated in honor of local food. Spoltore boasts of several *feste*: The town hosts the annual Easter tradition of the *Madonna che corre* (Madonna who runs toward a risen Jesus), and in September, the parade of the Madonna del Popolo statue from San Panfilo Chiesa. The chapel housing the statue, opened in 1906, was designed by the architect and engineer Antonino Liberi from Spoltore, also known as the brother-in-law and collaborator of Gabriele D'Annunzio. In my parents' hometown of Lorain, a parade with a replica of the statue from Spoltore was repeated often in the 1940s and '50s, organized by my grandmother and others through their Abruzzese Club and St. Peter's Catholic Church. Dollar bills were attached to the statue as honorariums. For decades, the church has continued to mark the first Sunday in September with a remembrance of the Spoltorese who came to Lorain. However, the statue is nowhere to be found.

My maternal grandmother, Raffaela Scurti, was born on May 16, 1898, in Spoltore, Italy, to Francescopaolo Scurti (1839–1898) and his wife, Annantonia d'Onofrio (1853–?), who had married seventeen years earlier. Raffaela was the youngest of nine children. Raffaela's father died two months after her birth, which was the beginning of many long hardships. Her siblings included Anna Domenica, and Concetta Appignani, whose great-grandchildren responded to my plea on the Spoltore news site. Concetta's son, Peppino, would become a popular, twice-elected mayor of the town. Three of Raffaela's siblings died an early death due to unsanitary and harsh conditions in the town. Two brothers, Giovanni and Leone, would depart first for Ohio, leaving three siblings, including Concetta, behind. Another brother, Panfilo, would leave and return.

In the early 1800s, most Italian towns adhered to the Napoleonic Code, which required all births, deaths, and marriages to be witnessed and recorded. Thankfully, those records still exist today to help determine genealogy and family history. Raffaela's parentage can be traced back to the early 1700s in Spoltore, with Michele Scurti at the helm. According to one local genealogy report[3], Scurti is a rare surname, and the family was one of the largest and most ancient in Spoltore. Originally there was one family with more than twenty-five members. Each line was identified with a nickname. Rafaella's family was *Ciavajune* in Abruzzese, translating to "stammerer," from a relative who stuttered.

Raffaela was a young woman with lush dark hair and a sturdy disposition, standing at just four feet, ten inches, and had only attained a third-grade education. In her hometown, she was a wool spinner and produced many other works using the intricate lace-patterned practice of tatting. She married a hometown boy, Vincenzo Giuliani, at the age of twenty-two. For several years, he would traverse the raging Atlantic waters to secure wages in the states and carry his earnings to Italy. Raffaela toiled alongside members of their families in homes where livestock bleated and moaned on the lower level and residents above. She awaited his final return, and the decision that would remove her from the beloved hillsides of green rolling into the seas.

My maternal grandfather, Vincenzo Giuliani, was born in the rural Contrada Mezzogiorno area of Spoltore on November 5, 1892, the son of Domenico Giuliani (1842–1898) and Concetta Di Iuliis (?). Vincenzo had six siblings. Two sisters died young. His other two sisters, Rosina and Angiola, stayed behind in Spoltore. His brother, Tommaso, immigrated to the United States in 1907 and headed to Steubenville, Ohio. We know little about the rest of the family's life other than their roles as *contadini*, peasant farmers. But the Giuliani name in Spoltore is known by the nickname *Masemucce*, meaning "little Massimo," possibly linked to the progenitor Massimo Giuliani. By the early 1990s, when my mother wrote to a cousin in Spoltore, the cousin observed there "weren't many Giulianis around town much anymore." Though this name would become well-known in the United States, it was often misspelled as "Guiliani," even for my mother, which makes searching records challenging.

As a young man, Vincenzo boasted a tall and thin stature of five feet, five inches, with full lips and piercing brown eyes. A *bracciante*, or laboror, he served in the Italian Army in the 114° Reggimento Fanteria "Mantova" during WWI, a regiment based in Tricesimo, 650 kilometers from home. His brigade fought in the Battle of Vittorio Veneto, where the 144th regiment took the lead in breaking through Austro-Hungarian lines. The war was a win for the Italian state and the Allies, though the aftermath did little to improve the lives of those living there.

By the late 1910s, my ancestors' lives in Spoltore were marked by misery and migration. After the 1898 riots that struck most of Italy, Mussolini had risen to power, declaring himself prime minister in 1922. An agricultural crisis had begun. Grain prices had fallen. There was no market for fruit. And phylloxera and downy mildew had hit the grape vines. To locate work, my grandparents might have gone north to Germany, rotated internally to the larger Abruzzese cities of L'Aquila or Sulmona, or transferred to the wider geographical areas such as Rome. However, in some municipalities, it was declared that peasants would forfeit property if absent for more than three months. Some workers set their sights on America, thanks to the appearance of *padroni* (recruiters for labor), the popularity of the steamship, bold advertisements by overseas employers, and citizens who returned with tales of the opportunities to be had. In 1921 the United States instituted a policy to limit immigration from eastern and southern Europe. My ancestors, sensing oncoming regulations, began making plans. What counted most, above all the other considerations, was the chance to break away from the tedium of migration loops and settle into one locale.

Departing from Spoltore in the early-1920s, Vincenzo Giuliani and others probably trekked through dusty hills on donkey carriages or clapped their heels along an old sheep track for several days before arriving in the port of Naples. A more expensive steam train (sometimes called *jo ciuff-ciuff*) was also available from various locales, connecting along the Adriatic railway lines and into Naples. Once arrived, the travelers were subjected to the ill will of a *gabbamondo* (swindler) who spoke a hyper-local dialect, were forced to undergo strict medical exams, and had to pay around two hundred lire for passage, when an average annual salary might have been five hundred.[4] Landing at Ellis Island, they stood sweaty or chilled, huddled together in long, intimidating queues to be counted as "southern Italians," when oddly enough their region was more in the country's middle. They bumped into more Abruzzese following the same resettlement lines, which led to the East Coast, to Philadelphia, to Pittsburgh, to Steubenville and Salineville, Ohio, and on to Lorain, certain that they would be reunited with the ones who carried the same blood through their veins.

They never returned to the columns of rich Abruzzese limestone rock, which would become a well-known wine growing region as time slipped in between the sands of the Adriatic at their base. Whether for financial reasons, or simply because they knew that forging ahead meant survival, Raffaela and Vincenzo never looked back.

By early 1915, nearly 175,000 Abruzzese had left their beloved fields and hills in a four-year span.[5] And from 1901 to 1920, Abruzzo had the highest number of emigrants leaving every year: 33.7 per thousand.[6] According to his ship's manifest, Vincenzo Giuliani had already visited the US from 1911 to 1913 to stay with a man who was a close friend *and* Rafaella's oldest brother by sixteen years, Giovanni Scurti. Giovanni had entered the States nearly ten years earlier. Steubenville, Ohio, was Vincenzo's destination for a portion of that time. He would return to Italy to serve in the Italian Army from 1913 to 1918, prior to his next documented immigration passage in 1920. On May 1 of that year, Vincenzo Giuliani married Raffaela Scurti in Spoltore's San Panfilo Chiesa. Seven years later, it is believed Vincenzo paid for the steam train to Naples, with my then pregnant grandmother, and departed on the ship *Dulio* for a two-week passage overseas. They left the temperate spring conditions of Abruzzo in exchange for similar ones in the States. Vincenzo arrived in the

US with sixty-five dollars in his pocket, presumably money accumulated from army pay, earned prior to that voyage, or raised following the marriage ceremony. First attending to a friend or cousin, Giovanni Morelli, in Astoria, NY, they rode on Pennsylvania Railroad trains running west from New York through Pennsylvania and into Ohio. Vincenzo and Raffaela joined Giovanni Scurti, who was already living in the small town of Salineville, Ohio, located twenty miles northwest of the Steubenville train station and thirteen miles from the Ohio-West Virginia border. That entire area would soon become home to over fifty ethnic groups working in its many mills, especially wool mills, along the Ohio River.

With Ohio as his locus for home, Vincenzo was a man who roamed. Records for "James," a name he used on occasion, point to a salary of $1,047.83 by 1923 in Schenectady, New York, known as the "Electric City" and home of GE and the American Locomotive Company (ALCO). Vincenzo stated his work as a trackman in various census and immigration records, so we can assume he was employed by ALCO. Likely recruited by padroni, as a trackman, he was given room and board. Rooming may have consisted of being locked into a boxcar at night, allowed to buy food for a 50 to 100 percent markup, and expected to toil all day long—conditions crueler than those back home.

A disciplined laborer, Vincenzo had become a "bird of passage," someone who carried his earnings back to Italy. "In 1896, a government commission on Italian immigration estimated that Italian immigrants sent or took home between $4 million and $30 million each year, and that 'the marked increase in the wealth of certain sections of Italy can be traced directly to the money earned in the United States.'"[7] For example, Vincenzo brought his earnings back in person in 1924 and 1925, before immigrating to *L'Merica,* as those in Italy called it, for good in May of 1927.

Soon after the couple dragged their trunks down the planks of the steamer, Raffaela traveled by train from New York to Salineville to join her brother, Giovanni. Vincenzo was employed as a laborer—again mostly likely engaged by padroni—at Bethlehem Steel's Sparrows Point, putting in backbreaking ten-to-fourteen-hour shifts. He would have been given two unpaid holidays a year and worn pajamas and work clothes that Raffaela had sewn for him out of blue and white ticking print fabric carried from Italy. The company town of Dundalk where he lived was known for its crowded and crumbling two-story track homes. Throughout suffering summer months, he shuttled by train between there and Salineville. Only six months after planting himself for good in his new country, with Raffaela glowing rosy as a child blossomed in her womb, Vincenzo died alone on November 7, 1927, in Baltimore, of encephalitis lethargica, in the same month as his birth. The world was experiencing an outbreak of this disease, known as "sleeping sickness," which caused swelling within the brain and led to respiratory distress. With unidentified friends or extended family members standing over his coffin, dressed for chilly temperatures, Vincenzo was buried in Baltimore in a grave that would remain unmarked until my mother changed that in the 1980s. He would never realize his ambitions to become a naturalized citizen of the United States, to embrace *la dolce vita* of any sort, or to see and hold his baby girl, my mother, Jean. That duty would fall to someone else from Spoltore. However, his premature death would give his granddaughter, me, the opportunity to reclaim Italian citizenship to honor my ancestor's toils.

Salineville is situated in Columbiana County, Ohio, in the valley of Yellow Creek, seventeen miles west of the town of East Liverpool. Squished into place by the borders of Pennsylvania and Ohio, this northeastern region of Appalachia was known first for its salt mines and coal, and later became a draw for its ceramics and pottery industries. Here, Raffaela's brother Giovanni (Uncle John) had established himself as the patriarch of the family after leaving Italy, and my grandmother's family, including Raffaela and her brothers Leone and Panfilo, embedded themselves there with him.

Salineville acquired its name thanks to its salt (saline) mines, where the first well was dug in 1809. By 1835, the area was populated by twenty wells. The Pennsylvania Railroad line had been constructed from Cleveland in 1852, thus connecting my ancestors to this curious region. The woolen mills and flour mills of the Faulk Brothers and F. H. Falloon came next, as well as tanneries. By the late 1880s, the ceramics industry began attracting laborers from across the Allegheny region, with companies like the

National China Company, J. W. Winterich, which produced ecclesiastical ceramicware and art, and the American Chinaware company drawn to the region's abundant clay deposits.[8]

Founded by Quakers, Salineville also supported six other denominations in the mid-1800s, including St. Patrick Catholic Church, where my mother was baptized and welcomed by her godmother—Uncle Leone's wife, Cristina—and a godfather, Luigi, who would later take on an even more important role in her life. By the late 1910s, the town's nine coal mines had diminished. Its population shrank from 2,700 to 2,100 residents in the span of a decade between 1920 and 1930. While some, including my mother and her mother, left for cleaner air and verdant hope, Uncle John, married to Eurichetta Scurti, stayed put, as did Leone, who by 1920 worked in the pottery industry as a kiln fireman. Older brother Panfilo returned to Italy by 1926, where he married and lived out his life until the 1940s. After joining the US Army and fighting as an American in World War I from 1917 to 1918—while his friend and my grandfather, Vincenzo, fought as an Italian—Uncle John eventually settled at 30 Lincoln Street and worked for the Pennsylvania Railroad Company. Working as a "trackman," he lost an eye in 1943 and returned to his employer unable to "work alone." Uncle John had no heirs, but he would take an interest in his new niece, Jean Giuliani. As he aged, for a short time, John lived with Raffaela and my mother and their eventual new family. My mother inherited the remainder of his estate and settled his affairs after his passing in 1959.

Raffaela, meanwhile, had found herself in rough circumstances as a widow and a new mother after her husband Vincenzo's death. No one wanted a single mother as a drain on the household, though she would never see herself that way or want to inhabit that role. In the tradition of naming newborns after a recently deceased member of the family, Rafaella named her daughter Vinzenzella, but the four Burns sisters who lived next door insisted she also crown the baby with an American name, Jean. Thus, her signature—which we forged plenty—was V. Jean Januzzi. The sisters' goal of protecting my mother by Americanizing her name had erased what was rightfully hers, something many Italians experienced and a duplicity that would chase her for nine decades.

Here, I must introduce Luigi DeLuca, born March 3, 1891, in Spoltore. (The Abruzzo-Molise region contained one of the highest concentrations of surnames beginning with *Di-* or *De-*, and patronymic surnames like *Di Francesco, Di Giandominico,* and *DeLeonardis* would eventually fill the D section of the phone book in Lorain.) Luigi's parents, Antonio and Rita (DeLeonardis), married in Spoltore in 1886 and produced four children: Luigi, his brother, Vincenzo ("James"), and two sisters, Rosa and Annina.

With the people of Abruzzo always, as Eide lengo states in his study of emigration from this region, "on the edge of financial disaster [in] an area of hunger, sickness and misery,"[9] Luigi departed once in 1909 with his father, Antonio. Again in 1920 after he presumably traveled once or twice to Italy and back, he and his brother James, departed from the port of Le Havre, France, in 1920, destined for Lorain to join Antonio. They left his mother, Rita, and the two sisters behind. By 1926, their father was working in the steel mill. According to city directories, both Luigi (sometimes called Louis) and James started a bakery called *DeLuca Bros.* in the rear of a building along East Avenue near the bend in the Black River. They lived a few doors down from there with Antonio. Antonio was widowed by 1930 and deceased by 1947. Rita most likely never immigrated. No Ohio census records exist with her name nor was she buried alongside Antonio in Lorain. In their tight dwellings on East Avenue, Luigi and James developed distinct plans for their future. Luigi left the bakery business, though eventually they would all reside together at 1722 Washington Avenue, along with Antonio and their wives, including someone new in the mix.

Given the confines of their small Italian hometown like Spoltore, the DeLucas, Giulianis, and Scurtis surely knew one another. Luigi was one year older than Vincenzo Giuliani, seven years older than Raffaela. Oddly enough, he resembled Rafaella's older brother, Giovanni, in his cheek and jawline enough for me to have confused their sepia-toned photos on occasion. Giovanni was also friends with Luigi's cousin John. When Vincenzo died, word traveled to both ends of the migration chain by notice in the news, letters from Italy, gossip, and word of mouth at Lorain's Abruzzo Club.

After a week of bitter cold, my mother was born on January 7, 1928. The unfamiliar name listed as godfather on her baptismal record was *Luigi Vanukki*— probably a corrupted name for Luigi DeLuca, who seems to have been in the lives of this mother-daughter duo from the start. According to county records, Luigi and Raffaela married one year later, after a year of mourning had passed. *The Evening Review* newspaper in East Liverpool announced "a very pretty wedding at St. Patrick's" and "a wedding breakfast served at the home of the bride's brother," John, along with plans for the couple to reside in Cleveland. From Salineville, or nearby East Liverpool where the report was filed, one might suppose everything north was Cleveland if counting only on train connections. Instead, Lorain awaited their arrival.

From Calabria

My father was named Ettore Anselmo Januzzi, though the family surname was originally spelled *Iannuzzi* and pronounced "ya-nootz-i." He was sometimes nicknamed Ette or ET, and his grandfather Vincenzo, whom he didn't know but affectionately referred to as "Papu," called him *Vincenzino* in letters from Italy, and so both my parents would be similarly named or nicknamed for a father figure in their lives.

Ettore had a deep, rich brown mop of hair and dark skin that he was often teased or demeaned for, which could have been influenced by a variety of ethnicities, Greek included given his maternal side of the family. His deep brown eyes could darken more when angry. Roundness of ears that allowed him to hear his kids as he waited for one of us to break curfew were said to symbolize his wisdom, and if there were stories to be told about Calabria, he was always listening. Unlike my mother, who possessed less knowledge about her lineage to learn from, he proudly professed his love for the Iannuzzi family's hometown of his father: San Donato di Ninea in the Cosenza province of Calabria. He came to know the scent and taste of the homeland through his grandfather's letters to his father, Enrico. He would eventually travel there and witness it, writing of a land "where you could see millions of stars at night." He met the *zii* (uncles and aunts). They fed him; he broke bread with them. Despite the little awareness he possessed of his mother's family beginnings in the town of Caulonia, my father carried his longing for the people of his parentage with him wherever he went.

Calabria, like other regions of Italy, contains a mix of coastal communities and the four mountain ranges of Aspromonte, Pollino, La Sila, and Serra.

Here, my ancestors were of both land and water. Out of 110 provinces in Italy, approximately half touch the coastline, half don't. There are several ways to travel to the familial provinces to locate San Donato di Ninea in Cosenza or Caulonia in Reggio Calabria, the origin of my paternal grandmother. One could fly into Naples or Lamezia Terme, book passage on a train, and eventually rely on a rental car or the kindness of cousins to pick you up. Superb state, province, and local trains and roads involve tunnel travel and produce a wistful scenery of smooth seas and groves of trees at most turns.

The name *Calabria* comes from the Byzantine term *kalos-bruo*, meaning "fertile earth," and the region has historically been host to a mix of ethnicities: kinships of Albanians who escaped Turkish prosecution with their *gjitonìa*, neighborhood homes arranged in small semi-circles around a "mansion"; Grecanico communities in the Reggio Calabria province; and the Occitans of southern France and northern Piedmont, who emigrated to Calabria to escape religious persecution in the thirteenth and fourteenth centuries and continued to be persecuted as Protestants (Waldensians) by Church authorities. Their last enclave exists in the Cosenza province. (In fact, our bed and breakfast in the town of Cosenza was positioned atop of a Waldensian church.)

The food of Calabria reflects the flavors I most long for; the flavors my father revered: fennel, sausage, chestnuts, and figs, and anything spicy. Every September the Calabrian borgo of Diamante marks the coming of autumn with a Festa di Peperoncino, and today, Calabrian chilis flavor dishes all around the world. 'Nduja, a spreadable pork sausage from the town of Spilinga, has also become a staple on charcuterie boards. Like other delicacies that are now celebrated worldwide, 'nduja was once a necessary provision for poor people, a way to stretch pork trimmings to last for weeks. In addition to pork, goat meat, lamb, and of course, wild boar, or *cinghiale*, are popular meats. A wide variety of fish is served in coastal towns, including the *panino di pescespada*, swordfish sandwich, in the quaint fishing town of Scilla. Sardines are preserved in terra cotta containers and the sauces are served with buttered bread. Peppers, sun-dried tomatoes, zucchini squash, and wild mushrooms are popular (porcini as big as a steering wheel were in season during our visit), and eggplant is another regional favorite, served pickled, fried, and in lasagna. Bergamot is a growing industry, but according to the guides of a local museum, only

View from Spoltore toward the Adriatic, 2022

View toward Convento di San Panfilo Fuori le Mura

Raffaela Scurti Giuliani DeLuca, circa 1910s

Raffaela Scurti Giuliani DeLuca, circa 1920s

Vincenzo Giuliani, Italian Army, 1913

Vincenzo's burial in Most Holy Redeemer Cemetery, Baltimore, MD, with unidentified persons in attendance, 1927

Raffaela Scurti Giuliani and Luigi DeLuca, wedding day, 1929

Vincenzo Giuliani, passport photo, circa 1920

several "families" or consortiums control the product in the supply chain as it is transported to perfumeries and other outlets, similarly to the way the Mafia controlled the citrus trade in the far south for years. Calabria contains a museum dedicated to this citrusy fruit and its offspring, as well as Museo del Cedro, the museum of *cedro di Calabria*, citron, in the town of Santa Maria del Cedro, where a sect of Orthodox Jews has planted themselves alongside the growers to secure only the purest fruit for their traditions. A strange fruit, the nespole, is a loquat grown in olive oil vineyards to protect the trees. Beans remain popular, and occasionally I experienced a sighting of lupini beans, the yellow ones found pickled in jars in Italian American stores. The Tropea red onion is highly sought after by Mediterranean chefs, and not to be missed. Adding a sauté of these onions to any pasta dish elevates the taste buds and the chef's reputation. Speaking of pasta, Calabria's comes in simple forms: tagliatelle and maccheroni, from which the American "macaroni" takes its name. Here, the pasta is made into long tubes. When we were served some for lunch, a cousin mentioned, "it's maccheroni," with a casual air. As if I should have known.

The sellers of *arancini*, fried balls of carnaroli or arborio rice, line the streets of many tourist beach towns. These arancini are not to be missed. The balls are stuffed with a variety of fillings, including mozzarella cheese, 'nduja, and red onions. Similar fried snacks, also called arancini at times, contain an outer layer of cooked potato filled with similar ingredients and deep fried. These are popular street-food snacks in Calabria—their version of mozzarella sticks.

For drinks, Amaro Silano, with its distinct pine scent, is hard to pass up, though plenty of other commercial and local amaro varieties are served. And granitas are served everywhere, including ones made with bergamot or chocolate. The region's wines have different names depending on the specific terroir and local spelling preferences. Cirò is the most important wine-making area in Calabria, where Gaglioppo grapes for this red wine are grown. Red wines include the dark grape of Nerello Mascalese (sometimes known as Nerello Calabrese), a deep ruby-colored Nerello Cappucio, and the indigenous Greco Nero. A sampling of white wines includes the Guarnaccia Bianca variety grown in the Cozenza province, and a straw-colored Pecorello Bianca. A few rare passito wines (sweet dessert wine from grapes dried off the vine on straw) are made from Zibibbo, also known as Muscat of Alexandria. The Zibbibo of Calabria is a dry wine, while that grown in Sicily is sweeter. Others include a rare Moscato al Governo di Saracena and a passito from Greco Bianco.

Today, the town of San Donato di Ninea is part of a grassroots movement (Pro Loco Ninea) to promote, as the Latin translates, "in favor of the place." The organization lends its logo—a native black squirrel—to local products that have secured a *denominazione comunale d'origine* (De. Co.) designation, including the chestnuts (*castagne*) that are a key part of the local heritage. In a country where chestnut trees cover eight percent of the country's forest, San Donato hosts the Sagra di Castagna, a chestnut festival celebrating the nuts of *nzerta, curcia e riggiola* varieties, during the Festa d' Autunno. Other delights featured at the festival include *bocconotti* with chestnut cream (similar my mother's pecan cups), *cassatelle con crema castagna* (think of these as cream-filled fritters), *taralli, turdilli* (similar to my mother's twists) and a traditional *Turdiddru Santunatisi*, a fried dough shaped with a three-dimensional spiral-ladder appearance, whose shape is said to reflect the solstice and the continuation of the seasons. "This is where everything smells of tradition," Domenica Assunta Dominianni writes about the festival itself—a tradition that was carried far and wide by the area's emigrants.

Every winter holiday in Cleveland, aligning with the festival of chestnuts in San Donata di Ninea, my father would carry home a sack of sweet chestnuts from the Italian mart, recalling his mother's recipe for a chestnut puree similar to mashed potatoes. My mother made chestnuts into dressing or roasted them in the oven. My father used a quick clip of the nutcracker to shell them while warm, peel away the skin, and eat the nuts, for a taste of the homeland.

The Iannuzzi hometown of San Donato sits on the southern edge of the Pollino Mountains. At four thousand feet, the Piano di Lanzo plateau in the municipality connects Cozzo del Pellegrino, one of Calabria's highest mountains, to the Esaro Valley. It's home to the Italian roe deer, and hikers pass through this area for the views and the solitude. Further along the way are the favored chestnut trees. The eye rises toward the gray and green mountainsides and falls over a territory heavy with a canopy of *pino loricato* (Bosnian pine), a thick tree whose branches and needles form a protection from the winds. (*Loricato* translates to "loriated," like the metal plates of medieval armor). Other canopy woods are cedar, alder, and beech. After a brief stint of warmth from the high sun, evenings cool off fast, especially when fog approaches off the ocean.

Luigi Bisignoni, local historian and editor of the online *L'Ecco Sandonatese*, calls the town "small in size, big in the past." San Donato di Ninea—formerly called Ninea after Ninevo, leader of the Enotri colonizers who founded the town—was mentioned as early as the fifth century B.C. by Hecataeus of Milan in a description of land. While most Italian Catholics will recognize San Donato as a healer of epilepsy (*il male di San Donato*, as the condition is known) in the south of Italy, the town's modern-day name was chosen in 1864 by the council of San Donato, who added the ancient "Ninea" to distinguish it from other municipalities with similar names.

San Donato's upper town square is known as Motta, and was once called *Morta*, because one might be killed crossing it. From there, you can enjoy a nearly 360-degree view of northern Calabria, and as in other hill towns, Motta was developed first for its protection. Soon the lower region was filled with people too. After settlement in the lower valley was interrupted due to Turkish and Saracen invasions, residents moved to the higher part of the ridge, where the village currently sits with its buildings nestled up to each other like sheep on a hill. It's said when San Donato became a municipality, its lands were sold to local gentry, which created dissension among the gentry and peasants. As one historian wrote, the San Donatese were "tenacious in affection, proud in hatred."[10]

Banditry occurred on a frequent basis following the country's 1861 reunification, when it was decreed that only lords could own land. Not all work was heroic, sometimes, they struck at locals. Among others, Saverio Iannuzzi (a possible relation in a town bursting with Iannuzzis], nicknamed the 'Prishente,' joined other bandits fighting against local lords, as did another possible kin, Domenico Iannuzzi, who abetted Saverio's banditry. Saverio was later murdered due to the high bounty on his head and therefore became an unofficial folk hero for the town.

Because the former hamlet of Policastrello was incorporated into the town of San Donato di Ninea, this unique area has two historic centers.

The outline of the commune's border slightly mimics that of Italy's boot, so perhaps it's no surprise that shoes would become our family business. San Donato di Ninea boasts of two churches. The first, Santa Maria dell'Assunta o della Motta, dates to the tenth or eleventh century. Stone altars and sanctuaries with frescos give one a sense of how present the past is here. From the piazza of the church, a mosaic compass points in the direction of other towns. The second church is L'arcipretura della S.S. Trinità, also called Chiesa Madre del Casale, constructed in 1500 in the village center and officially completed in 1631, along with its preserved frescoes. Coats of arms for the Caracciolo and Sanseverino families, owners of large fiefdoms across southern Italy, still hang on the exterior. My grandparents and great-grandparents attended to their marriages and births there. The Iannuzzi roots in the comune can be traced back to the early 1800s.

In my father's words, the town contained "homes [he walked to] over cobblestone streets...the homes clustered one over top the other and close." Photos from my grandfather Enrico's return trips in the 1950s and my father's only venture there in 1960 contain remnants of mines from when the village was known for its basin of metals. Donkeys trekked along rocky passages, dusty streets, and the stacked homes typical of hilltop towns, along with some of the last known family residences in the Strada Coste or Via Stellata neighborhoods. On the outer edges, one can still hike the perimeter paths to see evidence of abandoned mines and the municipality's cemetery.

San Donato is a town still relatively unknown, not unlike its region. In 1869, Baedeker, the guide used by the well-traveled, advised voyagers, "The length of the journey, the indifference of the inns and the insecurity of the roads, which has of late increased, at present deter all but the most enterprising." Some books note San Donato di Ninea wasn't known about outside of the most provincial circles until the 1970s, a decade after my father would have made his trip.

Southern Italy is nicknamed Mezzogiorno, a word that translates to "midday." According to legend, it's because the amount of eye-shielding sunshine splashed across the fields makes it appear like the time is always noon. I can attest to this, as I was surprised by the amount of warmth when at sea level. However, residents there lived meagerly, thanks to a history of poverty, sharecropping, the phylloxera outbreak that cause wine production to go bust, and the effects of the *'ndrangheta*, Calabria's Mafia, whose name loosely translates to "manliness" or "courage." According to John Dickie, author of *Blood Brotherhoods: A History of Italy's Three Mafias*, "from the 1880s onwards... overwhelming evidence for the 'ndrangheta's existence appeared. But how and why did the 'ndrangheta come into being? Traditional explanations tended to blame violence, familism and patronage politics of Calabrian society for generating the region's mafia." The absence of a unified power during the struggles for unification left a vacuum in most quarters of Calabria, including in the penitentiaries and penal colonies, and in the centers of the other two Mafia circles in Naples and Sicily. In other words, there were plenty of inside jobs. For instance, by April of 1944, 45 percent of Allied military cargo was being stolen, the locals as desperate to make a mark as the Mafia. They were also desperate to survive. *Chi si fa i fatti suoi campa cent'anni.* Those who mind their own business live a hundred years. As recently as 2011, there was controversy in opposing the mafia in San Donato, where a former mayor voted against hanging a plaque hung that read "The 'ndrangheta does not enter here, the Municipality repudiates the Mafia in all its forms." He was quoted as saying, ""if things continue like this in San Donato di Ninea, sooner or later someone will die" (which he later corrected to mean die a "political death" after the unfortunate declaration was recorded in the minutes).[11]

The rise of the railroads in the 1880s created additional opportunity for crime to thrive, and the syndicate not only used a family structure, but familial bonds and psychological abuse, to grow in power, which left behind plenty of carnage in families and small towns. Today, the 'ndrangheta is considered the largest, wealthiest, and most dangerous crime syndicate.

As a result of many factors, by the time my ancestors lived in San Donato, deplorable conditions were prevalent. Someone living in San Donato might walk miles to access their family's plot of land to work, and again to return to their secure domicile at day's end. According to Angelo Pellegrini, a successful immigrant who later wrote about his sharecropping family, "The central, dominating fact of our existence was continuous, inadequately rewarded labor.... Education beyond the third grade was out of the question.... At eight or nine years of age, if not sooner, the peasant child is old enough to bend his neck to the yoke and fix his eyes upon the soil in which he must grub for bread. I did not know it then, but I know it now, that is a cruel, man-made destiny from which there is yet no immediate hope of escape."[12]

Are these factors what caused Grandpa Januzzi, having reached only an eighth-grade level of education, to leave? Or was it Mussolini's rise to power, about which Enrico reflected on forty years later, "I didn't think any good would come from it"?[13] In the village there is a dialect expression, *Cùlu rùttu e sènza ciràsi*, that indicates "a defeat with damages, an adventure in which it was better not to embark."[14] Was this how Enrico saw his decision to immigrate? The losses would tally up regardless? Land ownership, food scarcity, resource depletion, and lack of opportunity likely all played a role, as did a correspondence and closeness with Zio Raffaele, Vincenzo's younger brother by sixteen years. Raffaele arrived in Beaver Falls, Pennsylvania, in 1889, worked as a tailor, and at the age of sixty-five, wrote, "I may have to die with a needle in my hands with all my 12 children. I feel as if I have just now come from San Donato di Ninea" (meaning he had just as little money as before he emigrated). Ironically, one of his children, Eugene, would lead a major steel company in Beaver Falls and become a writer, while daughter Leda was a professor at a local college.

My paternal grandfather, Enrico, the last of five boys and one girl, was born on March 2, 1901, to a San Donatese, Vincenzo Iannuzzi (1854-1936), a *vigile dei boschi* (forest guard), and Maria Concetta Ponzo (1862-?), a *filatore* (wool spinner). Concetta, as she was known, was already twenty-three years old with her father deceased when she met Vincenzo. Their marriage came quickly after, tying the knot at San Donato's S. S. Trinità Chiesa in 1885. *Iannuzzi* is a patronym for Ianni (John), and the name was altered over time by immigration, transcription error, or choice. People in Calabria were often identified by nickname rather than surname. For instance, in San Donato, there existed many others with the same name as my great-great-grandfather, Francesco Saverio Iannuzzi (married to Paolina Panebianco). One of seven nicknames for Iannuzzi known in town, such as *Francesco i jacipu* or *Francesco i lucia*, would be enough to identify him. The *soprannome*, or nickname, for our line was *cicchiianuzzi* (chee-kee), which according to my cousin, Rico, meant rigid and serious people—or a lot like me and my family. I bumped into several other Iannuzzis in

Altomonte and Aiello. Thankfully, the nicknames worked to distinguish lines, though I wouldn't have minded a connection to the *gelatiere* (gelato maker) in Altomonte.

Enrico's father, Vincenzo Iannuzzi, was a landowner for many years. However, *landowner* simply meant one who was self-sufficient by working their land; it did not denote an accumulation of wealth. In 1890, after the birth of their fourth son, Vincenzo became known in records as a country guard (*bosco vigile*). Theft was prevalent in many mountain towns, so most likely this position meant that he was sent out to monitor the countryside. By 1901, Enrico's family, now with six children, migrated north for a brief time to work for a contractor in France, turning stands of oak and pine into charcoal. It's possible that interactions with the Occitans living in the Cosenza region influenced the decision to seek work in the French Occitania region. There, in Saint-Mathieu-de-Tréviers (south of Montpellier), Enrico was born, and as a young boy, hiked in the forests with his father. Seven years later, the family returned to San Donato, content to settle into what life offered with five boys and a girl. In the heart of every immigrant, and of every Italian living in the far southern reaches of Italy at the time, there is a struggle between the desire to be free of monetary worries and foreign attacks, versus the longing for home, the ache for the grounding the mountains bring.

Once Enrico and his family had returned from France, his mother Concetta became afflicted by an undetermined disease that caused distress and debilitation. She was bedridden for many years as her family suffered from punishing poverty and her adult children began to undertake their own endeavors.

The oldest boy in Enrico's family, Amerigo, was born in 1876, and it is possible this occurred in Spain, for reasons that aren't clear. He married Angelina Ponzo in San Donato. Amerigo would later depart for Argentina, leaving two children, Concetta and Vincenzo, about the ages of three and one, behind. According to his father, Vincenzo, Amerigo left the family in disgrace, but nonetheless the father entreated Enrico in his later letters to Ohio that Amerigo should write home. As late as 1936, Vincenzo begged Enrico, "please tell me if Amerigo is still with brother [Francesco]." His pleas were released to the winds.

The next oldest, Francesco Iannuzzi, born in 1886, married Clementina Iannuzzi in San Donato di Ninea on February 14, 1915. Ten years older than his wife, Francesco and Clementina departed for San Isidro, Buenos Aires, sometime after 1925, according to Enrico's letters. In August of 1926, Clementina wrote to Enrico on half-torn sheets of paper inserted into purple tissue-lined envelopes, "So, my dear affectionate brother-in-law, who knows what you thought about my rudeness for not answering your letter personally and for not thanking you for your kind gesture. It didn't matter that I had lost two children before because I was still comforted that I had Concettina. Now your brother goes to work and I stay alone in the house crying all day." Not only had two of her children perished from the plague during their voyage, their remains cast to the sea, but the last of their girls, Concettina, was now dead too, at the age of eleven, of diphtheria. After several visits to the hospital, Clementina wrote, "Concettina was unable to recover, and we were left penniless and deprived of our own flesh and blood." Another son, Orlando, born in 1928, became a barber by trade. Records for him were not located.

It's unclear what took my grandfather's siblings to Buenos Aires in the first place, but plenty of Italians sought work and refuge there in the early 1900s. Italian laborers helped build Buenos Aires and laid most of the railroad lines. Work was work. Amerigo and any Argentinian offspring would evaporate from traceable family records, and Francesco would disappear from communiques back home, having experienced an early death in 1949 that left Clementina a widow.

Their sister, Paolina, remained in San Donato, married into the Notestefano line, raised a family, and died in her hometown in 1954, after which Enrico returned home to settle her affairs.

Next in line, Vittorio, resided in Lorain with his younger brother Minotti, who had immigrated to the states by 1910. Vittorio arrived in 1912. Five years later, the two moved to Allegheny County, Pennsylvania. Allegheny County was only forty miles from where their uncle Raffaele, or Ralph, had settled in the early 1900s, married Teresa Silvestri, and raised their ten children. There, Minotti (Mike), 25, met Cecelia Carmella Barrella, 16, at her older sister's boarding house where she worked. A boarder there, he worked for the Pittsburgh mafia with the accompanying gold cuff links and nice shirts. According to family interviews with his granddaughter, Anita Dwyer, the couple, now married, went to a park with their daughter where Minotti 's car had been pushed over a cliff. His wife told him they had to leave because "it was too dangerous." Enticed by a friend already living in Lorain to move there, he and his family packed up and left, possibly along with Vittorio. Cecilia's parents soon followed. Minotti wrote in letters to Italy about several dire situations he experienced, but appeared to eventually right his finances and family.

Vittorio disappeared from the records in Lorain for a time, but reappeared in Italy, based on letters to Enrico from Vincenzo in 1925 and 1926 asking for money. "My hand has been in bad condition for three months" and "I beg you I have debts to pay," he wrote to Enrico, possibly after a stint in jail, which also put his father in debt. He later married Maria Consoli di Innocenzo and raised a healthy family of two children and three grandchildren. Not immune to the impact of Italy's current events, Vittorio surmised in a letter to his brother, "at least we won the Abyssinian war," a war of aggression between Italy and Ethiopia, and added, "and mother has improved." He died on January 15, 1963.

As for Minotti, he was widowed in 1953. According to Anita, "your grandfather, Enrique [sic] arranged for Minotti to fly to Argentina and bring the now widow Clementina to Ohio (without her son, now 25) and marry her so she would have financial security. It suggests your grandfather wanted her taken care of, and since Minotti was alone, he agreed to the arrangement...in 1956 they were married in Lorain....Clementina did not speak any English." Rumor was Minotti's three adult children were not fond of her. This, despite that during her time in from Argentina, Clementina may have given or offered her family home or some housing help in San Donato to the Iannuzzis in some form, with Franscesco fuming to Enrico in a letter, "aren't they all exploiting my wife's property?" Anita wrote to me, "Minotti never learned to read or write. He was a good provider, worked at the steel mill. An avid hunter and fisherman, and a wonderful father." His hunting would be partially responsible for his death years later—Uncle Mike died the year of my birth, of heart failure in a hunting accident while Enrico ran to the road and called for help.

The youngest of five boys by nine years and scheduled to enter the Italian Army at age 19, Enrico followed in step with two older brothers, left the mountain's protective embrace, and arrived in New York in December of 1920 with little knowledge of Lorain's lake effect winds that could not shield the cold. That would be the final time he marched behind his brothers. Noting on the ship's manifest his *years in the US* as *always*, meaning he planned for permanency, Enrico carried with him a dream, plus $40 ($650 today) in his pocket lent to him by the village priest. He would *always* have money. And would *always* carefully give it away.

If ever anyone had left Italy for adventure, Enrico was that young man. His sister-in-law, Clementina, wrote to him in Ohio in 1926 from San Isidro, Argentina, following the death of her young daughter, *Ti essere padrone. Ti un Vincenzino.* "Be a master of yourself. Be a young Vincenzo" (like their father). Enrico was troubled by taking care of his family, yet did not shy away from the forty-plus letters—out of sixty-five in my archives—his father penned from San Donato to him over the course of ten years. The youngest of so many boys, he was unafraid, and he set out to prove it. With his sometimes-gruff disposition, he would exhibit a commanding presence at the shoe store he started, but at home would soften up enough to rumble around with stories of the old days, with grandkids seated on his lap. He inspired me to travel more, reach higher, aim for more out of life.

※

To understand the journey of my paternal grandmother, Stella, we must look another generation back at her parents, Antonio Mazzà and Carmela Maiolo, and at the lengthy ancestral lines that can be traced back to my great-great-great grandparents.

According to the town's marriage records, Antonio was born on March 19, 1875, in Caulonia, in the Reggio Calabria province of Calabria. Destroyed once by the Romans in 200 BC after siding with Hannibal during the Punic Wars, the town was originally known by the name Castelvetere until 1863 (and referred to as Caulonia Superiore). Following unification, the town changed its name, a frequent choice by people seeking to liberate themselves from the past. The people there wanted to pay homage to an ancient Greek city thought to be in Castelvetere's territory, though archaeologist Paolo Orsi later proved this to be untrue.

In the early-to-mid-1800s, Antonio's father, Guiseppe, and mother, Caterina Finis, along with his grandparents, Illario and Anna Mazzà and

Biagio and Rosa Finis, belonged to families of shepherds who looked after goats and possibly sheep. All attended Chiesa Santa Maria in the *susu*, or upper part of town.

The ancient town where they lived, thought to have been founded in the early second half of the seventh century, was comprised of three hills that were once home to plenty of oak, chestnut, fir, and pines, as well as mines, where the Roman invaders condemned criminals to work with a penalty called *damnata ad metalla*.

The town's churches and other buildings often take on an ochre or red color, the color of earth and sand, when the sun reflects their sandstone construction. The Byzantine influence on Caulonia's architecture can be traced to Greek origins. This area, along with other towns that ring the Ionian Sea, was a part of Magna Graecia, a name given by the Romans to Greek-speaking coastal towns of southern Italy. This Greek influence would eventually inform my perspective on my three great-aunts and my grandmother, whose appearances ran closer to Greek origins.

The four gates of the city's medieval walls are still visible, and Asciutti-Hyeraci Palace, known as "palace of the devils," boasts a façade with monstrous figures in relief. Caulonia Marina, a more populated outpost, contains several of the 339 towers built along the coastline by a viceroy of Naples and the marquis Fabrizio Pignatelli in the 1500s to protect from invaders. It is said even women and children were responsible for their watch. Every August, the town gathers to celebrate the birth of the tarantella, dancing to rhythms of a lyre.

In 1783, news of a 7.0 earthquake felt throughout all of Calabria was cause for alarm. By the late 1800s, with iron foundries in existence, railroads were built to link sea to sea, allowing easier access for anyone to leave. Antonio considered the accumulation of events an invitation to better himself and his family.

His wife, Carmela "Nellie" Maiolo, was born on April 15, 1880, in Caulonia in the Vergini neighborhood. Her father, Illario, was a laborer, and her mother, Concetta (Panetta), was a spinner. Their families all married or were baptized at the nearby Chiesa San Silvestro in the *jusu*, or lower neighborhood. Nellie was fifteen and her mother was already deceased when she and Antonio married in 1895. The couple moved to the neighboring Placanica, a commune known for its manual-loom textiles, clay-colored houses, and colorful tiles, which was their final home before they left for the US. The town was made famous by Edward Lear, who wrote in his journal, "This place has no depth, but it is as if it were only a surface, being the houses built one above another on the edges and in crevasses, on the façade of a large rock raised in a summit, its highest pinnacle adorned with a modern building [...] seems built as a marvel for the passer-by."[15]

Lear's words could have applied equally well to most towns of that sort in the southern reaches—charming to look at, but agonizing to live and prosper in. Following Nellie's marriage to Antonio and their departure to the US, the earthquake of 1908 damaged much of Caulonia. We know little about the families left behind, but by the time the couple had birthed one son, Michelangelo, in 1898, each of them had lost one parent. We can assume the remaining family in Calabria continued to struggle, based on accounts like *Gente d'Aspromonte* (Revolt in Aspromonte) by Corrado Alvaro, which examines the day-to-day poverty and exploitation of Southern Italian peasants on their wild, hostile, rural lands.

From Pennsylvania

Antonio and Nellie Mazzà migrated to the United States in August of 1899 on the ship, *Spartan Prince*. (Birth, death and immigration records for the next decades would use Mazzà, Mazzo, and Matts interchangeably.) They planned to meet Nellie's brother, Tomasso, in Pittsburgh, Pennsylvania, already the site of a burgeoning iron and steel industry, into which Antonio and Tomasso were recruited by padroni. "Because of their size and employment needs, the coal and steel industries hired their own recruiters. These labor agents or padroni were a significant factor in channeling Italians to these industries. Padroni were important and powerful figures especially during the early years of Italian immigration before family networks took over their functions. They secured the most crucial commodity for the immigrants—a job. They sometimes also paid the fare for passage and located suitable food or housing. Because padroni often extracted a fee from wages, it was difficult for the worker to save money."[16]

Antonio and Carmela were the earliest of their families' immigrants. Unable to read and write, they would begin a series of moves over two decades dictated by a black rock found nestled below the earth's surface, a rock that would define "industry" for the United States—and still does, depending on geopolitical winds: coal.

Before coal, the use of charcoal, was prevalent, but charcoal is made from trees, and not even America's vast forests could sustain the country's greedy consumption. In the 1700s, coal mining helped ignite the States' Industrial Revolution, which would grow to support the iron industry, the steel-making ventures of Andrew Carnegie, the generation of electricity, and eventually power plants. Pennsylvania was home to two types of coal mines: bituminous, found to the west, and the higher-ranked anthracite, which is nearly pure carbon and contains a lower percentage of volatile matter, mined in the northeast quadrant. While the race for coal brought hundreds of years of pollution to the state, and the money it generated was concentrated as always with the wealthy—an idea Italian immigrants thought they had escaped—the mining industry did produce jobs. Word of these jobs made its way to Antonio and Nellie, who left Caulonia and traveled, by way of the trains that now crawled through the region around the Ionian Sea and north to Napoli, where they exited Italy bound toward the west with $20 in their pockets.

The Monongahela River runs along the spine of western Pennsylvania, and about twelve miles away, in Fayette County, Uniontown lays out flat in a valley where smoking ovens, used to bake coal into coke, were prevalent. This area was known as the Connellsville District within the Pittsburgh seam (a seam is a dark banded deposit of coal visible within rock layers). In the late 1800s, Uniontown was the center of the coke region, where "Any time of year [the smoke] range[d] from pinkish lavender to gun metal tinged with purple at evening."[17]

The people who lived in Uniontown and the surrounding smaller territories gave thanks to a gentleman named J. V. Thompson for the rise—and fall—of their fortunes. An owner of the coal land in that region, J. V. Thompson worked as a broker and banker, growing his father's First National Bank, also known as the "Honor Bank," where customers could get loans without security if necessary. Miners placed their funds and invested their monies in more coal land through his bank. He generated wealth for many through this operational model. He was a titan during the heights of growth from 1890 to 1915, which paralleled the years Antonio and Nellie spent there.

The initial prominence of Uniontown, known for its bituminous coal, was attractive to Antonio and Nellie. The birth of my grandmother, their second child, Stella Marie, would come to signify this new life they'd begun there. Stella was born in 1902, during a time when municipalities and churches were responsible for record-keeping. The state of Pennsylvania began keeping records after 1904. Archdiocese records and other official sites have come up short in locating Stella's birth record, likely due to a switch in names—the local records include variations such as *Matts*, *Matt*, *Mazzo*, *Massa*, and *Mazzà*.

Antonio worked in the mines and with his family lived in the squalor of track homes for the opportunity to "have more," but he also encountered hate there daily. The whites—which, at the time, did not include Italians—did not like the Italians and Slavs who had begun taking their jobs in the late 1800s, as the labor situation was always in flux. Hungarians and Slavs and Italians were already ticketed to work at such sites as the Frick Coke Company. "It was the wholesale dumping of aliens"[18] that alarmed the native population, who considered them visually different from whites.

Little did these immigrants know they were arriving just as labor and financial issues were coming to a peak, and they would witness and participate in history. Only a few years earlier, a strike in the bituminous coal regions had occurred as wages were forced down and men were crammed together like sheep in their living conditions. Those in the anthracite region, where men could go months without pay, hoped to achieve better conditions too. But the key difference in the anthracite region was a "natural monopoly heavily concentrated in a few hundred square miles in five counties in Pennsylvania."[19] If the workers didn't live in company track houses, their jobs might go to someone else. Bribes were not uncommon to secure a job.

On October 23, 1902, a 163-day anthracite coal strike by United Mine Workers of America ended, thanks to Theodore Roosevelt's interest and intervention and the well-regarded Clarence Darrow, who argued the case for the workers. "He made labor and industry accept the fact 'that the third party, the great public, had vital interests and overshadowing rights' and so set a precedent for the Federal Government to intervene in labor disputes, not as strikebreaker but as a representative of the public interest."[20]

Surely news of the 1907 explosion on the Monongah mines of West Virginia had also traveled to the workers in Pennsylvania. Over three hundred perished in the West Virginia fires. Over half were Italian. With explosions, fires, collapses, and the dangerous chemicals they had to inhale, the coal miner was never safe.

Undeterred or unable to move out of their circumstances, Antonio and Nellie stayed in Pennsylvania and next gave birth to Frank, Ella, Gustave, and Mary. They moved northwest to the "patch town" or coal camp of Brier Hill, a captive mine/coke works of the Youngstown Sheet and Tube Company in Ohio and once a bustling tiny village. After, they transitioned to Redstone Township (now a National Historic District) on the Redstone Central Railway. By 1910, Antonio had become a merchant at a company store, possibly at Brier Hill or the Thompson 2 site, which was listed as their residence at the time another son, Giuseppe, died. Here, keen-eyed Stella would begin to develop her business acumen. By 1911, when Palma was born, they lived in Allison but remained in the same county of Fayette. Had they gone northeast instead, they might have found themselves in Connellsville, one of the wealthiest, but short-lived, coal districts of all time.

In 1913, J. V. Thompson's bank failed due to malfeasance and a bad divorce contract with this second wife, Hunny. This set off a series of events detrimental to anyone in the area who had trusted him with their money, including my grandparents. He lost his 42-room mansion, and took his patrons, and the miners, down with him. Those misfortunes reverberated throughout the industry and the coal districts.

By 1920, Antonio worked as a coke miner and the family made their home at Allison Works No. 2. The family's last known residence was in Lamberton. Over twenty years, they had followed the work through a triangle of moves, never moving more than twenty-five miles away and never escaping the harsh conditions of mining life. Meat, fish and dairy were sorely lacking in their diets. Their oldest son, Michelangelo, died of pernicious anemia in March of 1920 in nearby Brownsville, the former junction for those coming to and from Pittsburgh along the river. His death would set their feet in motion once more.

For those two decades, the family made their home within what would become known as an Appalachian culture and society, blending in with others. As Shepphard writes, "Life has always been violent here and unpredictable here, sometimes sordid, but never monotonous. After a while one gets a taste for it."[21] It's no secret that Italian men, as a newer ethnic community, were often hired for the lowest paying jobs, and the dirtiest ones too. Mostly, they would taste coal on their tongues. They did what they could to taste home in their bellies.

And even as they struggled, they knew who they were. The predominant white population would not allow them to forget. Their Italian connections created a strong community, with a home in the Italian congregation at St. Therese in Uniontown. The church itself was conceived when they arrived in the area, though not completed until the late 1920s, and services were held to embrace the Italian community.

At their centennial in 1906, neighboring Connellsville held a parade in which the Italian *società* was over two hundred strong, many carrying an American flag.[22] The area west of the town was known as Little Italy. And on a website that gathered data on immigrants from the town of Calascio, Abruzzo, a Sons of Italy photograph depicts a healthy gathering of twenty-some men in Fayette County.[23] Today, a mural in Connellsville itself, painted in 2019 on the former Italian Independent Social Club building, depicts a thriving Italian American family seated at a table clad in white with plenty of wine to share. While every proud Italian dressed their best when possible, including a suit coat, vest, gold pocket watch, and bow tie or knot tie as wide as a tablecloth—and while Stella's family certainly aspired to this image, given her attention to detail and style—the depiction of a prosperous Italian at that time couldn't be further from the truth.

By 1901, Andrew Carnegie had since sold his Carnegie Steel to J.P. Morgan for millions of dollars. In 1901, U.S. Steel was formed through the merger of Carnegie Steel, Federal Steel, and American Steel & Wire. About the same time, Lorain (Ohio) Steel was absorbed into U.S. Steel. Antonio had tired of moving his family from mine to mine while the coal industry declined, and black dust permeated their lungs. The prospects for steel loomed large for his growing young family.

As Professor Francesco Filareto of Rossano Calabro said, speaking to the Italian Cultural Institute in San Francisco, 2016[24], "Calabrians are different from anybody else, as they have always felt the 'need' of migrating somewhere else." Between 1876 and 1925, along with my grand- and great-grandparents in the Iannuzzi and Mazzà families, nearly 272,000 inhabitants of the province of Cosenza departed for North and South America. The number of inhabitants who remain in the province's urban core today, 260,000, is close to the same number of residents who left over a hundred years ago.[25]

In the Italy they left behind, a series of earthquakes rocked the foot of the boot, including the one in 1908 that nearly wiped out the entire town of Reggio Calabria, with 80,000 dead. While the powers that governed above ground were always invading the people's lives, so too did those beneath.

In 1943, Allied forces landed in the country. Only a few years later, in 1946, Italy pressed its citizens together like dozens of tomatoes pushed through a sieve. They abolished the monarchy through a referendum, passed a 1951 land reform law that helped many farmers and broke up the large estates (latifundia), and began looking toward more profitable agriculture and tourism too. By then, it was too late for both sides of my family. Their fates had been sealed by their own drive to break away from home for the sake of self-worth and survival.

In America's growing immigrant communities, it took a while for the flavors of the many provinces to blend, if they did at all. While "white" Americans would develop their own ready-made perceptions of Italian immigrants who largely originated from the southern region, lumping them all together, Italians busily disparaged one another, even in the States. When I asked my mother why we didn't eat much polenta, she recalled, "Your grandmother fried leftover polenta and wrapped it around salami. That's what I ate for lunch." My mother was ridiculed by schoolmates for eating this meal that had been perfected by centuries. Her peers may or may not have known that their jeers echoed the slur of *polentoni* ("polenta eaters," those from the northern provinces; "a heartless and cold people") that were slung out five thousand miles away. Further south, the complementary word *terroni* was used to denigrate "persons from the land," who were considered noisy and rude.

The referendum that blended the Italy my parents and ancestors knew, loved, and fought for, against, and over, was a reason for the country to celebrate the *Festa della Repubblica* every June 2. Yet today, Italy is still defined by and divided into those twenty boastful regions, with 110 provinces among them. A tour guide in Calabria once confided, "the Abruzzese and the Calabrese are known as the two most-stubborn peoples in Italy." As such, the regional dynamisms of Abruzzese and Calabrese pride, of people "strong and kind" and "tenacious in affection, proud in hatred," that had accumulated across two Italian provinces, across five hundred kilometers representing half the length and nearly the full breadth of the peninsula, would collide on the streets of Lorain, Ohio.

San Donato hillsides, 2024

Concetta (Ponzo) and Vincenzo Iannuzzi, early 1900s

Piazza Mese, Caulonia, 2018 *

The five Iannuzzi brothers. Enrico Iannuzzi is second from the right. Late 1910s.**

Antonio and Nellie Mazzà, circa 1940s

The Mazzà family, with Stella in background, next to Carmella (Nellie) and Antonio, circa 1930s–'40s.***

Enrico and Stella Januzzi, wedding day, 1925

Four Mazzà sisters

COMING TO LORAIN

The reasons for fleeing Italy were plentiful in the late 1800s and early 1900s. By why did so many of those who disembarked ships and trains arrive within the community of Lorain, Ohio? The reasons had to do with chain migration, and with the allure of better wages and working conditions than could be had in the mines. There was work in foresting and farming. Factories in Lorain built up staffing. Shipbuilding was increasing thanks to a land grant accepted by Augustus Jones and William Murdock out of the Northeast, and the fishing industries were trying to establish themselves too. The steel mill was recruiting immigrants from southern Europe, and well after World War II, paid for recruits from Mexico and Puerto Rico as well. Clean air might also have been a factor.

First settled in 1787 by Moravian missionaries, the town was established as Black River Village, renamed Charleston or Charlestown Village, and subsequently incorporated as Lorain in 1874. Lorain is situated at the mouth of the Black River twenty-five miles west of Cleveland, along Ohio's northern border with Lake Erie.

In *A Standard History of Lorain County, Ohio*, published in 1916, the editor writes Lorain was, "a dense, almost impenetrable forest of trees of immense size, covered every acre of the territory. The heroism of the families who plodded their way thither from New England, some on foot, some on horseback, and others in slowly moving carts, occupying more days in the journey than it takes hours now, is worthy of all praise. The rapid clearing of homesteads, and establishment of educational and religious institutions, scarcely find a parallel anywhere else in history."[26]

We too, could not imagine Lorain in its original wildness, knowing only how the land cleared along the Black River's banks served another purpose. Running somewhat parallel to the course of its water from north to south, Broadway Avenue was developed as Lorain's commercial thoroughfare. The road bisects parts of town from one another, and is home to many of the city's businesses. There, along a stretch of forty-eight blocks bustling small enterprises including my family's, Januzzi's Shoes, would thrive to serve the greater community.

The city's access to Lake Erie has always been its real attraction—for shipbuilding, for moving steel, for me, and, I suspect, for my grandparents. The water must have been a welcome sight to those who had once woken to long-traveled wafts of wind off the Italian sea, or the distinct scent of elicriso emanating off heated rocks. Though much of the Lorain waterfront wasn't available to ordinary citizens for their own dreams, as railroad companies and other entities bought up land along the water, plenty of them found some respite along Municipal Beach, as well as through ice sailing on the frozen lake and yacht clubs that organized as early as the 1920s. In 1916 and 1917, the mayor of Lorain, Leonard M. Moore, spurred the effort to purchase acreage along the north and south sides of West Erie Avenue for $53,000. The city named the parcel Lakeview Park and added a public bathhouse, diving board, and slide, the latter two of which no longer exist. In 1924, a tornado plowed through the park and up Broadway and forced reconstruction of the bathhouse. Its historic rose garden, a thriving destination still, was developed around the same time, in 1932. Years later, in the late 1970s, we would be cautioned away from the prolific use of drugs in the park. But it was our beach, and we inhabited it all the same with our own set of dangers at hand.

The city's shoreline at the Black River mouth also features a lighthouse, named the Lorain West Breakwater Light or Lorain Harbor Light, built in 1917 by the US Army Corps of Engineers. Once emitting a beacon for 18-25 miles, one can only imagine how this served as a steady, comforting light to any new arrivals. A community that cared. Its last light shone in 1966, 12 days before my birth. The lighthouse is listed on the National Register of Historic Places and offers tours during tranquil seas.

The first arrivals to the area included those of German, Scandinavian, Scottish, and Irish heritage. Lorain had been attracting immigrants since its youth—in fact, the city was named after Lorain County by Herman Ely, who thought the city reminded him of Lorraine, France. Perhaps this weak French connection attracted Enrico to Lorain. As industry steamrolled its way into Lorain, mostly because of its access to the lake and proximity to Cleveland and Pittsburgh, with it came the jobs, the recruiters, the immigrants, and the correspondence back home.

And as in other areas, with immigration to Lorain came xenophobia. The Sheffield Land Company supervised the development of South Lorain, where thick forests once stood, to house workers at the steel mill. However, the company also "pursued a policy of blatant containment of foreigners," with "American" districts between Pearl and Grove and "foreigners" located between Vine and Pearl. After the company went into receivership, these policies were disregarded, but not the discrimination they planted in the minds of immigrants.[27]

Industry

The first sailing vessel launched from Lorain in 1819. But soon trade entities included the B&O Railroad, such as the ten-mile line of the Lake Shore & Tuscarawas Valley Railway, which opened in 1873 with a northern terminus at Black River Harbor in Lorain. The city's population would grow "230% in the course of ten years (1890-1900)"[28] thanks to The American Shipbuilding Company, begun in Cleveland in 1888 and opened in the Lorain yard in 1898; Hayden Brass Works on Elyria Avenue, which in 1883 was the town's largest employer; The Thew Shovel Company; stove companies including the

American Stove Works, plant built in 1894; and the steel plant, established in 1895 by the Johnson Steel Company to produce steel pipe and rails. One steel company become another, from Lorain Steel to United States Steel Company (U.S. Steel) and by 1904, the mill was run by the National Tube Company, a subsidiary of U.S. Steel. National Tube built settlement houses for many of their workers and families, especially immigrants, to aid in learning a new language and adjusting to life in the States. Their employment offices often posted news in six languages, accommodating for all. Fortunes rose and fell with the mill, whose property ran along the river and the city's south side for about three miles. For decades, residents grew accustomed to the grit, the "hells' aroma," as poet Harry Youtt once called it, and the orange smoke that permeated every clothesline. Over a hundred years later, by 2008, the furnaces were silenced. The mill, by that time named Republic Steel, closed in 2016. But not before helping to generate thousands of jobs, as did the Ford Motor Company, for immigrants and their families. That sustainability in employment helped many other supporting businesses to thrive—after all, the mill workers needed shoes, steel-toed ones from Januzzi's Shoes, and bread, from DeLuca's Bakery.

In nearby Cleveland, the area of town now known as Little Italy was one of five original settlements of Italians in the city, including many from Abruzzo, as well as skilled artisans from Naples who worked for the Lakeview Marble Works. This area, often called "Murray Hill" after one of its cross streets, was the site of another important industrial occurrence: the invention of a macaroni machine.

The name Vitantonio, for many, brings to mind an electric pizzelle maker. But on his way to creating the pizzelle maker, tinkerer Angelo Vitantonio, a resident of the Murray Hill, also played around with a hand-cranked pasta machine. According to *Italian-Americans and Their Communities of Cleveland* by Gene Veronesi, infinite pounds of pasta were cranked out on this machine. Italian women still rejoice at the time it saves—then return to hand-rolling for *pici* and *strozzapreti*. Though Vitantonio's VillaWare manufacturing later also produced a pizzelle maker, my mother commanded an Imperia brand with a "three-year guarantee" which is now in my possession. Her mother's old cast-iron press remains in my brother's home.

While the influence of Cleveland as a destination for Italians cannot not be understated, especially given its larger railroad connections, Italians also reached for smaller towns in Ohio and Pennsylvania like Lorain.

For most, Lorain wasn't a reminder of Italy, though on a bright June day, Lake Erie might sparkle like the Adriatic or Ionic seas. Rather, it was an opportunity to support and feed a family, a prospect that for many Italian immigrants had been eliminated overseas and even in other parts of the US. It was a place where an unskilled steel worker might find opportunity in an industrial center, or a talented artisan might become a tailor, shoemaker, baker, or seamstress, and might live with elbow room to spare alongside people of other ethnicities attempting to do the same.

Italian American Mutual Aid Societies and Other Cultural Outlets

The immigrants who settled in Lorain were distrustful of handouts from governmental factions, so when they fell on hard times, they turned to one another. As they had in their homeland.

To aid the working poor in Italy, social associations were formed. "The Italians of Abruzzo were exposed early on in their original Italian villages and towns to a rich and sophisticated associational life. The workers association begun in 1880 in the small town of Spoltore, in Abruzzo, was open to men and women workers, offered sick and death benefits to its members and a constitutional structure that had 125 written rules of membership."[29] There existed class solidarity and care for the worker, as well as an appreciation for the value of work. And societies could meet under the guise of aid and shift suspicion away from what some might perceive as a political gathering. Membership in these associations, which my grandparents claimed, dwindled depending on the season, and eventually, on the working conditions. *La Società Operaria di Mutuo Soccorso di Spoltore*, founded in 1880, operates today on a smaller scale to bring the community together, demonstrating the motto about the Abruzzese as *forze e gentile*, strong and kind.

This instinct was also reflected in my paternal grandmother's and father's continued insistence, "family is everything." In Lorain's growing immigrant population, Italian social and mutual aid clubs and fraternal organizations, modeled on those back home, came into prominence. They were created out of necessity to help those in need, and were also a place to gather one's pride by joining hands with other Italians to honor the good works that had been done. These "fourth places"—for Italians, church was always the third space, after home and work—eventually became the site of weddings, fundraisers, community presentations, and holiday gatherings.

The Sons of Italy, founded in America in 1905, states in their bylaws that a member "propugnates (by means of defending) all those causes which can concur to demonstrate that Italians possess such qualities of mind and heart which compel to consider him not only a precious worker, but also an efficient factor of progress and social greatness."[30]

By 1922, the Italians of Lorain had begun to organize, and planned a celebration for Discovery Day in honor of Christopher Columbus. During the parade, American and Italian flags were displayed side by side as the Lorain Boys' Band, headed by a Cleveland Italian, led an assortment of Italian groups, including the Sons of Italy, through Washington Park. "The Italian band played the National Anthem of Italy" and later a large fireworks display would take place at the city field, accompanied by more Italian bands.[31]

In 1921, the Vittoria Lodge was formed, followed by Anchorian Lodge in 1932. Four years later, these lodges combined under one roof at 221 West 15th Street. Several Mazzà aunts would head up their auxiliaries. And the next set of members undertook painstaking work to document the area's history, identifying the earliest of bakery owners, Joe Galasso in 1896, the first macaroni factory, opened by the Gloriso Brothers in 1907, and the first shoe repair, by Angelo Trigilio in 1906. The Lorain Abruzzi Lodge, fashioned in 1935, formed a Ladies' Auxiliary, Società Femminile Abruzzese, open to all women natives of the Abruzzi region and their descendants. My grandmother, Raffaela DeLuca, owned medals marking her as a founding member. An early photo from 1934 shows hundreds of Abruzzese showing up in suits and dresses for a formal meeting outdoors with other Italian clubs.

In the early 1930s, "2,751 people of Italian descent resided in Lorain of which 1,137 were foreign-born. At this time, Italians comprised 9.78 percent of foreign-born ethnic residents of Lorain,"[32] out of a population of 44,000. Italian Mutual Benefit Society laid out plans for a lend-a-hand club, while directory listings for other Italian clubs in that era included the Mafalda social club, named presumably after Princess Mafalda of Savoy who went on to speak out against Hitler. Ella and Palma Mazzà were both active there. The Sons of Italy's Vittoria Lodge was located on Livingston Ave, along with the Salvo Lodge, a women's offshoot, the Italian American Citizens club on 17th Street, and the Società Abruzzesi on Broadway. Italian American veterans of

World War II met to apply for a charter to the Italian American Veterans post in 1945. And by 1948, the Montenero Society, organized by those originating from Montenero Val Cocchiara on the Abruzzo-Molise border, celebrated their one-year anniversary.

As of 1988 The Sons of Italy; the Montenero Club, the Abruzzesi Club; and the I.A.V. were still operating as places for Italian Americans to gather and celebrate their heritage.[33] Several Italian American media sources also carried forth news, including the Lion's Roar, IAV Local, and a broadcast on WCPN out of Cleveland for *Italian Hour with J. Giuliano*.

The Abruzzesi Club played a large role in my mother's and grandmother's lives. My grandmother was a 1935 founder and active member of the Società Femminile Abruzzese, the women's branch of the social aid club. She won a baking contest in the early days, went on to become vice president in 1942, and three years later, chaired the tenth anniversary dinner and a 1945 victory day celebration, to no one's surprise. Spoltore itself had a strong tradition of helping families, and all that goodwill instilled in her by the Spoltorese had translated overseas. Decades later, after Raffaela had died, the Società Femminile Abruzzese would be issued a twenty-one-day suspension for "Sunday sale and consumption of liquor and sales to a non-member." [34] Under Raffaela's watch, that would have never occurred.

My mother's presence at many of those spaghetti dinners started her on the journey toward the kitchen. In her belongings years later, I discovered a pile of aprons with an explanation attached: "aprons I used when serving Italian dinners at the old St. Peters when I was in my twenties." She would become a one-woman Italian social and mutual aid society through her connections, correspondence, and conversations with friends, and through her contributions to church rituals and to her family.

This kinship between Italians extended to other cities as well, such as the Alta House in Cleveland, which was once a social settlement home for immigrants. The conception originated from Joseph Carabelli, a marble importer who helped find work for artisans.[35] Italian life was thriving in the early decades of the twentieth century, with Italian Americans contributing to the country's progress, the arts, and to the "social greatness" referred to in the Sons of Italy bylaws, for which Italians and their progeny are still known.

Italians, of course, were not the only immigrants in this new land, and benevolent and fraternal organizations like the Daughters of Scotia and the

Knights of Malta helped to unite and ground those of other backgrounds. At one time, Lorain boasted fifty-five such entities, and the gathering of so many representative cultural backgrounds was noticeable enough that in 1967, the city formed the Lorain International Festival. As Americans and Italians, all we knew of the other ethnicities was in the context of eating gyros, pierogies, pastelitos, and baklava. But the specialties on display at the festival represented Polish, Greeks, Bulgarians, Czechoslovaks, Croatians, Puerto Ricans, and many others. We bothered none with the geography, and greedily ate up all the culinary stores. My memories of that festival, coupled with my mother's and grandmothers' cooking, defined my early perspectives on food and the way taste connects us to time.

An Italian's Two Religions: Faith and Food

Along with its diverse cultural social organizations, Lorain also saw the rise of a wide variety of religious denominations, with churches such as Saints Peter and Paul Orthodox Church, St. John the Baptist Ukrainian Catholic Church–Byzantine Rite, Saint George Serbian Orthodox Church, and many others. The Roman Catholic congregations were no different, with each group seeking its own soulful solace.

The oldest Catholic church in Lorain, St. Mary's Roman Catholic Church, was founded by a reverend who, in 1873, began to serve residents living near the mouth of the Black River, visiting monthly. St. Joseph's Roman Catholic church's first service was held in the chapel of St. Joseph's Hospital, no longer in existence. The Church of the Nativity opened to serve the Catholic Polish demographic near the docks and the rolling mills. Next came Hungarian denominations looking for a spiritual home, followed by the Greeks, and with them Sts. Cyril and Methodius Parish, organized in 1905, and Holy Trinity Church. In 1900, St. John's Roman Catholic Church laid its cornerstone. But for me, it's hard to imagine other Catholic churches existed outside of St. Peter's Catholic Church. The church was central to my parents' upbringing and to the remainder of their days living in northeastern Ohio.

While in larger cities like New York City, many immigrants operated within colonies of people from the same origin, in a smaller city like Lorain, bumping up against the rituals of others helped Italians to define and cement their identities as Italian Americans while crossing over to other cultures. In the traditions of food and faith, Italian Americans found a home in Lorain where they could live within themselves without sacrificing everything once more.

St. Peter's Church, where both sides of my family belonged, was founded in 1909. Reverend John Salerno, of the southern Italian Basilica region, aided as community members organized and raised funds, through the diocese and surrounding Italian enclaves of Cleveland and Akron and through the Italian mutual aid societies, to build a new structure. It was completed in 1914 by Italian immigrants hoping to recreate their faith in this new land. The church sat on the 800 block of West 17th Street[36] three blocks from my mother's home. In the late twenties, my grandparents boasted that the church had a membership of one hundred families, according to former journalist Jim Mahoney in an undated *Lorain Journal* column.

My father was baptized at St. Peter's, and my siblings and I were, too. (My mother was born and baptized in Salineville). Both parents often returned or "snuck back" to Old St. Pete's in their later years to recapture a time when their ancestors thrived and the Italian community was strong. In 1936, Fr. O'Dea was named lead reverend. He went on officiate at my parents' wedding and remained a fixture at our family's home for many years. In 1951, parishioners received a statue of *Madonna del Popolo*, a replica of the one in Spoltore. We know Spoltore was an important origination point for many Lorainites, as the newspaper would often print news of arrivals from there, such as Aunt Mary DeLuca's sister, who arrived from "Spoltore Village." Residents in Lorain marked the *Feast of the Madonna del Popolo* in the "second annual observance of the statue's arrival." Out-of-town guests came from Spoltore to participate, and the night was capped off by fireworks shot over City Park.[37]

In 1962, before my parents moved from Lorain, they celebrated Christmas, possibly Midnight Mass, in the new church erected on its current site at Oberlin Ave and West 25th. When the Mazzà, Januzzis, and DeLucas died, the congregation observed their passing at Old St. Pete's.

The history of the Italians in Lorain, though, is intertwined with more than just one religion. There is the religion that fed my ancestors spiritually, and the one that fed them corporally; the religion of food.

Often, the two were celebrated together, as when St. Pete's held regular spaghetti dinners, where my grandmother Raffaela would join with other women of the parish to provide sustenance and generate funding. One of my mother's meatball recipes called for twenty pounds of ground meat to produce 240 meatballs; the quantity necessary to feed large bands of hungry Italians. When they weren't eating at home, at church, or the Italian social clubs, they were eating at any number of Italian establishments that also carried plenty of Italian *alimentari*, goods from Italy or imported from New York. One pizza and sandwich shop was owned by Pete D'Agnese, who in an interview told a local journalist: "Women have been seeking the fountain of youth at their drugstores ... It really lies in their food stores. The inner glow that they seek comes from within, not from a powder puff."[38]

In 1926, approximately twenty of Lorain's 150-plus retail grocery shops were owned by Italians, and the Italian population and stomachs would only grow from there. With the influx of Italians into Cleveland and the growing availability of goods from New York, Italians added to those local Italian resources with Pat Manaco's Grocery, the Manhattan Market, and the Four Winds Drive-In. In 1954, Louis Fuervando, Jay Telloni, and Yala Armelie opened Yala's Pizzaria (as spelled in *Lorain Journal* ads), which would later become our family's favorite, along with Eliseo's, because of its proximity to the shoe store. In the 1957 business directory, a few others were added, including my mother's stepfamily's bakery, DeLuca Bakery, where it's possible her pizza dough recipe originated.

But we know the best cooking started with memory and flourished in the home.

Società Abruzzese of Lorain, with Raffaela, Luigi, Jean, and Tony Deluca, 1934. Author believes two children to the far-left, middle are Jean and Tony. Raffaela is seated in black with back to camera. Luigi stands to right of Societa Abruzzese flag.

BECOMING ITALIAN

Layers of Ancestors

When Rafaella and Luigi moved to Lorain, they lived beneath the eaves of the home of Luigi's father, Antonio, along with Luigi's brother, James, and his wife, Catherine. Seven inhabitants were nestled inside a home of 1,200 square feet. The baking still occurred in the back of someone else's home up the street, while Luigi split off from the upstart bakery to pursue his own interests at the steel mill. Antonio, now widowed, remained head of the household. Somewhere around 1935, Luigi, Raffaela, Jean, and their new baby, my Uncle Tony, moved to 1132 West 17th Street. That home would continue to be occupied by members of the DeLuca family for the next eighty years.

Rafaella made the new house a home, with long tablecloths tatted with intricate flowering patterns, as well as smaller doilies, covering the furniture. This artwork—and it was art—was reminiscent of what one might see in the town of Scanno, Abruzzo, where thanks to wealth accumulated in ancient times, shops have always created and sold a variety of lacework in fabrics and jewelry. Because the town borders the national park of Abruzzo, sheep were often herded through seasonally, which helped such handicrafts to expand to other *paese*, or small towns, in the region. The nearby town of Pescocostanzo also lays claim to a focus on pillow-lace or bobbin lace. "Perhaps the most curious of all lace techniques, tatting has morphed from simple knots on a thread to one of the most expressive and personal of all textile techniques. Without needle, bobbins, or frame it requires only a single thread and a shuttle to hold and guide the thread as it is supported in the hand."[39]

Every woman from the area was expected to learn these ageless methods of weaving and to add to a collection of embroidered cloths. Raffaela was no exception. While the oversized steamer trunk in which she carried these precious fabrics now resides in my office, her trousseau takes up a home in my mother's cedar chest, where they remain sacrosanct. The collection includes lace-adorned aprons, a honeymoon nightshirt, and the tablecloths that always reappear at holidays, with several red wine stains as proof of their use. In sewing circles today, crafters are refashioning tablecloths like these into dresses and skirts, carrying this tradition into the next era.

Raffaela was a woman who knew how to work with her hands, and her knowledge did not go to waste. In addition to her lace handiwork, she also became known for her dedication to the Società Abruzzesi. She cooked to aid others, both there and at her church, and this feeding by faith had a profound influence on my mother. Of course, Raffaela also saw it as her duty to push my mother to succeed, in school and in work outside the home. Perhaps this is the reason my mother married later than her peers.

In 1939, Raffaela became a naturalized citizen of the United States. Soon, World War II loomed. Camp Perry, an hour's drive away, was activated in 1943 and eventually housed some two thousand Italian POWs. Certainly the knowledge of others from back home who had fought on the Italian side being held nearby as prisoners must have hung over any nearby Italians heads.

During wartime, women were needed to work. My mother, only seventeen, was finishing school, but Rafaella went to work at the Weitz Clothing Company as a seamstress—a natural outgrowth for someone whose hands once carved art out of string.

Given that she had lost ties to her family in Spoltore and her brothers remained in Columbiana County, for Raffaela, socializing revolved around the Abruzzesi Club and the Abruzzese customs that were refashioned there, like the *Madonna del Popolo* procession. Neither Raffaela nor my mother ever envisioned that I would one day carry my grandmother's prayer card from the original church as I tread on the stone walkways where that ritual of *Madonna del Popolo* parades originated. Or that I'd meet the cousins who had taken part in those processions and breathe in the same air as her parents did inside the Baroque-style San Panfilo. There, the Madonna's golden statue stood surrounded by walls and columns of bas relief. The sculpture sparkled with an Adriatic light and caused tears to flood my eyes. I imagined my eyes connecting me to my grandmother's similarly warm brown ones when she first caught sight of the statue. That same perspective linked me to my mother, as she worshipped the *Madonna del Popolo* into her late years.

My step-grandfather Luigi was handsome, with a roundish face, elfin ears, and sleepy, dreamy eyes. His cigarette smoking gave off an air of being cool; little did we know the damage it would inflict later.

Stepfamilies are now as they were then—hard to define. While Italians like to say everyone is family, it didn't always feel like the case. Two years after my mother, Jean, was born, Raffaella and Luigi bore one son together, our beloved Uncle Tony. It must have been challenging to decide on methods of discipline when raising children in a blended family, and at times, my mother recalled overhearing Luigi say, "she's your daughter, you decide." The "she" and the dispossessive "your" hurt. But she never turned away from the opportunity to learn from her mother's adopted kin—Uncle James and Aunt Catherine and their children Rita, Leo, and Leonard, as well as cousins of Luigi's, Uncle John, Aunt Mary, and their children Linda, Bobby, and Frank. While a stepfamily may be separated by blood and genes, cultural traditions can and do tie them back together, as does what eventually becomes an enduring love, especially for food.

Growing up, the DeLucas were family in the same way we were tight with our godparents' families. These "cousins" were my best friends, and sometimes first crushes. And we revered Uncle Tony for his fandom of the Cleveland Browns and the jokes he told in our ears. My mother's stepfamily was no different, and my father, who always touted a philosophy of "family is all," learned a new definition of family and loved them as his own. We appeared at their homes and sat next to them at the table every Sunday, every holiday, and on vacations.

Funny and tender, Luigi protected and supported his family through his dedication to work. A longtime employee at National Tube, over the years he would progress from machine operator to mechanic to boilermaker, while also minding the roses that vined alongside the western edge of his property. In the back of their eventual home on 17th Street, a run of Concord grapes grew. Our family referred to Concords as "Italian grapes" mainly because Luigi grew them for wine, proudly sharing with relatives and friends. Luigi worked for thirty-eight years at the steel mill and retired with a tidy pension. For someone who had flitted off from Spoltore as a bird of passage and married a hometown girl, he had achieved an existence worthy of an immigrant, surrounded by his brother, father, and their families. An existence many would emulate over the years.

Luigi and Raffaela's backyard also contained a rectangular brick oven, a feature with Italian origins. How much she utilized the backyard oven is unclear. However, given her service to her community, it's no surprise Raffaela turned out bread daily, inspired by her in-laws' bakery. No longer in use by the time we played kickball behind the house, the oven became home or second base instead.

I have no recollection of my mother baking bread, though she wrote out a recipe for large quantities, so bread must have been had in the household. Of course, with her uncle's bakery a mere ten blocks away, the importance of supporting her family always had to be balanced with going it alone. DeLuca's bakery bread was a centerpiece at the family table.

When my older sister, brother, and I were little, my mother signed us up for swim lessons at the YMCA in downtown Lorain. Despite my abhorrence and fear of the water, I overcame the odds and learned to swim, most likely because I knew at the end of each lesson, we would be treated to a stop at DeLuca's Bakery.

The business that began in 1926 as *De Luca Bros.* continued to grow with James at the helm. Eventually, with his father widowed and living with him, he relocated to 1512 Broadway, where by 1945, the business was listed as *DeLuca Bakery*. When his two sons came along, he renamed it *DeLuca and Sons*. We only knew it as *the bakery*.

The location we frequented, at 8th and Reid Avenue (former home of the Herman F. Probst Confectionary from 1945 to 1958 and the Handy Pantry Delicatessen from 1958 to1959), opened in 1960. By 1965, the bakery also celebrated the grand opening of a new branch, with a carryout buffet, at 38th and Oberlin Ave. Surely, my mother learned how to feed the masses not only from her own mother, but also by watching the bakers do so. The buffet included the bean salads we Italians always ate, lasagne, gnocchi, stuffed peppers (for which my mother never even had a recipe), chicken paprikas, stuffed cabbage, ravioli, and more. Many of the recipes my mother inherited from her mother, from Aunt Mary, and from Aunt Catherine DeLuca probably originated from their work cooking for crowds at their clubs, the church, or the bakery. Though Luigi did not have a financial relationship with his brother's bakery, my mother recalled standing in line for their famous Italian bread often. She was highly influenced by Raffaela's baking prowess and the bakery's sheer output of bread and Italian pastries—cannoli, gnocchi, lemon squares (named *Lemon Squares DeLuca* in my mother's archives), biscotti by Cousin Frank. The nut rolls showcased in old DeLuca's ads are instantly recognizable to me as my mother's, reminiscent of Czech and Slovak kolaches. This adoption of new family, this assumption of the identity of others, could be seen as a loss, or a gain. If you've ever eaten one of my mother's nut rolls, you'll know my answer. When I say we were *something Italian*, we had a little *something* of everyone else in us too.

According to the Lorain Historical Society, the bakery was eventually sold to someone who renamed it *Avonti's*, after the well-regarded Studebaker the owner admired. The new owner obviously wasn't Italian enough to know the car model was spelled *Avanti*—meaning forward, onward, or after you.

Raffaela and Luigi DeLuca in their side yard with homemade wine, late 1950s

Lorain National Tube postcard, 1950s

ONE TASTE

is worth a

Thousand Pictures

DeLuca's "ITALIAN BREAD"

One delicious bite reveals a new world of taste sensation — with this unique, individual flavor. DeLuca's Italian Bread captures the continental cuisine at its finest. Zesty, tangy .. yet full - bodied and mellow — Italian Bread is delightfully different. For the life of your meal .. and the meal of your life — try Italian Bread — it's the only real Italian bread made by true Italians.

Open Sunday — 7:30 'TIL 2:30

DeLuca & Sons Bakery

Stop In After Church

1512 Bdwy. CH 5-4081

Closed Wed.

OPEN SUNDAY   OPEN SUNDAY

DeLuca Bakery ad, Lorain Journal, May 16, 1959

Family and friends gathered for Jean Giuliani's First Communion, 1935

My father's father, Enrico, arrived in Lorain on a cold December day in 1920, about three years before Stella's family landed there. Tall and erect, with chiseled features and daring brown eyes, he was nothing like the London Office of Civil Affairs' description of Calabria Zone men: "dark and whiskered, short and wiry."[40] Enrico lived at first with his brother, Minotti ("Mike"), and although in San Donato di Ninea he boasted about working as a cobbler since the age of 11, in Lorain he was first employed as a railroad trackman/section hand for B&O. He later worked at National Tube as a repairman in the 1920s, earning $1,594 per year. Mike worked as a repairman too, presumably for the mill. By 1925, Mike and Enrico lived at 3002 Caroline Avenue under the name Jannuzzi, in a Sears and Robuck–manufactured home with two bedrooms upstairs where boys and girls shared a room. Sometimes, as stated by Anita, "when cousins visited, there were four to five children to a double bed."

According to my grandmother Stella's accounts, she lived in Lorain in 1923 with Antonio and Nellie, though her marriage certificate claims Lamberton, Pennsylvania as home while working at a bank. Her two sisters, Mary and Ella, were also listed in the Lorain business directory, having found work as a machine operator and teacher, respectively. In the 1930 census, Gus (aka August), Palma, and Frank also appear on record. All four sisters were expert seamstresses and later went on to work in that industry, with Ella meeting often with the Gemm Tatter's club. Stella's father retired from National Tube in 1938. Her parents would live for another decade or so, celebrating their 50th wedding anniversary at 3127 Denver Avenue, before both died of chronic pulmonary congestive failure. It's not hard to draw a line from the coal mine dust they had inhaled in their youth to this respiratory disease. I have no additional information on Frank, but Gus married Bessie Johnson in 1930, eventually moved to Cleveland, and died in 1966. Palma, who once declared to the school newspaper she would "take up story writing," also moved to Cleveland, where she lived in Little Italy, and today, her son lives there as well. Ella eventually moved to Wooster, becoming more active in politics as a congressman's committee chairperson, while Mary, once known for her jigs at social events, remained in Lorain. When I look at pictures of me with my sisters, I'm often reminded of the photos of these four aunts—astute, determined women whose roundish faces reflected the Greek origins of their family's Caulonia home. My father shook his head at the arrival of each of his female progeny, knowing what he was up against.

In Lorain, Enrico and Stella crossed paths, perhaps through an Italian connection, a Calabrian association, a link to Pennsylvania through his brothers, or the fact that her father, Antonio, now worked at the steel mill too. An interview with my uncle, Albert, in 1997 describes how Enrico had seen Stella a few times around Lorain, and observed her close to home to see if she could bake.[41] The answer was "yes." Stella, a petite bookkeeper with piercing brown eyes and stark cheekbones, married Enrico in August 1925 at the age of twenty-three at the original St. Peter's in Lorain, ministered in faith by Fr. John Kubicki. In an interview years later, she would tell a reporter how she thought Enrico "was one of the most handsome men I'd ever seen." When the two wed, Stella had already assimilated into American culture, while Enrico stubbornly and proudly held tight to his Italian roots—my siblings and I absorbed that *testa dura* (hardheaded) trait from one of the best. He studied English at his new wife's insistence in "good time, by listening to others and through marriage," as he said in the same newspaper interview.[42] Though he didn't look much like the London civil office proclaimed a Calabrian should Enrico and his family members did embody their personality description: "a man of few words, and those straight to the point. He is scornful of comfort and luxury, which never enter his own life, and indifferent to pain and suffering."[43] We were often told our family's name change had occurred at Ellis Island (where a misspelling occurs on the ship's manifest and other documents). At first, Enrico and Stella used both family surnames, Iannuzzi and Jannuzzi. By 1936, Enrico had become a naturalized citizen as "Jannuzzi" and by the 1940s he casually went by several spellings. Oddly enough, in 1951, my father, Ettore, submitted paperwork for his own official name change from Iannuzzi to Januzzi as well. The fate of the family name had been sealed—a decision I understand, and regret.

At their home at 506 West 28th Street, an early residential building in that locale, Enrico and Stella began their shoe enterprise in the basement, replicating Enrico's skills from back home by repairing soles. Soon after their marriage, my grandmother gave birth to two children: my uncle Albert in 1926, and my father, Ettore—whose name translated from ancient Greek meant "loyal" or "holding fast"—in 1928. A month before Albert's birth, the couple disseminated a printed flyer advertising *Enrico's Electrical Shoe*

Repair Shop. Despite his early reasonable success, Enrico's father, Vincenzo, wrote that he was saddened to hear Enrico had been "unwell with *melanconico.*" Melancholy. How could he not be, given the number of troubling dispatches exchanged between father and son? Enrico was distressed by the imposing need to work harder and the burden he put upon himself to provide, both for the one family intact in Lorain, and for the family that had scattered.

The year my father was born, Vincenzo wrote to Enrico about the high prices in Calabria. The letter contained mostly a list: "meat 4 lire/kg, wine 4 lire, cheese 20 lire, macaroni 4 lire, flour 2 lire/kg, bread 2 lire/kg. I do not remember a bad time like this." Meanwhile, Enrico was sending money home by the hundreds of lire, and Vincenzo begged of him, "your mother hopes to see you soon in Italy." Instead, Enrico sent lire home for the family to purchase a pig, according to a letter Vincenzo sent in 1925. In the early 1930s, Vincenzo told his son, "you see the people and the famine and you won't believe it." Oddly enough, Enrico's sister, Paolina, had disobeyed her husband—something about not doing his wash—and soon the brothers banded together to buy her a home. Francesco remained in Argentina with his wife, his son, Orlando, and his brother Amerigo, too, who by now had contributed to the San Isidro household, which was somewhat of a surprise given how he had fled. He and Stella also sent money the family Amerigo's had left behind in Italy. Many years later, Concetta Macrini, Amerigo's great-granddaughter, shared with me that my ancestors' letters referred to Amerigo as *nasconi*—a nickname for "big nose," but also a derogatory term for the man that had evaded his family, abandoning his children, Concetta and Vincenzo. Several in Vincenzo and Concetta's lineage would be named *Enrico* or *Stella* after the beneficence of my grandparents. And the letters of gratitude from Vincenzo to his son for monies sent were too numerous to count.

By 1933, with a good deal of shoe business to be had, the shoe cobbling and repair shop was moved to a four hundred-square-foot building at 2839 Broadway (later the home of Lusca's Pizza). In a location teeming with other small businesses, such as Woodlings Confectionary and a barber shop, Stella "womaned" the counter, took in orders, and sewed while Albert and Ettore attended to school. Enrico returned home from the mill to repair shoes at night, competing with other shoe repair shops that proliferated the strip. He hired his godson, Orlando Petrillo, as his first employee.

Amid Enrico's early starts, his family back home still experienced trouble. There was some battle fought between Francesco and a brother he alluded to as "he doesn't deserve to be named." There's no indication as to whether this was Vittorio, back in Italy, or Amerigo, perhaps having fled once more. The letters from Italy ended in 1936. In his last letter, Vincenzo wrote, "the money you sent me is almost finished because as soon as it arrived, I bought some coal, after which I felt bad but God will take care of us too. Warmest regards also from your mother." Vincenzo died in 1936. It's presumed Enrico's mother died shortly after.

The '30s weren't so kind to Enrico either, working in a shop with no running water, challenged by the Depression years. He used a government loan to quickly repay debts on the home they lost. During one Easter, Stella required hospital admittance. With no insurance, the family went door-to-door soliciting funds.

In contrast to my mother's family with tight-knit social clubs that might offer aid, my grandfather was proud. And everyone else struggled too. While his son, Albert, was stationed with the Army in Texas during World War II, overseeing German POWs who repaired shoes, others back home used war ration cards and were forced to decide on shoes—or food.

By the 1940s, amidst dust from sanding of shoes and leather particles, Enrico had moved the shoe repair to 26th and Broadway, where he and his wife leased a storefront with a brick-front and cement-block-side from 1948 to 51 for $70/month and began to sell new shoes for the first time. The year prior, in 1947, Enrico had earned $500 from National Tube, and made a net profit of $1700 from the shop. Soon, he purchased the building that housed the store and the lot to the north as well, to construct a combined shoe and shoe repair business under one roof, for a tidy sum of $23,000. In the early fifties, after the boys had graduated from high school, they were included in the company name—*Enrico Januzzi and Sons*—but Stella would not yet get her due.

From there, the family continued to expand their literal and figurative shoeprint. By the 1950s, coming out of the recession, and the '60s, they owned three lots. The city directory confirmed the existence of a retail shoe store, where Enrico put in an average of sixty hours a week. They promoted the enterprise as the largest independent shoe seller in Ohio at the time, and one of their frequent customers would go on to fame as a writer of poems and greeting card verses—Helen Steiner Rice. Here, as they incorporated into Januzzi's Shoes, my grandmother finally got her due. With Enrico serving as president, my still-single father as vice president, and my recently married Uncle Albert as secretary, Stella was named treasurer. It wasn't uncommon for women in those days to perform bookkeeping tasks, and to be charged with the keeping of the change. As much success as they enjoyed, in the early '60s the business received notices from creditors like International Shoe Company asking to see a 40 percent profit instead of 27.5 percent. Couldn't the shoe store see to raising their prices a little more? "Hardly anyone in the community would notice it," they wrote.[44] My grandfather or one of his sons wrote across the typed letter: "Januzzi's will continue to sell for less—always has, always will." I'm certain this was Enrico's creed.

By the 1970s the business was comprised of two locations: the main Januzzi's Shoes, and Januzzi's Downtown, located further south on the same thoroughfare at 440 Broadway and run by the oldest male cousin. That was always how Italian families operated—the oldest and the males came first.

The brothers and father would continue their expansion to Jaeco Shoes in south Lorain in the late '70s. That store became the sponsor for my bowling team in my teen years, and was also where my sisters and I were highly influenced by the fashion preferences of the Puerto Ricans who lived in the area and demanded high heels and platform shoes. Later iterations included a new store, Januzzi's Select-A-Shoe (think DSW before its time), in Sheffield Center in 1981 and partnerships with Jax Men's Wear, a short-lived outlet in Elyria, and others.

Through the early years of establishing himself and his family, Enrico wished to return to San Donato to see his father, but Vincenzo insisted it was too soon. He worked hard to establish himself and instead, sent lire. The money never stopped, with 250 lire, 150 lire, 1,000 lire making its way overseas until his father's death sometime around 1936, fifteen years after Enrico had left to shop for his fortunes elsewhere. Grandpa Enrico did return to Italy in 1953 on a grand tour, along with Stella and his friend Al DeSantis, my father's godfather, to handle his sister's estate. My father later accompanied my grandfather on another trip in 1960, where he recalled, "Pop made Kool-Aid for all" as the relatives kept coming to meet them.

Ettore, Enrico, Albert, and Stella Januzzi in the shoe repair shop, 1940s

Enrico and Sons store window, 1950s

Enrico's Electrical Shoe Repair Shop, May 8, 1926

Januzzi's Shoes building, 1950s

Enrico Januzzi with his original sewing machine, 1980. ****

Stella Januzzi, Florida, 1960s

My memories of Stella are rooted in my father's tales of her influence. As the fortunes of the town, the nearby steel mill, and the shoe store rose and fell, how did Stella have time to devote to cooking arancini (rice croquettes) and her famed fried twists, advising my mother while managing family and business affairs, and keeping her foot on the pedal of the sewing machine that kept the Januzzi family cobbling soles for years? Though Stella appeared with her husband and sons in black-and-white photos, she never seemed to receive the credit she so deserved. Years later in her death notice, all her accomplishments, from the family's move from the far regions of Italy to the coal mines of western Pennsylvania to working nonstop to raise a family and manage a store, were packed into one single phrase, recognizing her as "co-founder" of Januzzi's Shoes.

Born in 1928, my mother, Jean, possessed a sense of propriety, perfectionism, and vivaciousness that grew from the dictates of prior times—out of the Great Depression, two world wars, a birth father dead, a mother separated from the homeland for good. If "Spoltore, near Pescara, in Abruzzi" was always in the back of her mind, in the foreground was her mother's early mantra, "You no speak Italian at home. Only English." Taking on the role of teacher at an early age, she would also learn, as an American, to never shrink away from her chance to shine.

Her early years were spent among many other young Italians, related or not. She excelled in school, where she joined the a capella choir and was a member of the National Honor Society at Lorain High School, graduating two years ahead of another famed writer, Toni Morrison. She taught summer school at St. Pete's, and participated in the Young Ladies Sodality, the church group responsible for crowning May Queens, in her twenties. My mother had a flair for the dramatic, pushing us into summer stock theatre. She also possessed a voice all her own, a mix of Keely Smith and Julie Andrews. With facial features that were not as hardened as those of her immigrant parents, she was well-known for her smile and for her short stature, which she veiled behind long coats, hats, and heels with an impeccable style of dress. Her skinny legs were a direct descendent of her father's. No hair or hem ever moved out of place, and yet, the passion my siblings and I have for sports and competition also originated with her.

During high school she worked at King's Shoe Store part-time, and following graduation, spent a year at the American News Company bookkeeping and packaging magazines. In 1946, the same year Italy became a republic, my mother started her official working career. She was employed as a clerk (typing and shorthand) for American Stove Company in Lorain, a company whose name was later changed to Magic Chef. For decades after the factory's closure, one of her many social groups was the "Magic Chef girls," who met for dinners and what one newspaper called a "gabfest"— a description to which my siblings and I could attest. With a buoyant personality, she collected friends easily along the way, and socialized not only with Italians, but also with many others who would become her closest friends and club members. After a few years at Magic Chef, she was sent to learn key punching on IBM machines in Cleveland. When Magic Chef closed its local operations, she moved on to employment at St. Joseph's Hospital. In a podcast interview in 2024, Adriani Trigiani, the Italian American author of *Big Stone Gap*, said that young Italian women were drawn (or pushed by their mothers) to working in office settings. Their mothers would have admonished, "if you want to clean, clean our house. Otherwise, go find work that's productive." In an office environment, Adriani said, "They could be in charge. And dress up." Nothing summarized my mother more.

The 1950s brought political and social changes that resulted in expanded federal education funding. The US government funded programs to attract more teachers to the field, such as Kent State University's Cadet Teacher Program. My mother enrolled and attended extension classes part-time from 1958 to 1963 in a satellite classroom at Elyria High to earn a teaching certificate. After that, she found herself daily in the front of a class, reading to a group of precocious first graders. Her final teaching stint, for which she was paid between $3,600 and $4,200 a year, was spent at St. John's Roman Catholic Church on 36th Street. Formerly St John the Baptist, the church kept records in Latin until 1950, and had originally been established for the area's Germans, Hungarians, Croatians, Slovakians, and Irish. By the time she taught there, a blending of cultures had occurred. Her students called her Ms. Jean Giuliani, and were lucky to have her as teacher—though they may have felt unlucky, as we did later, whenever we slacked on our schoolwork. Her school supervisor, Sister Augustine, once wrote to her about my mother's home with Ettore, *I'll bet every crack and crevice are in perfect order.*

Though we never had passports as kids, my parents stamped travel into our being. My mother's itineraries as a young woman included a dude ranch at Lake Luzerne, New York, and high times in New York City in 1951, where she took in the follies, attended the taping of TV shows, visited Coney Island, drank cocktails at the Piccadilly Circus Bar, and ended her journal entries with "out like a light." Though she was in the same city where her mother and father had first landed in the New World, a visit to Ellis Island didn't enter her mind. After all, what would be the value? That was everything they had tried to leave behind. Besides, the immigration depot was rapidly falling into disrepair. In 1957, my mother and two friends drove the famous Route 66 to California, with stops everywhere along the way. Her lone regret was not seeing Frank Sinatra perform in Vegas, since he wasn't on the road at September's end that year. These experiences seemed to feed her desire and love for the glamorous, something her mother had never dreamed of.

Cooking at home wasn't necessarily a focus—she wasn't married, and besides, Raffaela and her many step-aunts were still alive to cook for the family. Aside from the father she'd never known, she had yet to experience anyone missing around her table. To conquer cooking, she would first need to experience that loss, of missing the people who once prepared meals for you; missing those you once prepared them for. Until then, she deemed the important task to be bringing a paycheck home, contributing to the household, knowing how much her parents struggled. And she never let go of that sparkle that originated from within. In another year or two, that trait would catch the attention of a man the *Lorain Journal* called one of the county's most eligible bachelors in 1956, who proclaimed, "I think all girls are wonderful."[45]

Born January 15, 1928, Ettore had a bit of a sweetheart face, with a pointed chin and a pudge to his cheek. He owed his countenance to the diverse ethnic influences in Calabria, and his profile resembled his mother's, whose family had lived closer to the Ionian Sea. He was baptized at St. Pete's, and his godfather, Orlando Petrillo, would become one of my father's idols, having flown thirty-five bombing missions during World War II and been awarded numerous medals.

Ettore played the bass drum at Lorain High and also excelled at mechanical drawing—later, we would turn to him whenever we needed a map drawn anywhere, or when we needed cardboard cut for school projects. An excellent student in his own right, he was literally born into the shoe business. One might think that was a blessing, but in later years, he confesssed that he would have liked to be a history teacher. He was always interested in the military and, of course, in Italy's history, from its centuries of dominance by others to its modern independence. I'm certain this propensity was driven by his travels, and when I was a child, our family trips weren't just to the beach or amusement parks— time with my father always contained some element of learning about the past, whether from historical sites, battlefields, or even phone books. As we embarked on the Spirit of '76 tour and trips to Williamsburg and Washington, DC, he would page through the phone books in every dingy motel room, looking for Januzzis. Maybe, he'd call them. Or he'd say to us, "See there, how they spelled this? This might be your great-uncle so-and-so's second cousin." Oftentimes, he was right. *Remember your roots* was the rally call no matter where we traveled or what game we played.

As a teen, Ettore brought money into the home by riding his bike to Speigelberg Orchards to pick peaches. The fields there are nonexistent now. And of course, he worked at the shoe store. His rise there and his prowess at running a business would grow in parallel with the store as it expanded. Like his mother, he treasured the bookkeeping work. The dance of numbers in the columns. The *click-click* of the mechanical adding machine. Outside the store, he treasured nothing more than the outdoors, small game hunting with his father and his two young beagles. When he came of age, he enlisted in the draft. By the time the US entered the Korean War conflict, he had served for two years stationed in Ft. Knox, had been promoted to PFC, and had applied to officer candidate school.

What little we knew of Ft. Knox as kids involved gold bricks, so naturally we assumed our father served to protect the gold. However, that wasn't the case. He was part of the 3rd Armored Division, where more than three hundred thousand soldiers would be trained before assignment to their

Jean Giuliani, in coat and hat, circa 1932

Jean Giuliani, school picture, 1930s

DeLuca Family, Left to right: Jean Giuliani, Raffaela, Tony, Luigi DeLuca. 1930s

Jean Giuliani, Picadilly Circus, NYC, 1951

Luigi DeLuca, Jean Giuliani and Raffaela DeLuca, 1950s

Jean Giuliani, at work, 1950s

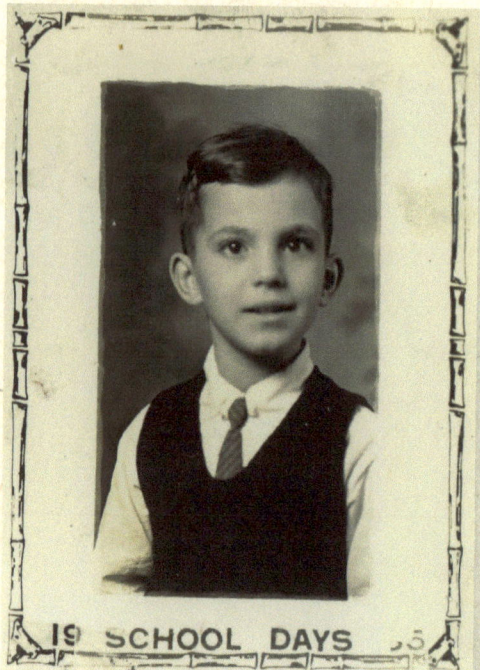

Ettore Januzzi, school days, 1934

Albert and Ettore Januzzi, 1930s

Ettore Januzzi, high school graduation, 1946

Ettore Januzzi, Oldsmobile Convertible, 1950s

Ettore Januzzi in Rome, 1960

Ettore Januzzi, far right, with Enrico Januzzi, second from left, at the famed Checco er Carrittiere in Rome, a trattoria where the poet, Trilussa, made his second home. 1960

permanent stations. When the Korean War began in 1950, those armored trainers from the 72nd Tank Battalion fought with distinction in Korea until the cease-fire in 1953.[46] My father would serve for two years in the supply division stateside, where he learned skills that would later serve him well as he managed a large household with four girls (enough to "spend all the gold in Ft. Knox," as he once said). He was released in 1953, rescinded his application for officers' school, and returned home, where he would remain on reserve for five years.

I once heard my father reminisce about the long drive from Lorain to Ft. Knox in his mother's borrowed 1950 Plymouth Special. He wasn't nostalgic for the wartime, only for the drive through the rolling hills of Kentucky. Like his father, he was drawn to places where the eye might wander and the mind might dream. He was a man born with an artist's heart into a world that asked otherwise. But he was tough, too. Once, when working in the family's store, he was approached by a young boy with a gun. It wasn't until he attempted to wrest the gun out of the youth's hands that he realized it was a toy gun.[47] The boy cried relentlessly while pinned to the wall of the shoe store. Dad would go to great lengths to protect what was his.

Back in Lorain, in 1956 Ettore was voted one of Lorain County's most eligible bachelors—a little like the famed Casanova, who also spent time in Calabria. He proudly wore this mantle for some time, but eventually something else lodged inside of him. Possibly his mother had tired of him living at home, or perhaps it was just that the right Italian girl came along.

Recollections differ on how my parents met. At Lorain High, they were a half-year apart, with my father graduating in '45 B and Mom in '46 A. Probably they knew each other through St. Pete's, or through their Italian connections. Perhaps Jean needed a shoe repaired. Lorain was small enough. Everyone knew who the bachelors were, and who the most eligible young women were too. My parents enjoyed dates at the Lorain Palace, the Tower Drive-In theatre, and most likely, riding in my dad's powder-blue convertible to The Hoop drive-in or to Lakeview Park, where the colored fountain had "60 changes of water design and color effects every six minutes."[48]

In the summer of 1960, in a voyage that might have been seen as his "last chance" at being single, my father departed Lorain for several weeks. Together with Enrico, he made the trek to Italy. For years, he'd heard the stories. Now he lived them. He was in the audience with Pope John XXIII at his summer home in Castel Gandolfo. He saw Rigoletto, and walked the steps of Rome's Scala Sancta, which pilgrims climb on their knees. He ate at Checco Er Carettiere in Trastevere long before the neighborhood became cool. His travel journal, though somewhat unreadable due to his handwriting, included a steady recitation of train trips between Rome, Florence, Venice, Verona, Padua, Pisa, Napoli, and San Donato di Ninea, as well as his marveling at the architecture and history intertwined all around him. His shopping list for those back home included *tablecloths, bristles, onion seeds,* and *one purse.* On this, his only journey with his father to the family's ancestral foundations, he maintained a distinction important for many Italians, proudly proclaiming his provincial roots. It was this yearning he instilled inside of me and my siblings. Like him, I too would reach for the tales he knew of people he never had the chance to love.

While in Italy that summer of 1960, Ettore sent postcards to Jean nearly every day. "Tonight the ocean rages, the swells are pretty in the moonlight," he wrote from Naples. "Saw Pompei. Going to see the uncles." Which uncles were unclear, since Amerigo had disappeared, Francesco and Minotti were deceased, and Vittorio was the lone uncle on the Iannuzzi side. The connection to the Mazzà and Maiolo side overseas had all but ceased to exist in modern records. Ettore signed his cards and letters, "as ever, ET."

My parents were engaged on April 28, 1961, and married two months later. For their wedding on July 4, 1961, at St. Peter's, the church was decorated with white gladioli, and forever after "glads," as we called them, would rise above marigolds and zinnias in my father's garden in tribute to this greatest love. Ettore and Jean entertained invitees with pride at the Italian Mutual Hall with one of the first catered weddings of their extended family and friends. The caterer's tagline was *Be a guest at your own party.* It was the only time my mother did not play host to an affair where both she and the food were the stars. The fare included the traditional candied almonds, or *confetti,* as they're known at their original shop in Sulmona, Abruzzo. With a list of nearly three hundred attendees, mostly Italians, the reception at the church's parish hall was no small thing. A day later, they left for a week in the Poconos at the aptly named Chestnut Grove Lodge, my mother wearing a yellow linen suit dress with black patent accessories.

Try as she did to hang on, having completed two years of Elementary Education courses, my mother left teaching for good after her marriage. Another of her former school superiors, a nun, wrote, "in the distant future when your family is raised you might want to come back," but she never did. She and my father moved into the upstairs of a rental home in Lorain. In the cramped kitchen was a dormer window, through which lake breezes floated in. They would become a necessary balm for the young couple.

Imagine you have crossed an ocean, endured harsh working conditions, and set aside your own yearnings to achieve a better life for your children, and then, just as they stand on the cusp of that life, your children are met with tragedy of their own. A year after Jean and Ettore's nuptials, their firstborn son, David Ettore, died of pulmonary hyaline membrane disease two days after his premature birth. This condition was a common cause of death of premature infants at the time. Baby David existed in our household as an aching, *la mancanza*. Our evening prayers at the sewing machine turned altar, asking him to "help us be a good, kind, and loving family," were proof. His death prompted my parents to move to Amherst, a smaller town next door with very few Italians and a younger, rapidly growing demographic (between 1950 and 1960 census, Amherst's population grew by 6,750, a jump of 90 percent). For my parents, the town offered distance from the daily demands of the shoe store, their grief, or both. Following David's death, five more children followed: Laura, Paul, myself, Beth, and Jeanne. My mother claimed she gave us names that couldn't be shortened into nicknames, but my siblings and classmates in Amherst found ways around that rule.

Over the course of my first eighteen years, our family life, other than school, revolved around three things: church, the store, and of course, food. My parents had switched their allegiance to St. Joseph's Catholic Church in Amherst, a sandstone building originally dedicated in 1868 and rebuilt in 1955. Amherst called itself the Sandstone Capital of the World,[49] a fact we would proudly proclaim whenever we traveled from home. Our home backed up to a former tuberculosis sanitarium, named Golden Acres due to its sandstone construction, which offered convenient access to a sledding hill and woods. Though we were public school children, given Amherst's excellence in education, our Saturdays were spent in CCD classes at St. Joseph's, where Jean taught every Saturday before driving us to bowling leagues. Sundays revolved around church and the obligatory visit to Calvary Cemetery, my mother's scrumptious brunches, and dinner at home—a prototypical Italian weekend.

Italian clubs fell under the umbrella of church. About this time, my parents also made a switch from the Abruzzesi Club to the I.A.V. According to the *Lorain Journal*, "The Italian American Veterans Post No. 1 was born in 1946 and moved to its current location at 4567 Oberlin Ave. in 1968. It was founded with the goals of aiding and assisting veterans and their families and fostering social, civic, historical, athletic, patriotic, musical, and scientific activities, and more."[50] The I.A.V. was the site of many of their New Year's Eve outings with my godparents and parents, as well as countless spaghetti dinners.

At the store, there was always conflict between the two brothers, Uncle Albert and my dad. They both married strong Italian women who bore four and five children respectively. Each served their churches and communities. They shared ownership and leadership of the shoe store, and both had been trained as salespersons and knew how to take a shoe apart and sew or glue it back together faster than one could open a jar of canned tomatoes. They, along with other Januzzi employees, had trained with a renowned podiatrist, author, lecturer, and research director for a children's shoe line, Dr. Ross A. Tenant, who said, "I don't know of a store anywhere else, in any town comparable in size to Lorain, that carries as complete a selection as Januzzi's."[51] My older siblings and I learned, too, at the foot of our paternal masters or under the scrutinous eye of Enrico. The refrain "get busy" was not lost on any of us, and it would instill that same work ethic I would find later woven into my great-grandfather's letters, as he praised Enrico for monies sent back home. In our home, a blue children's shoebox contained all we needed before church outings—Kiwi shoe polish in a rich brown or black stain, a few soft yellow cloths, a wooden bristle brush, and extra heel plates, tips and nails. Our father insisted we know how to properly polish our shoes and make repairs when necessary. Rarely we were allowed to be the proverbial shoemaker's children. To this day, my adult son will ask me to check his toes when fitting shoes.

That constant tension between the two men, evidenced by Stella's insistence in her final letters "for everyone to get along," ultimately brought about the store's demise. Due to irreconcilable differences, the Januzzi Shoes corporation was dissolved in 1984, the year I graduated high school, fifty-six years after Enrico and Stella set up shop. The immigrant dream had died, torn apart by—what else?—family.

Stella did not live to see its end; she had succumbed to death in 1974 following brain surgery for her anemia and convulsive disorder. Those health issues were a common thread in a coal family, though no compensation would ever come for the victims who suffered. Her hospitalizations and stays in sanitariums were our first up-close look at the frightening sights and sounds of a nursing home in the '70s. But Stella remained resolute. In the last letter she could write, six years before her death, she left instructions for her family: "No masses after death." Her favorite charity was Shrine of St. Anthony's in Italy. "Always give to the poor, the really poor. No splurging. I want a pretty lacey hat, plain simple dress and shoes. No jewelry on me. And teach your children to always remember their grandchildren."

Enrico remarried Carmella Scardamaglia Medaglia. A spry Italian woman who had worked as a seamstress in the 1940s and '50s, she was six years younger than my grandfather. What I remember most is that she loved to boogie in our basement with us, and could knock your socks off with her crème horns. That recipe does not exist in my mother's books, but the confections served her well. She lived long into her nineties. Enrico's death came in 1984 of adenocarcinoma of the prostate, and, though it would take my dad nearly twenty years to grasp, his passing was the impetus my father needed to let go of the blood bonds created through the decades at the family business and allow the business to disappear from his life. Other than a brief stint at the JCPenney footwear department, he would not pursue shoes again. My parents had two kids in college, with me on the way there and their two youngest still at home. The years of summers and weekends I spent at the store, filing customers cards, checking inventory, fitting shoes, lunch with my dad, were dear times. I learned less about leather and more about who gets what, and why. I had hardly known if my vocational path would include the shoe business or not. My older sister and brother might have railed at the decisions being made to exit the shoe business, but I stood on the precipice of college, my prospects still unknown. Gossips around town stood at the ready to spread rumors about the company breakup. Getting out meant getting away.

My father felt the strain heavily, especially as my uncle and his oldest son would restart a new shoe enterprise. He was not the face behind the business, choosing to remain the background. He was that type of person. His practical actions took precedent over the pretense all was okay, no matter the situation. He threw himself into real estate, like two of my sisters would later, while serving as chairman on the Lorain Metropolitan

Housing Authority Board for twenty-five years, serving the community as his mother had taught. That was no easy feat as Lorain County continued its economic and industrial slide. The city itself was known for carrying the bulk of the burden of affordable housing, and at the helm of LMHA, my father knew the city needed to extend its services county-wide. It was his devotion to this work, along with his love of gardening, that rescued him during a most challenging time for our family. Both our family homes had contained large lots for him to plant apple and sour cherry trees, seckel pears, and grow a fig tree grafted from a branch of his father's. His crops of green beans, long zucchini, near-black eggplant, and bursting tomatoes flourished in his sadness, proof that our food carries emotions with it to the plate for others to consume. He handed my mother a bounty with which to work her magic. She did so famously, with him at her side. We consumed all we could.

My mother, meanwhile, had long been without her parents. Her mother, Raffaela, had died in December 1964, about a year before I was born. Sadly, I have no first-hand knowledge of either of my mother's birth parents. Rafaella was in and out of the hospital during her final years before falling victim to carcinoma of the lung related to the cigarettes and pipes her second husband had enjoyed.

Luigi himself died of congestive heart failure and pulmonary emphysema in 1976. He too had been overexposed at National Tube to the orange-colored fumes that rose above the plant where he worked. The stale smoke off his pipes and cigarettes in the house aided his demise. The night of his visitation, our home was burglarized. I'll never forget entering with an adult neighbor and hearing the plodding of footsteps running to escape out a back window. My mother had lost the last of her familiar ties to Abruzzo that night, and precious jewelry belonging to her mother. Another sadness reigned over her roof. In typewritten sheets left behind, she documented over seventy-five Italians who had donated a mass in Luigi's name. And lest we forget about food, there was plenty to be had, including banana nut bread, cherry cheesecake, roast beef, and a cheese plate.

As my parents had moved from Lorain and gradually lost the family ties that rooted them, Americanism had become their way of life.

When my parents introduced acquaintances and friends to their children, they started with my brother. "This is our son, Paul." That was easier than what came next—a lineup of four daughters to run through, *the Januzzi girls*, seven years apart in age.

"This is Laura, Annette, Beth, and Jeanne," my mother would say. We braced ourselves for the usual response from onlookers: "I can never remember. You girls all look alike."

It wasn't a lie. The pictures overflowing out of cardboard cartons inside my sister's garage prove it. They capture the sameness of four big-permed Italian American brunettes, with dark eyes and squiggles of hair on our forearms, growing up in the '70s and '80s. My brother, also present in most of the pictures, stood by with wisps of brown-blonde hair flapping in the wind. We joked that he was the most northern Italian one.

Our parents had created a dangerous mix of genes when they melded together families from two Italian provinces five hundred kilometers apart—a distance equal to half the length and nearly the full breadth of the Italian peninsula. As Mario Pei writes in the introduction to the 1950s translation of *The Talisman Italian Cookbook*, "A North Italian and a Sicilian, each speaking his own dialects, have no more chance of understanding each other than an American and a German each using his own language."

Mom and Dad had been born eight days apart at the same local hospital, graduated from Lorain High School a half-year apart, and lived about a mile from one another. They resembled each other so much in appearance, they were often mistaken for siblings, and not just as they aged—from the beginning. They were almost fated to be together. Yet their vows left their children with dueling regional provenances. What part of Italy they had come from was an important distinction for many Italians who proudly proclaimed their provincial roots, and still weren't completely enamored with the unified country.

And it was crucial to us.

Was it this merging that created our persistent need for individuality, or was that my requirement alone? We argued furiously, as on our family trip to Italy, where we can recount fights we termed the Battle of Assisi or the Venice Inquisition. On our honeymoon, my husband and I overheard a couple in an argument. The woman smacked the back of one hand into the palm of the other. "*Cento è cento*," she said, her hands speaking louder than words. "One hundred is one hundred." *Cento è cento* is still used in my household today as a metaphor for arguments that rage on. However, when Laura's boyfriend moved to Cincinnati and she did too, I didn't hesitate to follow. Beth joined us next, and when my parents were ready to transition to the final stages in their lives, they decided on Cincinnati for no other reason than some of us lived here. Like our ancestors, we understood the importance of chain migration. Cincinnati was a place that came to feel like home, not because of the Ohio River rocking through the city, and surely not because of its German immigrant population, but because *family was everything*, even if we ourselves had torn the unit asunder at times.

And no matter what region you were from or where you were in the world, being Italian was being Italian. Especially in our world. Though the boundaries between my hometown and my parents' hometown were also the city limits between being Italian and being American, between the old ways and the new, throughout our many years living in Amherst, Lorain never seemed like separate town.

As kids, we easily identified with the home country's regional struggles; conquered by many, unified by few. Pulled away from the grubby hands of ancestors squeezing our cheeks, we also diverged from classmates whose pale skins burned, who didn't know what calamari was. But that rhythm of ethnicity that my parents pumped through our hearts, the same rhythm that wove itself through international festivals and parades and foods and friends, was never foreign to us. We straddled two worlds, moving one giant step further away from the first-generation Italian American experience of our parents while centering ourselves in the meager tidbits of their stories, crumbs that lodged themselves in the cracks between leaves in the family table.

That *la mancanza*, as the Italians called it, the yearning or missing, the "why" I needed to understand, came only after my parents were gone.

A Reverse Migration

I was born in 1966, the middle child in a family of five living siblings, plus our oldest brother, David, whose death held sway over us all our lives. In the long line of hash marks we left behind in the family home, five feet tall was the highest my permed brunette hair might reach. My hands are small like my father's, but their makeup, their structure, is that of my mother's. I boasted about having inherited my mother's lighter complexion, emblematic of families from the central regions of Italy. Like my Mom's, my skin reddens before deepening into the tone of someone more Italian. But I hardly cooed over carrying her ancestors' squared-off shoulders and hips.

My first husband, Devin, understood the dynamics of our family as much as one could, having witnessed me and my siblings together most often. He also understood my need to stand in the silent hills where I could hear my own voice and those of my ancestors, too. One of his last wishes was that, after his death, I would take my parents to Italy, following my mother's hip surgery and my father's heart bypass surgery. It was the beginning of the end of my need to find that place. And the beginning of my desires to know it. Five years later, upon completion of that trip, I wrote in a photo book gifted to my parents, "it was a dream to live in every waking moment" with them.

Writing now about our family's time-honored Italian American food traditions, I have been reminded of my siblings' shared love for my mother's Christmas rosettes, a variation on *caviciuni*, fritters sometimes filled with chickpea or chestnut paste and flavored with chocolate or cocoa. The grinder whirring through bags of nuts...or pizzelle—also known as *ferratelle*, from *ferra* (iron)—the "zz" on the tongue like the sizzle of dough in the iron press where the waffle-like treats are formed. The sounds harkened back to my parents work in the basement kitchen. What would it be like to eat these same confections, made with a similar whirs and sizzles in the background, on their parents' homeland?

It's hard to describe to anyone with parents still alive the rootlessness I felt in the early years after my Mom and Dad's deaths. Hers, from complications from dementia; his, from Parkinson's. Uncle Tony and Uncle Albert, the only and last of their siblings, had already died. That restlessness was the same my mother had felt in her premature losses and the predicted ones. The same my father felt after the shoe store closed, though some reconciliation occurred before his brother Albert's death. My grandparents had also felt this when they pried themselves from the family pastures. An unnamed melancholy lived beneath the surface of the immigrant life and never disappeared. If our *Italianità*, that faithfulness to being Italian, had been erased by the forces that Americanized my parents and grandparents, I was desperate to reclaim it.

In 2022, my murmuration about "becoming more Italian" was about to be realized. My first husband had been deceased for two decades, the family trip with my parents was long in the rearview mirror. I remarried, folded my new husband's three teenagers into the family with my son, Davis. Pushed them all through college. Lost my parents, and persevered through a global pandemic.

I had an elementary grasp on the Italian language. Cousins' names were doggedly chased and now in hand. An in-depth reading of my Abruzzese mother's recipes books had been completed.

In August of that year, Mark and I had married off the last of our four adult children.

One month later, tired from our overnight flight to Rome from Cincinnati, I inched the rental car off the autostrada ramp and toward a ticket machine lane that read *Speedpass*. Twice I approached the arm. Twice, the arm didn't raise. Forced to back up to the tune of a honking, irate driver, Mark and I argued. It's good to argue in Italy. You know you've adopted the passion of the people if you're doing so.

Mirella Ammirati had helped launch my search for relatives. In Spoltore's town square, Piazza di Marzio, I met Mirella and a local historian who would accompany our tour. Who else would join us? A distant cousin of Vincenzo Giuliani, my mother's father, and three of my mother's Scurti cousins from Spoltore: Viola, Luigina, and Antonio, whose wife had died only weeks prior. Amidst a chilly morning, we immediately embraced, though our conversations in Italian never reached beyond my kindergarten level.

After a lengthy discourse by the historian, including a visit to the family church and a look at a plaque for the inventor of dentures, the cousins arranged a private lunch for us. To our surprise, they were friends with the owner at Luca Remigio's La Bella Addormentata (Sleeping Beauty). The restaurateur had opened for us on a Tuesday when they were normally closed. Our table overlooked rich blue skies with grassy olive groves, tilting farmhouses, and the view toward Chieti tempting us. It felt like gazing at heaven—though I would have been denied entry due to the gluttony that followed. One by one, the lunch plates arrived. A sliver of raw tuna topped with slice of green apple. Fish crème inside a crisp wafer served on a rock from the local shore. Each dish cascaded into the next, fortifying my connection to people and place. The meal closed out

Ettore Januzzi and Jean Giuliani, engagement, 1961

Jean Giuliani with Raffaela DeLuca and Stella Januzzi, wedding day, July 4, 1961

Wedding feast at the Italian Mutual Hall, 1961

Mr. and Mrs. Ettore A. Januzzi, 1961

Annette Januzzi, age 4, at nursery school, 1970

Wedding of Annette and Devin Wick, plus Januzzi family, 1994

Annette Januzzi Wick with Jean and Ettore Januzzi, Siena, 2005

Ettore and Jean Januzzi, Roman Coliseum, 2005

when we heard a clambering of feet and realized we weren't alone—the cousins and their families had arrived to celebrate our appearance. Shots of espresso and glasses of genziana and ratafia, the *apertivo* made with local sour cherries, were delivered to the table.

The afternoon sun set and brought the brood of cousins and their grandchildren back to us in a new light; the soft, orange light prevalent in Italian movie scenes. I was lacking in language and so much more, but tried to hold on to the blessing of the present moment. Here, what I sealed in my heart was a sacred love for my origins.

Antonio drove us back to our B & B, the sun long since chased west. There's a selfie picture of the three of us there, Antonio leaning large over Mark and I, holding on to us. I could feel the weight of his grief. Perhaps for a moment he had allowed it to fall off him; allowed us to grasp it for him for a while, as his family had held, in their cells, the grief of my grandparents' departures many years ago. He offered a final embrace that said, *Come again soon, be with us in our own ways.*

"It's a kindness that the mind can go where it wishes," Ovid of Abruzzo wrote. I concurred.

During our remaining travels around Abruzzo, we discovered one *proprietà* had an uncle in Pittsburgh. A visitor we met in Sulmona, Abruzzo was from Hinkley, Ohio, and one of our guides in Spoltore wanted to connect the mayors of Spoltore and Steubenville, Ohio, birthplace of Dean Martin, or Dino Paul, Crocetti, to form a sister city. The chain migration to the Midwest had prevailed.

In 2024, after a flight to Napoli and a stopover with yet another rental car issue, we drove into Calabria, into the stirrings of the Pollino Mountains. Their limestone peaks protruded through the blue skies. We turned off the main highway and found ourselves winding along local roads, where signs for San Donato appeared.

Chimes beckoned us inside the family church. Red, white, and gold drapery hung across the ceilings, in startling contrast to the simplicity of the white walls of the church. The small piazza outside the church felt oddly familiar. The final home of my great-grandfather was located upon the same flat of land. Off to our right, a father and son making wine observed us.

"*Sono Annette Januzzi. Mio nonno era nato qui. Mio bisnonno Vincenzo Ianuzzi ere abitato li.*" My grandfather was born here. My great-grandfather Vincenzo lived here.

They informed us Cousin Stella's home was around the corner, and two other women up on a third-floor balcony pointed the way. As Stella met and ushered us into her home, we felt as if the entire town had taken possession of us. We had a timeline to stick to, but Stella informed me that would have to change. We would have lunch with her and her friends. And what of this hike? *Chiamo Ernesto. Gli dico che farai tardi.* I call Ernesto (our hiking guide). I tell him you will be late.

Stella had made a fig crostata with some peach preserves, and now made a mascarpone cream topping for it. We followed her down to the home of her friends, Maria Panebianco (a distant relative of ours), her brother Innocenzo and his wife, and their friend Giorgio. A lunch of homemade maccheroni was accompanied by a simple tomato sauce. Calabrian chili peppers were strewn across the table. Following our hosts' lead, we cut the raw peppers into strips over our pasta with a pair of scissors, learning there is such a thing as *too much*. The crostata, we ate with hands straight out of the pan.

Soon enough, Stella handed us off to Ernesto. Everyone knew Ernesto, a certified trail and trekking guide in the area's tourism industry. Prepared for the shift in temperature and deepening gray clouds, he carried extra fleece coats for us. And his mother's frittata, made with wild asparagus, which he also carried for sustenance? Necessary. Many people didn't see the mountain as a valuable resource. Ernesto saw it for what it was. A place to connect with the history of a people, a chance to draw the outline of a place from above, a place where nature existed at its finest with tall cedar trees, pines, and the occasional wild boar. My great-grandfather, a guardian of the forest. Being a nature girl, I appreciated the woods as a family birthright.

Physically exhausted, an entire evening lay ahead with Concetta Macrini, my first point of contact online, and my second cousin once removed. The light in Italy that day was still crowded out by clouds, but that didn't stop us from feeling the warm generosity of her family. We were welcomed into her home, a two-bedroom flat on the second floor of a café/restaurant. In the kitchen, a large dishcloth-lined pan was filled with mounds of fresh-rolled tagliatelle. The dinner table had been lengthened with another leaf, and was set with a plastic tablecloth that, funnily enough, I mistook for actual lace work. I was still getting accustomed to the language, and needed help from Concetta's daughter, Giada. Concetta showed off porcini mushrooms, as round and large as a steering wheel, that she had foraged in the mountains and on the family farm they referred to over and again—an *azienda agricola*.

Soon, a cell phone was handed to me. Did I know about the cousins in Montreal? One of them, Vittorio Capano, was on the phone. Vittorio and his brother, Antonio, lived in Montreal, and they also had a sister who lived in Torino, Maria. Vittorio had recently returned to Canada from Italy, and already he wanted to know when I would come back. A little later, Concetta's phone was handed to me again. This time it was Luigi, in Paris. Luigi was the son of another cousin. He too experienced a father, who, like Amerigo, had left his family.

Posso aiutare? Chi vengono a cena? Can I help? No. Who is coming for dinner? Stella, Giorgio, Maria, the ones we lunched with. Also, Concetta's father, Rico (my actual second cousin), her mother. Concetta's family. Cross talk flowed about us, around us, over us, and sometimes through us.

We learned more about the beneficence of my grandfather Enrico. The family spoke fondly of visits he had made in the years when the shoe business was still growing, or during the time when Paolina, Enrico's sister, had died. Enrico became godfather to Rico, and months later, in conversations with Vittorio, I would learn Enrico was his godfather too. My grandmother Stella, whose namesake had welcomed us to San Donato, had also shown her kindness when accompanying Enrico. The two bestowed many blessings on the extended Iannuzzi family.

The evening went long, as we feasted for hours and Mark and Concetta's husband, Giovanni, drank Peronis, then wine, then amaro. The tagliatelle was served with a tomato sauce that was rich and creamy, though not made with cream. Chicken, potatoes, homemade bread, another crostata of fig, crespelle made from a simple flour paste. Rico had brought his homemade wine. As in the lineage of Vincenzo Iannuzzi and his family living off the fields, everything was procured up the street, at the farm, on the land in this unassuming life.

Late in the afternoon the next day, after touring nearby cities, we received a message from Concetta, who always was busy farming, cooking, making. She told us to meet Nicola, her son, and he would lead us to her mother's house for her mother's birthday party that evening. Once there, Rico showed off his grapes that were *locale*. They drank the wine made from these grapes in the fields, at work, at lunch; to soothe aches, to calm nerves, to hydrate, and to mark time by vintage.

Shuffled off to ride in Rico's late-1980s Jeep, Rico, who spoke no English, drove us to the *cimitario*, the cemetery. There, we not only found graves of some ancestors, but could finally communicate with Rico in the manner of someone who has mourned. In Italian cemeteries, photos of the dead are common on the graves. We stopped for several minutes to pay respects to his mother who had been young when her father, Amerigo, left for Argentina. Also common, many markers with the *Iannuzzi* name. With our time consumed by lunches and dinners, I really didn't see the rest of the town or its grottoes and mines. *La prossima volta*—next time.

The last brightness of the day was snuffed out as we left, the wooded roads no longer clear to us. Rico entertained us with mainly hand gestures. Occasionally, we caught "Americani" or "politico" or other familiar words I could not string together. He pulled over to sip some wine, and then again for young Nico to unlock a padlock to the family farm. Finally, using only the flashlights on our phones, we passed through chicken coops and barns and were led inside the home that had been built in 1984 by hand.

Inside, *baratolli* of tomatoes and Calabrian chili peppers lined the shelves. Hammocks of prosciutto and sopresetta hung upside down, tucked safely into pillowcases. The state of the home made it appear as if someone had departed in a hurry. The work here was never done.

My phone rang once more. *L cena è già pronto*. Dinner is already prepared. Rico would be late for his own wife's birthday dinner.

My hair in tatters from the wind, we returned to a house stuffed full of twenty-plus guests, most of them relatives. This tableau surprised me. I excused myself to the bathroom to calm my nerves before facing the guests seated around a table laid with platters of tagliatelle, eggplant parmesan, and goat chops. There were no fancy plates of cheese, only slices of soprasetta, and Calabrian chili peppers, both salted and fried and a few for fresh use in the pasta. More plates held potatoes, pizzas, and slices of bread that were slung around like frisbees. Wine was poured, then Amaro Silano, anisette, limoncello.

On the day we left San Donato, Concetta was still prepping foods for winter stores, and the festival coming up soon. Over coffee and crespelles, she shared how she and her mother had helped build the homestead on the family farm, placed the rocks that lined the driveway, cleared away the long vines and immature trees, and run fences for the chickens. When I asked about the crespelle, she wrote out the recipe for me and within minutes, showed me how to make them. Everything—*prodotti tipici*, wine, the Calabrian chilis—was at her fingertips, ready to be made into something else—including us.

Layers of rain descended as we prepared to leave. With Concetta standing outside her doorway, I was reminded of my parents, who always walked us out of the house and waved from the garage. The gesture had come naturally to them and to Concetta, and somehow I knew to wait for that gesture before driving away. Leave, but don't say goodbye.

"*Tornerò,*" I said. "*Ci vediamo la prossima volta.*" We see each other next time.

Stella, Enrico, and relations in San Donato. At the Iannuzzi family home, San Donato di Ninea, 1954

Anna Buonvivere, Spoltore, 1970s

A Scurti-Giuliani family wedding, Abruzzo, Italy

Letter from Anna Buonvivere to Jean Januzzi, 1970s

Violetta Giuliani, Antonio Dottore, Annette Januzzi Wick, Luigina Dottore, and Mark Manley in Spoltore, Abruzzo. 2022

Stella Macrini, second cousin, name also inspired by Stella Januzzi, 2024

Original Madonna del Popolo, Chiesa di San Panfilo, Spoltore

Annette Wick, Rico Macrini, second cousin named after Enrico Januzzi, and Mark Manley, 2024

Fish crème inside a crisp wafer served on a rock from the local shore, Bella Addormentata, 2022

Concetta Macrini, second cousin once removed, with tagliatelle, 2024

Cravatta Friggere

Bow Ties #1

- 3 c. flour
- 3 T. powdered sugar
- 1/4 tsp. salt
- 1/4 tsp. lemon rind (optional)
- 4 egg yolks
- 1 c. sour cream
- 1/2 tsp. vanilla
- or 2 T. rum

Sift flour, sugar & salt together into bowl. Add lemon rind. Beat egg yolks well & combine with sour cream & vanilla. Blend with flour mixture. Knead on floured board. Roll very thin. Use spaghetti machine. Cut in strips 4 x 2. Make small slit in center & pull one corner thru. Fry in deep fat. Drain on paper towels & dust with powdered sugar.

Updated

Grandma DeLuca

Cannoli — my mother's

Use this 1/3 recipe

2	6 cups flour	3
1/3	1 c. crisco	1/2 c.
1/3	1 c. milk	1/2 c.
1	3 eggs	1 1/2
1/4	3/4 c. sugar	9 oz. 1 1/4 c.—10

This makes too many. For about 30 or 40 should make 1/3 recipe, on the left

Press edges together with beaten egg white.

Shells

Add more flour. For 1/3 recipe start with 2 1/2 c. Use flour on pieces. Roll & reroll. Then end with 2nd from last on machine. If you double pieces, it will stay together better on 2nd from last setting.

7/30/13

Rice Croquette

Cook together, 1 quart milk, 1 tsp. salt, 1 c. raw rice (regular not minute rice) stirring until rice is soft and all milk is absorbed. Remove from fire, add eggs (2) one at a time beating with a wooden spoon quickly and fast, or the egg will cook before mixed throly. Stir in 3/4 c. romano cheese, a little less if you wish, add some garlic or onion powder, and 1 tsp. celery salt. Some cut parsley and sweet basil.

Cool and refrigerate over night. Roll and dip in beaten 1 egg diluted with 2 tbsp. milk then in fine bread crumbs. Let stand while heating your oil in heavy frying pan about 1/2 inches of oil. Brown. Do not have oil too hot. Just like for doughnuts.

— Mother Jamugi

Biscotti di Lemone

Lemon cookies ***

- 1 c. margarine (2 sticks)
- 2 c. sugar
- 3 eggs
- 5 1/4 c. flour   2 c. 5 oz.
- 1 orange rind, grated
- 2 tsp. lemon extract
- 8 tsp. baking powder **
- 1 c. milk

1/2 Recipe:
- 1 stick
- 1 c.
- 1 1/2 or 2
- 2 c. 4 ½
- 1/2 orange
- 1 tsp.
- 4 tsp.
- 1/2 c.

Cream margarine & sugar. Add eggs and beat till creamy. Add dry ingredients alternately with milk. Add lemon extract & orange rind. Refrigerate.
* Shape in balls & roll in powdered sugar. Bake in well-greased & floured cookie sheet for 10 min. - 350°. These cookies will be light in color. Do not wait until tops brown.
* Upstairs oven – 10 min.

Part II

The Recipes That Held Us Together

THE FIRST RECIPES

RECIPES

Grandma DeLuca's Cannoli • Aunt Mary DeLuca's Biscotti •
Grandma Mazzà's Fried Twists • Bow Ties (*Chiacchiere*) •
Pecan Nut Cups (*Bocconotti*)

My friends alleged our family consistently—and insistently—attached *Italian* to everything: *Italian* bread, *Italian* cheese, *Italian* celery, as if simply doing so made it true. A sandwich of Italian bread might be jammed with Italian salami with bits of peppercorn or fennel seeds that stuck in our teeth, and squishy, salted Italian tomatoes, their juices flowing between our fingers. Like something sticky, something you couldn't rinse off, it was always *Italian* something.

We, too, were always *something* Italian, said my mother, who possessed the gift—and the challenge—of being a first-generation Italian American, and therefore existing closer to her roots. My parents' claims and the burst of backyard tomatoes should have been enough to convince me. But it wasn't.

Early in my first marriage, my husband Devin coveted whatever Italian meals steamed in the sauce pot on my mother's harvest-gold stove. He'd call her from our home in Cincinnati, his blue eyes sparkling at me, as he cozied up over the phone to the woman who filled his stomach like his own mother did. "What's for dinner, Nana?" he'd ask, already looking forward to whatever would greet us after our four-hour drive on interstate and rural routes to Amherst. In the background, I pondered how to reclaim this heritage I savored.

Once Devin and I moved to Oregon—and long before the federal TSA instituted strict security measures—my mother carried a Corning Ware casserole dish of *lasagna primavera* and boarded a plane from Cleveland to come visit. Our son, Davis, had been born premature. Recovering from a

C-section, I hardly ate my mother's meals. But Devin? He worshipped at the lip of that clear glass dish morning, noon, and night. Twelve months passed. Devin was diagnosed with leukemia. My mother (and his) stayed for days and weeks to cook his favorites. After my mother's death, I found her remarks on the lasagna primavera recipe: "A family favorite, especially my son-in-law." My tears tasted like alfredo as I read that missive from beyond.

We ate so much love in those days, I still feel satiated by the experience even now. For what was food but the greatest expression of joy and hurt in the world?

Mere months before Devin's death, he begged of me two things: "You should take your parents to Italy. It's one of my last wishes." And another: "You should also collect your mom's [handwritten] recipes."

For a time, I fell short in that assignment. Devin died. I married again, to Mark, whose first wife had also died of cancer. Mark had never tasted many of my mother's culinary treasures, due to the ravages of time that had slowed her. But he was a beneficiary of that inheritance, nonetheless.

In the summer of 2005, I finally planned that family trip to Italy with my parents, my four sisters, my brother-in-law, and Mark, though our brother was unable to attend. We offered my mother the option to attend a public papal audience, or to make a pilgrimage to her family's hometown of Spoltore, somewhere she'd never been, located about two hours from Rome. "I'd like to see Pope Benedict XVI in St. Peter's Square," she decided. I didn't know then about the correspondence she had stashed away, dating from 1973 and resuming in 1992, between my mother and her cousin, Marianna (Anna) Buonvivere. In 1992, Anna wrote, "I haven't heard from you in 19 years, and I was very disappointed. For this reason, I didn't contact you when my husband and I went to Baltimore and stayed there for 45 days. However, let's forget about it now, I'm just so happy to hear from you." My mother had inhabited her motherhood during those nineteen years, but by 1992, her kids had mostly dispersed across the state. Possibly known to my mother but confirmed during my travels to Spoltore, Anna's sister, Maria, had died in 1944 when she was 15, the victim of a tragic accident. As she ran through the hills of Spoltore where Germans had left mines, she had been struck by one and died instantly.

Also buried away, unbeknownst to me, were dispatches from her cousin, Peppino, or Giuseppe Appignani, from three years prior. She'd been trying out her Italian again through a friend, Lilian DiDonato, who acted as translator. "*Baci cari a voi tutti.*" Dear kisses to you all. Letters, Christmas cards, and cards wishing my mother a *buona Pasqua* (happy Easter) and *buona duemila* (happy 2000) had begun arriving in 1995, but by 2002, the letters had stopped coming. My mother never mentioned the invitation she had received: "We would be very happy to have you as guests in order to make our parental relationship more felt," perhaps out of disregard or a sense that she might never travel there. Her grandchildren had taken precedence, as did the needs of her own kids.

As she considered the decision to see the Pope or her people, then, was she torn up over the choice? It seems it was her preference that history remain in the past. Her parents had once made similar decisions. Once you shut yourself off from the past, you never want to give it the chance to seep back through and ruin what you might already possess, including your convictions about choices made.

Some might have considered this sojourn a vacation, but for me, it was an expedition made holy for many reasons. My father reclaimed memories of soaring architectural heights, the ease with which the train system whisked him through the land, and the dedicated time he had once spent with his father, now dead. For my mother, it was a time of trepidation. She'd been hospitalized a week prior. Had this planning been too much on the seventy-eight-year-old couple? Or was her anxiousness caused by the excitement of fulfilling a vision she didn't know she wanted to pursue? For me, I focused on the food and wine, and on ensuring that my parents' memories of this excursion, certainly their last, would be enduring. On ancient cobblestones baked by thousands of September suns, I watched as my parents venerated the Vatican and Michelangelo, the David statue, the Ponte Vecchio and its gold sellers, and most of all, the gelato. In the sear of a late fall heat, my father wearing his chauffeur hat, my mother's face shaded by her hand, they walked arm in arm up the Piazza del Colosseo. My blood pulsed with awe. One moment contained all I needed to know. I felt what they had been genetically predisposed to at birth—the sense of being part of a place that wasn't where you slept, but existed as the starting point of your dreams yet to come.

On our final drive to the Milan airport before leaving the now-familiar land, my mother sat in the front passenger seat. Autumn rains were occasionally pocking the windshield of our transport van. "*Piove,*"

THE FIRST RECIPES

she said, and smiled. *It's raining.* The miles we walked had been enough. She was no longer separated from her homeland by the years she hadn't traveled there, the long stretches when she'd lost touch with family. She had reverted to her first language. She had come home. I'd like to believe that in that same elongated lapse of days, my father also came to know his life once more. He'd chosen to follow in his father's footsteps during their trek together in Italy, in the shoe store business, and again during our 14-day outing. But no more. He was Ettore Anselmo Januzzi, a life well-earned and lived.

A year later, Mark and I traveled to Amalfi, a town known for its limoncello and papermaking. He bought a leather-bound notebook and presented the blank journal to me wrapped in a soft cloth. "Your mom can write her recipes in here." When I returned, I shared the journal with my mother. "What do you want me to write?" Pain vibrated in her voice. My father had begun tasting the meals as my mother's memory began to fail, her decline evident in forgotten ingredients and mistakenly salted pizzelle. "C'mon, Jean, you gotta get this down for Annette," he said, without conviction that she could perform the task. A packet of a dozen recipes neatly stacked arrived in the mail with the note: *More to come later.* But nothing came.

In the interim, I reread words of my mother that described what I could no longer touch—the crease of her pizzelle hot off the press, the bump of her moist meatballs, the warm, egg-washed crust of her Easter bread. My hands hovered, shook, over her hands in written form. My fingers curved as if to trace the gentle rise of knuckles that still knew how to knead.

Tracing my fingertips along the recipe titles contained in the recipe notebooks inherited from my mother after her death, I could feel the press of my mother's pen as she had entered her culinary record into a trio of three-hole-punched fabric binders.

Threads frayed at the bottom of the first binder, colored tomato-red with bowls of fruit and vegetables dotting the cover. A scrap of fabric pulled away from the spine as if some recipes had tried to escape, but I wouldn't let that happen. The dedication was located three pages in.

To Jean - Cooking is an art, and one of the best hobby [sic] I know.

The binders had been a wedding present from her mother-in-law, Stella. Had my mother been fully prepared to turn away from teaching, from her friends, from freedom, to welcome this gift into her life? She was driven by her heritage—not just the convention of dishes from both Abruzzo and Calabria, but the tradition of adhering to guidelines to produce the perfect plate. Stella taught my mother how to turn food into art. Inside Mom's copy of *The Talisman Italian Cook Book*, Stella wrote a quote from Grace Noll Crowell's poem, "I Have Found Such Joy." The opening of the third stanza reads: "Oh, I have found such joys I wish I might— Tell every woman." Stella's gesture meant, "I see something in you that is in me." Both ran their kitchens with the adeptness of a Michelin five-star chef: smoothly, efficiently, and with the goal of bringing joy to everyone at the table. Now, these recipes were telling me how to do the same.

The *pomodoro*-red binder contained the heart and heartiness of a meal along with the recipes for pastas and pizzas. A play dough recipe for Mom's grandchildren sat alongside her breads and pies, and recipes such as apple cake, gnocchi, and ravioli dough from her mother, Raffaela. My mother hung on to the scant rewritten remains of her mother's instructions, the same way she cherished the collection of handcrafted tatted pillowcases she spread wherever we lay our teenaged heads. The recipes, the linens, said who Raffaela was to her daughter. Someone who had endured hardships and taught Mom to instill her food with just enough vibrations to penetrate the soul.

Ink drawings of cheese graters, lobsters, and mushrooms swam amid a turquoise sea on the second binder—possibly the newest of the bunch, or the most precious. The blue book contained a treasure trove of the recipes for which we best remembered my mother—her cookies.

On the final binder, images of flour sifters, garlic bulbs, and asparagus spears bubbled across the expanse of cover the color of an amber sunset. Duct tape embraced the spine and held in its contents. In this binder, Stella had written: *Silence is a true friend who never betrays.* A quote from the Chinese philosopher Confucius, offered from one Italian woman to another. My mother took this to heart, and never betrayed much of who she was, either.

THE FIRST RECIPES

My mother didn't leave behind specific requirements for these files as part of any inheritance. No asterisk in the will told us what to do with them. If possible, she would have stipulated only that she never be replaced. So what had she tried to conquer in keeping these kitchen records? "*Dove c'è l'amore le montagne sembrano pianure,*" the Italians say: "Where there's love, the mountains seem like plains."

Mom learned to write in the Palmer method of the 1930s, with letters that leaned right, as if blown sideways by the harsh winds that swept across the landscape of her life. The *stop-start* movement of her hands across paper could be attributed to her precision. Her lettering was tight and controlled. Her life was tight and controlled. She set herself up for success in the kitchen however she could. But between the strokes of handwriting where she and my grandmothers had exchanged their archaic instructions on life, my mother's volumes spoke to something more. Cooking proved to be her way out into the world, despite the real and imagined boundaries of the space in which she prospered. Her recipe repository became a diary where she begged, *come find me between the lines.* The pen was her tool to realize her culinary gains. She wove the long, handwritten threads of her kitchen existence in with vining notes from her mother-in-law, Stella; a copied-down recipe that had belonged to Stella's mother, Nellie; hints of my father; and echoes of her own mother's recipes, once scrawled in Italian, attributed to *my mother, Raffaela.*

In my analysis of an Italian American woman at work, in this catalogue developed by hands rubbed with Vaseline in wintertime, I find an archive of my mother's thoughtfulness, her intention to get something right for herself, and to demystifying the culinary inheritance she had received from her ancestors. Between the lines, she had left extra space; room to think, change her mind, or manifest her own creations. In those blank spaces, I heard her voice and felt an emotion she rarely expressed out loud: the desire to be known.

If I flayed open the thin pages, with the mere touch of my hands, a *whoosh* of air brought my mother, Raffaela and her mother Annantonia, Stella and her mother Nellie, and the other *parenti* into my kitchen, with the memory of so many meals stuffed with laughter and salted with tears. Their soft arms muscled through turns at kneading dough, while their big Italian hearts burst open with every dish consumed by someone they loved.

Raffaela DeLuca fourth from left, with other Italian women cooking for a wedding, 1947.

Jean Januzzi's three binders.

GRANDMA DELUCA'S CANNOLI

My mother's binders contained three different recipes for cannoli, but this one belonged to Raffaela. The notes she included throughout her recipe binders—"Grandma DeLuca," "my mother's," "Raffaela"—were telling. Raffaela was everything to her, and remained a puzzle to be solved, a little like herself. The suggestion of wine is derived from my godmother, Sarah Magazine. The filling used in this recipe originated with Aunt Mary DeLuca and was made with ricotta, but you can substitute mascarpone cheese. Also, this filling calls for powdered sugar, which gives it a coarse texture. You can substitute granulated sugar instead.

SHELLS

- ⅓ cup vegetable shortening, softened
- ⅓ cup milk
- 1 egg
- 1 teaspoon dry white wine, for binding
- ¼ cup sugar plus 2 tablespoons
- 2 cups flour
- 1 egg white, beaten
- Vegetable oil, for frying

FILLING

- 15 ounces ricotta cheese, drained, overnight if possible
- ½ cup powdered sugar
- 2 tablespoons finely chopped citron or candied orange peel
- ½ teaspoon vanilla extract
- ¼ teaspoon ground cinnamon
- 6 ounces semisweet chocolate pieces (mini chocolate chips work best)

1. In a large stainless-steel bowl, combine shortening, milk, eggs, wine, and sugar. Add in flour and blend all ingredients together using a hand mixer. Roll out dough to less than ⅛ inch thick and cut into rectangles about 3 x 3 ½ inches, or use a round 3 ½-inch cookie cutter. Roll each piece of dough around a cannoli shell form. Press edges together with beaten egg white.

2. In a large pot or deep fryer, heat 2–3 inches oil over medium high heat. Working in batches, fry cannoli shells until golden brown. Remove to paper towel-lined cooling rack, taking care to drain oil from inside forms when removing from pot. Cool for 24 hours at room temperature. Store in a cool, dry place until ready to fill.

3. For the filling: mix all ingredients except the chocolate chips together using a hand mixer. Refrigerate for several hours or overnight before use. Use a piping bag to fill shells, then sprinkle both ends of each cannoli with chocolate chips. Double recipe for filling if serving cannoli in one setting.

4. Makes 28 cannoli shells

AUNT MARY DELUCA'S BISCOTTI

Aunt Mary was married to John, a cousin of my mom's stepfather, Luigi DeLuca, and his brother James. Therefore Cousin Frank, her son, was a younger, sort of second cousin to my mother. Frank and his mother held competing versions of biscotti in Mom's binders, though the preparation was the same. Like my mother, I've merged the two into one. However, the proportions belong to la donna più saggia e anziana. A wiser, older woman.

My mother baked several kinds of biscotti over the years, including new variations like breakfast biscotti and pumpkin and maple pecan biscotti. I also tasted other types of commercial biscotti on a trip to San Francisco and after moving to Oregon, and referred these to her. But this recipe has always been the standard bearer. I substitute dried cherries for cranberries for an updated taste.

---

1 ⅓ cups sugar

1 cup vegetable shortening

6 eggs, well-beaten

1 teaspoon anise extract or anise oil, or 1 ½ teaspoons vanilla extract

4 cups flour

3 ½ teaspoons baking powder

½ teaspoon salt

2 cups walnuts or pecans, chopped (optional)

⅓ cup dried cranberries or dried cherries, cut up finely with scissors (optional)

1. Preheat oven to 350°. If using nuts, spread them out on a baking sheet and roast for 2 to 3 minutes, then remove and let cool.

2. In a large bowl, cream together sugar and shortening by hand. Add eggs and extract. Stir in flour, baking powder, and salt. Add nuts or cranberries, if using. Mix dough thoroughly to avoid cracking during baking.

3. Roll out dough on lightly floured board and divide into four sections. Shape into four loaves, each about 12 inches long and 3 inches wide. Roll and pat each loaf with your hands to eliminate any air holes and create a smooth top. Roll once more across a light dusting of flour, then let loaves rest for several minutes. *Note: Don't flatten loaves too much; leaving some height will make them a little daintier and not quite as long when out of the oven.*

4. Grease and flour cookie sheets or line with parchment paper. (Loaves will not spread as much if the cookie sheet is floured.) Place one to two loaves on each prepared pan.

5. Bake for 20–25 minutes. Remove from oven. Transfer loaves to a board and carve immediately into ½-inch slices, using a bread knife if possible. Cut on a short diagonal, *otherwise, biscotti will come out too long and too pointy.* Place slices back on baking sheets on their sides and bake 5–6 more minutes, then flip and bake 5–6 more minutes on the other side. Remove from pan and cool.

6. Drizzle with icing or dip in chocolate for a sweeter version.

7. Makes approximately 48 biscotti

GRANDMA MAZZÀ'S FRIED TWISTS

In Calabria, there are many versions of a sweet donut, including nocatole in Reggio Calabria, where Stella's family came from, which closely resemble what we called "twists." Around Cosenza, similar versions like turdilli exist. The Mazzà version was a favorite in our home because you could truly taste the effort in making them.

- 1 cup milk
- ¼ cup plus 2 tablespoons sugar, and 1 pinch sugar, divided
- ½ teaspoon salt
- ¼ cup vegetable shortening
- 1 (¼ ounce) package dry yeast
- ¼ cup lukewarm water
- 4 ½ cups flour
- 2 eggs, beaten
- 1 teaspoon vanilla extract or anise extract or seed
- Vegetable oil, for frying

1. In a medium saucepan, heat milk over medium heat until small bubbles appear around edges of saucepan. Do not boil. Remove from heat. Add ¾ cup sugar, salt, and shortening. Cool to about 110° (otherwise the yeast will die and the dough won't rise). In a small bowl, dissolve yeast in water and add a pinch of sugar.

2. Place flour in a large mixing bowl and make a well in the center. Add cooled milk mixture, beaten eggs, dissolved yeast, and extract. Mix well, then knead until smooth. Add flour as needed until the dough is soft but not sticky.

3. Grease a large bowl with oil and place dough into the bowl. Turn to coat dough with oil, cover, and place in warm area to rise for about 1 hour. "May need a little longer on a cool day," my mother wrote. Punch dough down to eliminate air holes.

4. Cut off 2 x 3-inch pieces of dough and roll each piece *pencil thin* (about ¼ inch thick) into a long, even rope about 10 inches long. Here you can form twists or braids. To make a single-strand braid: first form a lower case "e," then thread the bottom of the "e" through the loop and pull straight. Twist the remaining loop away from you and tuck the end through the last loop. To make twists, at desired thickness, move one hand away from you and one hand toward, so rope remains twisted in between your hands. Hold ends in the air. Dough will twist naturally with 3 to 4 twists in the roll. Place twists on parchment paper–lined cookie sheets, tuck ends beneath the twist and cover with a cloth. Let rise about 30 minutes.

5. Heat two inches oil over medium high heat in deep fryer or large, light-colored pot (a light color makes it easier to determine doneness). Working in batches, add twists to hot oil. "Do not crowd," Stella wrote. Fry until golden brown with a lighter shade in the crevices. Drain on paper towels while you fry the remaining twists. Cool, then store in airtight container.

6. Makes approximately 35 twists

BOW TIES (*Chiacchiere*)

Bow ties were another standard family cookie. How many standards were there? We could argue all day. These are light and fluffy, and Italians might call this version of deep-fried sweet dough *chiacchiere*, like the word for the incessant chatter of Italians. With their basis in Carnevale, bow ties also go by different names in many regions. My mother clarified this was her updated version, which had evolved from a second, more traditional Italian recipe. In our home, this delicacy was fried only at Christmastime, because the oil that splashes everywhere when frying made them too messy for an everyday treat.

---

3 cups flour

3 tablespoons powdered sugar, plus more for dusting

¼ teaspoon salt

¼ teaspoon lemon zest

4 egg yolks

1 cup sour cream

½ teaspoon vanilla extract or 2 tablespoons rum

Vegetable oil, for frying

1. In a large bowl, mix flour, powdered sugar, and salt. Add lemon zest. In a medium bowl, beat egg yolks well and combine with sour cream and vanilla. Blend with flour mixture.

2. Knead dough on floured board. Roll into a rectangle about 8 inches long and 4 inches wide. If you prefer, you can use a pasta machine on the second to last setting to reach desired thinness. Add flour while rolling if necessary to prevent sticking. Using a pastry wheel, cut into strips about 4 inches long and 2 inches wide. Make about a 1-inch slit in center of each. Pull one short end most of the way through slit in center and pull lightly to open the short end you pulled through to create bow tie look.

3. Heat 2 inches oil in deep fryer or large pot over high heat. Add one or two bow ties at a time. They will immediately puff up. Using tongs, tip or turn over and fry for several seconds until lightly brown. Nudge with a fork so they will surface quickly. Drain on paper towels. Cool and dust with powdered sugar.

4. Makes approximately 48 bow ties

PECAN NUT CUPS (*Bocconotti*)

In Calabria, we discovered cookies called *bocconotii*, or *bocconotto* in the singular. Variations exist across regions from Abruzzo to Calabria, each made with a different type of filling, some with nuts, some with ricotta and black cherries. But the crust, a slightly flaky version of pie crust, remains the same. Below is my mother's recipe, influenced by both Abruzzese and Calabrian nut versions.

CRUST
- 1 cup flour
- ½ cup butter or margarine
- 1/3 cup cream cheese

FILLING
- 1 egg
- ¾ cup light brown sugar
- 1 tablespoon butter, softened
- Pinch of salt
- ¾ cup chopped pecans, chestnuts, or walnuts

1. For the crust: Using a pastry cutter, mix flour, margarine, and cream cheese until the consistency of pie dough. Form ball with dough and refrigerate for several hours. Or overnight.

2. For the filling: Beat together egg, brown sugar, butter, pecans and salt using whisk or wooden spoon.

3. Preheat oven to 350°.

4. Grease a mini cupcake pan, or use paper liners to line cups. Roll out dough to pie crust thickness, less than ⅛ inch. Using a small round cookie cutter (2 ½" in diameter) with scalloped edges, cut out circles and press into prepared pan. Use a ½ teaspoon measure to spoon filling into cups. Bake for 15 minutes until edges begin to brown. Remove to cooling racks.

5. Makes approximately 40 cookies

BASEMENT KITCHENS & COOKIE ALTARS

RECIPES

Italian Rolled Cookies • Caviciuni •
Bones of the Dead (*Ossi dei Morti*) • Totos • Nut Horns •
Lemon Cookies (*Agnetti*) • Nut Rolls

Like cooking a recipe from scratch, I could trace the corporeal and spiritual origins of my mother's culinary inspirations to the basement. Her beginnings as *capocuoca*, head chef, in our Italian American household were scattered across the dank, subterranean lower-level kitchens in northeastern Ohio she occupied over her nine decades of life.

At the varied stations downstairs, my mother yanked at dough with the same force she used when pulling stringy hair into pigtails. She pounded on veal cutlets with the backdrop of glass block bars lighting up her countenance. Ice-cold cement cooled her tired feet. A speckled green metal table with six chairs to sit in—before we needed seven—absorbed the blow of an aluminum mallet. Her mother's old cast-iron pizzelle maker and a shiny new Vitantonio one waited at ready.

Long ago, summer kitchens complete with fireplaces or hearths had been built into basements, or *cellars*, as we called them then. Servants would bed down there after preparing feasts for their employers living upstairs. Some homes possessed back-alley entrances to their cellars, a feature my mother would have loved so less dirt was tracked in.

Many of my American friends with Abruzzese connections shared enthusiastically about their basement kitchens. They were proud to have a "show kitchen" upstairs and the workhorse kitchen below, which was where tomatoes were canned and sausages made. Wine was fermented there too, in proximity to where it was sipped—parties were held downstairs, to minimize the mess upstairs. Some called it the *sugo* kitchen, because it was where sauce was made. Yet, even in the basement kitchen, my mother wrapped the stovetop coils in foil to save on cleaning later.

That a second kitchen was built into or installed in the very foundation spoke volumes about the countless Italian American women who found themselves down below. The cellar kitchen was a luxury, but it felt essential to many, including my mother. There, she stored the accumulated goods and appliances that were constantly plied to the modern woman (like the Presto Hot Dogger), hid smells her children considered odorous (tuna casserole), and kept the chaos contained, to maintain a certain level of *bella figura* upstairs, where all appeared to run smoothly. Every course she made for her family claimed the basement kitchen as its primary source. If you want to know the secrets to the culinary success of her and countless women like her, you'll find it there in the foundations.

⸺

As a youngster, my mother inhabited several residences in Lorain. At 1722 Washington Avenue, in a space with an extra-large cellar and dark stained wood–trimmed archways above, the home she encountered after Raffaela remarried Luigi was also filled with her new stepfather, and Luigi's brother and his wife, and soon, Jean's baby brother, Tony. Later, during birthdays, holidays, and Sundays, Raffaela and Luigi's next dwelling on West 17th welcomed us to our second home, that of Raffaela, Luigi, and Tony. At a time when twenty-four different dairies thrived in Lorain, the Lorain Creamery hummed in the backyard there. The cellar called for hide-and-seek, and homemade wine. When my mother and father first married in 1961, the young couple rented the second story of a twenty-year-old home on King Avenue whose address was 967 ½ That half was important—the old-fashioned ice box–style cabinetry in the kitchen offered my mother a meager hideaway in which to develop her expertise, but not enough space of her own for the job.

Upon moving to the neighboring town of Amherst four miles away, she finally gained the physical distance needed— from both her own roots and my Dad's—to grow into her own destiny as a cook. The basement of their small ranch home on a 2/3-acre lot along Ridgeland Drive was finished in

1950s brick block linoleum, and sectioned off into one large half and two smaller quarters where the temperature ranged from "cool enough for wine storage" to cold.

Here, my mother found peace in a lower level whose expanse was a cavern for her creativity. Its beadboard wainscoting offered padding for when she talked to herself, or for any solitude she sought. The closeness to the earth provided a sense of grounding, a weightiness that provided an anchor for the weightlessness of her ways. There her vast repertoire of recipes began to take shape.

We had no formal dining room above. Therefore, no baptism or First Communion after-party or priest dinner took place unless the antipasti all the way through to the cookies were served beneath the diffused light in the entertainment side of the basement. Recipes my mother accumulated over time were like the Bible cracked open. She read the lines repeatedly—*Keep mixing flour for a soft dough just until rolling consistency*—to understand the subtext delivered from on high; that is, from her mother or Stella. She put into practice these parables of food and family, over and again, hoping to achieve sainthood someday. In that undercroft, serving and feeding became part of her faith.

The basement on Ridgeland Drive held many contradictions: It was a place of work and play, a place of celebrations and silence. And a place that would inspire starting over, after a blizzard pounded Amherst the night of my tenth birthday slumber party. The basement flooded that night, and by morning, my parents had decided to move about a mile away. We rode our bikes each day or went for drives in the station wagon to witness the spectacle of a new home being built on Lincoln Street. Of a family being reshaped by concrete footers and rebar reinforcements. What went into the basement there helped distribute the weight of everything that house would hold, which in time would be much more than a steel Imperia pasta maker or extra sacks of flour.

Despite the pristine nature of the new kitchen, considered "gourmet," Mom plotted out a second kitchen in the basement that she could dirty without worry. There, stores of canned tomatoes (the only kind she used in her sauce), jarred peaches from Speigelberg Orchards, or pints of homemade raspberry jam with green tomatoes and eggplant in jars were hidden in the cupboards next to the old stove.

But nothing took precedence over the ultimate goodness that exuded from this covert space: Her cookies. Once, when my mother was hospitalized, she prayed the rosary while I busied myself at her side, listing the entirety of the Christmas cookie repertoire she would have baked in the cellar. A meditation on the names and their makeup was like meditating on the Mysteries and Glory Bes.

Taralli. Holiday cornflake wreaths. Warm, gooey frosting poured over sour cream chocolate drops. Lumpy chocolate logs rolled and cut into marshmallow church windows.

The size of each of those cookies expanded or shrank based on the humidity lurking in the northern Ohio air, and their numbers fluctuated too, depending on who was present or absent in the household at the time. But the one constant was that there would always be cookies.

In the basement, the hallowed tradition of baking began the instant my mother finished scrubbing the turkey roasting pan. Maybe she cheated and started baking after Halloween, beginning with *ossi dei morti*, bones of the dead. Pinwheels and cherry winks. Peanut butter cup tarts, which her notes said "Betty did not refrigerate." The crunch of *fiore di Natale* from Grandma Januzzi's sister, Aunt Palma. For *biscotti di lemone* [sic], she suggested in her binder to use the half-recipe because "there will be others." There were always others.

In the background, my father sweat while the fried twists twined in vats of oil and splattered his sleeves, adding to the sunspots already dotting his skin. *Caviciuni* (which we also called rosettes) stuffed with ground nuts or chickpeas floated around the fryer. My father saying *ca-vi-choon* became a train in my mind's tracks. Over the stove, he flipped old-fashioned pizzelle in their iron like a pizzaiolo. My mother never forgot he was the brawn behind her feats. His sole reward was to lick the bowl and eat the burnt ends.

When the chance was granted to us or when we wanted to borrow the car, we impatiently crushed walnuts in a grinder or stuck a raisin in the bellybutton of a snowman sugar cookie cutout to await an answer. We pushed faded fuschia-colored spritz dough through the press, or sprinkled a cutting board with flour for pecan nut cups, or were asked to "listen for the timer on the rolled powder sugar balls" or "plate some the wedding cookies for me, would you?" She delivered those petitions in the vernacular of her generosity. "Please, you do such a nice job with the gingerbread men." Or "Company is coming"...or "here"...or "leaving soon." And before she could finish, the green-and-red metal platter checkered with Christmas symbols, cold to the touch, was shoved in the hands of someone she was forced to trust to make up the cookie tray. If an empty space on the tray appeared due to snacking, laziness, or fear of freezing our fingers off in the freezer storage, she demanded, "What do you mean, 'it's all out'?," turned us around, and banished us to the rear of basement to stack more on the tray, never revealing the yields that existed in the ledger in her head.

For my wedding in Cincinnati, ten family members relayed boxes of biscotti, pizzelle, nut horns, and Italian rolled cookies with icing, nestled in clothing boxes between crumpled sheets of wax paper overhead, and wobbled through Cincinnati's Oktoberfest celebration to arrive at the rented banquet room ten stories above the public square. My mother stood by with pride to confirm the ceremonial cookies were safe from harm until their time came to be demolished after the meal.

It seemed there would *never* be a time when her supply ran out. Totos. Chocolate crinkles. Cannoli from Grandma DeLuca which she wrote, "makes too much." But she kept her production as special as Saturdays in winter when our bellies ached for that warmth yet to come, and as clean as the new year, after all the guests were gone. And she never forgot the Italian rolled cookies with no Italian name.

Hail, Holy Queen, Mother of mercy, our life, our sweetness, and our hope.

But yes, there were messes in the basement. One pivotal event, the Grease Fire of '94, occurred in the basement as Mom and Dad fried Christmas rosettes in hot simmering oil. Flames leapt from the burner, surrounded the pot, and jumped from the stovetop onto the vinyl flooring. My father called the fire department. Thankfully, no one was hurt—except the stacked-brick vinyl flooring. It didn't go unnoticed that a speck of singed flooring in the kitchen area required an all-new cream pattern to be laid downstairs. "I never liked that other flooring anyhow," my mother confessed.

"Oh, you should have heard the sirens," my father bragged. "The whole town probably wondered what was going on." No, they knew who was at work.

Despite my mother's expert instructional abilities, in the basement, she was culinary teacher and student alike in a classroom of one. She had no greater imperative than to excel at inventing the banquets to be served, like those young chefs who trained at Villa Santa Maria in Abruzzo. She would emerge with, perhaps, a plate of Roma tomatoes, perfectly sliced as if she'd been in the shop with a circular saw, with olive oil drizzled over their gleaming bodies using only the pad of her index finger for a spout.

She absorbed the teachings of her elders and practiced at the perfection imposed upon the modern American woman. And she discovered how to be alone, but not lonely in that basement shrine, an unfinished hermitage for her soul. With recipes fanned across a table free of neatly piled clothes, no one came between her and her sacred acts.

CLOCKWISE FROM TOP LEFT Jean Januzzi, kitchen cleanup, 1980s; Ettore and Jean Januzzi's first kitchen on King Avenue, 1961; Basement kitchen, Ridgeland Drive; Basement party for Annette Januzzi's christening, 1966.

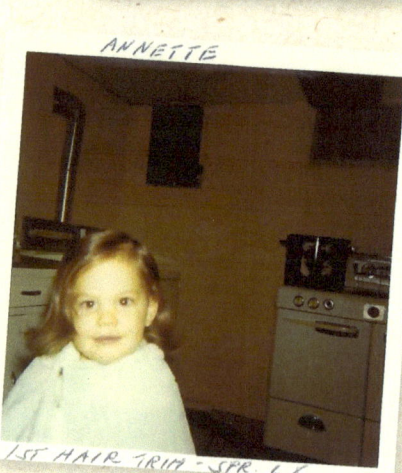

ITALIAN ROLLED COOKIES

There are a number of recipes like this one categorized generically as "Italian Cookies." Some versions are flavored with a hint of almond, but this recipe includes lemon or vanilla instead and resembles the taste of some typical Italian wedding cookies. This was a standard bearer for our family at wedding receptions, graduations, and celebrations of life, including my mother's final goodbye. The original recipe yields plenty and therefore is well-suited to cutting in half or thirds. In my family, we usually made only a half batch at Christmastime, which is the recipe listed here. But if you don't make a lot, it wouldn't be Italian, right?

DOUGH
- 3 eggs
- ¾ cup vegetable oil
- ½ cup milk
- 1 teaspoon lemon or vanilla extract
- 1 cup sugar
- 5 cups flour
- 1 heaping tablespoons baking powder

GLAZE
- 2 ½ cups powdered sugar
- 4 tablespoons milk
- 1 teaspoon vanilla extract
- food coloring and/or sprinkles (optional)

1. Preheat oven to 350°.
2. In a large bowl, beat eggs by hand. Add oil, milk, extract, and sugar to eggs. Beat again. Stir in flour and baking powder until blended.
3. Grease cookie sheets or line with parchment paper. Roll dough into little balls about ¾ inch in size and place on cookie sheets. Bake each batch for 8–10 minutes, until light brown on the underside. Cool on wire rack before glazing.
4. Mix all ingredients for glaze. Add additional milk if necessary to achieve thin, drizzling consistency. Glaze should drip off butter knife end gradually. Add food coloring if desired for a special occasion. Using same butter knife, drizzle across cookie tops to cover and allow glaze to slightly run down the sides. Add sprinkles immediately after frosting if desired.
5. Makes approximately 80 cookies

CAVICIUNI

Caviciuni go by many names in the Italian culture, including *cavazune* or "St. Joseph's pants," depending on the filling. In our household, this type of sweet was referred to as fiore di Natale (flowers of Christmas) or winter blooms, or simply rosettes, since they appeared like little flowers to us. Nuts were used for filling instead of the traditional combination of nuts and chickpeas in cavazune. The honeyed coating across the hardened, crispy surface gives them a crunchy texture, and we loved chocolate since it was Christmas, when chocolate flowed as freely as wine and coated the rest of the cookies in our stomachs. This recipe was adapted from Stella's, which was adapted from the version she received from her sister, Aunt Palma, who lived in Cleveland's Little Italy. Observe the use of chestnuts, as certainly Italian.

FILLING
- ⅓ cup chocolate chips
- ½ cup finely ground nuts (chestnuts, walnuts, or hazelnuts)
- ½ cup finely ground vanilla wafers (from about 14 wafers)
- ¼ cup honey
- 1 teaspoon vanilla extract

DOUGH
- 5 ½ cups flour
- ¾ cup sugar
- 1 ½ teaspoons baking powder
- ½ teaspoon salt
- 3 eggs plus 3 egg yolks (reserve whites for finishing; if halving recipe, use 2 eggs and 1 yolk)
- ½ cup milk, plus more as needed
- ½ cup oil
- 1 tablespoon white wine
- 1 tablespoon vanilla extract

FRYING AND FINISHING
- Vegetable oil, for frying
- 1 (8-ounce) bottle or jar of honey (a squeeze bottle works best)
- colored sprinkles (optional)

1. For filling: In a double boiler, melt chocolate chips. Add nuts, wafers, honey, and vanilla. Stir until blended, turn off heat and keep warm. Set aside. When cool, roll about 70 balls.

2. For dough: In a large bowl, mix flour, sugar, baking powder, and salt. In a medium bowl, by hand, beat eggs and egg yolks, milk, oil, wine, and vanilla. Add additional milk as needed to cover all ingredients. Add wet ingredients to dry ingredients one-third at a time and mix to form a stiff dough. Work dough until is evenly blended, then let rest until pliable enough to shape, about 5 minutes. Use a pasta machine to roll pieces of dough out into rectangles ⅛ inch thick (between second- and third-to-last setting on pasta machine). With a round cookie cutter about 2 ¾ inches in diameter, cut out 16 rounds at a time. Keep extra dough moist beneath a towel or wax paper while working on the first batch. Lay two rounds flat on a work surface. Place a marble-sized ball of filling on one round of dough, then top with the other round of dough. Press edges of rounds together with fork or baste edges with egg whites and press together. Repeat with remaining rounds.

3. Heat 2 inches oil in a deep fryer or a large, light-colored pot (a light color makes it easier to determine browning) over medium heat.

4. Cut six slits along edges of each filled dough round, up to the filling. Pick up every other petal, brush with egg white, and press together in the middle. Deep fry caviciuni in oil until lightly browned, 1–2 minutes. Some ends may open slightly, resembling a flower in shape. Remove to paper towel–lined plate. Drizzle honey on flowers and add colored sprinkles immediately, if desired. Transfer to wax paper–lined surface until cool. Repeat with remaining dough and filling.

5. Makes 70 cookies

BONES OF THE DEAD COOKIES (*Ossi dei Morti*)

Traditionally, Italians put their energies not into All Hallows' Eve, but into the Day of the Dead, November 1. In some cases, *Capotempo* (the beginning of time) was marked from November 1 through 11, during which Italians would follow rituals to get on the good side of the spirits and guarantee a plentiful harvest. They would visit their ancestors in old graveyards and make *ossi dei morti* (bones of the dead) to honor their past. One year, I had a "Mom" day and missed her beauty in my life. I rummaged through her cooking books and found two recipes for ossi dei morti. I used the one she had marked with an asterisk, shared below. Of course, what would an old family recipe be without a few "probably"s or "little bit"s. So much to figure out and learn about my mother in the making of a single batch.

In addition to Day of the Dead, ossi dei morti were also a tradition in Lorain in the 1950s for the celebration of Madonna del Popolo, when the Spoltorese residents served them along with wine.

---

2 cups flour

2 cups sugar, plus more for finishing

1 teaspoon baking powder

2 eggs, beaten

zest of 1 lemon

2 cups chopped walnuts or pecans

1. Preheat oven to 350°. Grease and flour cookie sheets or line with parchment paper.

2. In a large bowl, combine flour, sugar, and baking powder. Add eggs and zest and stir to mix, then fold in nuts. Knead until dough becomes a rolling consistency. Roll into logs about 1 inch thick and cut logs into 2-inch pieces along the diagonal.

3. Dip one side of each piece in water, then in sugar, to coat and resemble a fingernail. Place sugared side up on prepared cookie sheets.

4. Bake each batch for about 20 minutes. Watch carefully and do not let cookies brown. Remove from pan to cool.

5. Makes approximately 48 cookies

TOTOS

Totos were a popular cookie on the tray at all our family gatherings, especially among the adults. The surprise nutty flavor in a chocolate-based cookie was a turn-off to us kids growing up, until we acquired more refined palates. Following the lead of many other versions that call for warm spices, I added cinnamon and cloves to my mother's original recipe. The name *totos* (or *dodos*, another name for these) is thought to be derived from an Italian translation loosely meaning, "I give one to you, and one to me." Mostly, though, I save these for myself. At the bottom of this recipe, my mother made annotations for a larger quantity using 5 pounds flour, 1 pound of nuts, and so on. Presumably she used these when she and her mother baked for the Abruzzesi Club or the Church, the recipients of most of her kitchen endeavors after her adult kids had left town. I've cut her original recipe by half.

---

5 cups flour

1 cups sugar

½ cup cocoa powder

1 tablespoon baking powder

½ teaspoon ground cinnamon (optional)

½ teaspoon ground cloves (optional)

3 egg yolks

1 cups milk

juice and zest of ½ orange

1 ½ teaspoons almond extract

1 cups vegetable shortening, melted and cooled

1 cup chopped walnuts

GLAZE
2 ½ cups powdered sugar

4 tablespoons milk

1 teaspoon vanilla extract

1. Preheat oven to 350°.

2. In a large bowl, mix flour, sugar, cocoa, and baking powder. Add spices, if using. In a separate medium bowl, mix egg yolks, milk, orange zest and juice, and almond extract. Add egg mixture to flour mixture and stir to combine. Stir in melted shortening. Add nuts and mix well.

3. Form dough into walnut-sized balls. Place on greased or parchment-paper lined cookie sheets

4. Bake for 12–15 minutes. Remove from pan. Cool on wire racks.

5. Mix all ingredients for glaze. Add additional milk if necessary to achieve thin, drizzling consistency. Glaze should drip off butter knife end gradually. Using same butter knife, drizzle across cookie tops to cover and allow glaze to slightly run down the sides.

6. Makes approximately 60 cookies

NUT HORNS

My siblings and I all had our favorite cookies growing up, and this one belonged to my younger sister, Beth. My mother tested her recipes often, comparing them with friends' recipes or with whatever she might find in cookbooks. On this recipe, she was very clear to "Make recipe as is. Do not use egg white." The dough, which is similar to a pie dough, is made ahead of time and will need to be refrigerated for at least 4 hours.

DOUGH
- 2 cups flour
- 1 cup butter or margarine, softened
- ¾ cup sour cream
- 1 egg yolk

FILLING
- 1 cup ground pecans or walnuts
- 1 cup sugar

1. For the dough: In a large bowl, combine flour and butter and work dough together using a pastry cutter. In a separate bowl, combine sour cream and egg yolk. Add sour cream mixture to dry mixture and blend until it reaches a pastry dough consistency. Roll into one ball, then divide into four parts. Wrap each piece in plastic wrap and chill for at least 4 hours, or overnight. Let rest 5–10 minutes at room temp before use.

2. For the filling: Combine ground nuts and sugar. Divide filling into four parts and set aside.

3. Assembly: Preheat oven to 350°. Grease cookie sheets and set aside. Using one ball of dough at a time, divide dough into 16 pieces and use rolling pin to roll each piece into a 12-inch round on floured board or surface. Divide first batch of filling among rounds and spread thin layer, less than ½ cup, across each round. Using a pastry cutter with straight or scalloped edges, cut each round into sixteen equal triangles. Roll each piece from outside in to enclose filling. Turn ends of each roll in slightly to form a crescent and place on greased cookie sheet.

4. Bake at for 8 minutes on lower rack, then 8–10 minutes more on upper rack, until slightly brown at the edges. Remove from pan. Cool on wire racks. Repeat with remaining three batches of dough and filling.

5. Makes approximately 40 cookies

LEMON COOKIES (*Agnetti*)

"For many people, use regular recipe. For Christmas use half recipe because there will be other cookies," my mother wrote in her recipe's addendum. At last count, there were over fifty types of cookies my mother made over the course of holidays. She served about two dozen at any one time. Those of us who prepared the cookie platters throughout the season can attest to the freezer burn we suffered when stocking the plates. We can also attest to some additional carbohydrates consumed at the same time. Mom's cookies were *Mom's cookies*, even if they were frozen. To accomplish the enormous endeavor of her full complement of cookies, my mother utilized the upstairs "show kitchen" and the basement one. These cookies, with their light, lemony feel on the tongue, were special enough to be granted *upstairs oven* status.

My mother told me this recipe was attributed to Lillian DiDonato, her Italian translator. Liliana was born in Spoltore, Italy, on May 1, 1925; she immigrated to the United States in 1955. In 1956 she moved to Lorain, where she remained a resident until her death. According to her obituary, she loved her "family and Italy." My epitaph too.

- ½ cup butter or margarine, softened
- 1 cup sugar
- 2 eggs
- 2 ⅔ cups flour
- 4 teaspoons baking powder
- ½ cup milk
- 1 teaspoon lemon extract
- zest of ½ orange
- powdered sugar, for rolling

1. In a large bowl, cream butter and sugar together by hand. Add eggs and beat until creamy. In a separate bowl, combine flour and baking powder, then add to butter mixture a little at a time, alternating with the milk. Fold in lemon extract and orange zest.

2. Shape dough into 2-inch balls and roll in powdered sugar, then place on well-greased and floured cookie sheets and refrigerate for several minutes. Meanwhile, preheat oven to 350°.

3. Bake for 10 minutes. These cookies are light in color; do not wait until tops brown. Remove from pan and cool on wire rack.

4. Makes approximately 48 cookies

NUT ROLLS

Nut rolls are similar to *kolache* rolls in Eastern European cultures. The people of Czechia, Slovakia, Poland, Hungary, and Croatia all made their own versions of kolache, and trade between these countries and Italy was consistent across the Adriatic. Given that my mother's family lived near the Adriatic, it's not surprising that these nut rolls originated from her mother's side of the family. Lorain also contained a large Slovakian population, and newspaper archives reveal that DeLuca's Bakery and its successor were known for their *kolac* (kolache), which means "wheel" or "round." This recipe is a direct descendent of that one.

Nut rolls appeared at every holiday gathering, but they were never given away in the same fashion as the dozens of cookies packaged and sent off with guests and visiting college students. Perhaps because they involve time, energy, and patience, my mother saved them for the family. The recipe involves several steps, but the accolades and memories are worth the time.

NUT FILLING
- 2 pounds shelled walnuts, ground, plus ½ cup chopped for topping
- 6 graham cracker squares, ground
- 1 cup milk
- 1 teaspoon vanilla extract
- ½ teaspoon lemon juice
- 2 cups sugar

DOUGH
- 1 package dry yeast
- ¼ cup plus 1 teaspoon sugar, divided
- ¼ cup warm water
- 4 cups flour, plus more as needed
- ¾ teaspoon salt
- 4 egg yolks, room temperature, well beaten
- 1 cup half-and-half
- 1 cup butter or margarine, melted and cooled
- ¼ cup milk

FROSTING
- 2 ½ cups powdered sugar
- ½ cup butter or margarine, softened
- 1 teaspoon maple extract
- 3-4 tablespoons milk, plus more as needed

1. For the dough: Dissolve yeast and 1 teaspoon sugar in warm water and let stand for 15 minutes. Combine flour and salt in a large bowl, then add remaining ¼ cup sugar. Add beaten egg yolks, cream or milk, and yeast mixture. Finally, stir in melted butter and mix well. Knead for 5 minutes, adding a little more flour as needed if sticking. Separate dough into 6 pieces (or 4 pieces for longer nut rolls), wrap each in wax paper, and refrigerate overnight. The next day, roll each piece out into a rectangle about 12 inches long and 4–6 inches wide. Spread one portion of nut filling across each rectangle and roll up lengthwise. Set on parchment paper–covered cookie sheets and let rise 2 hours or longer in a warm location.

2. Preheat oven to 350° for 20 minutes. Brush tops of loaves with milk before baking. Bake for 20 minutes, then check for a light brown crust. Bake 5 minutes longer if necessary. Allow rolls to cool slightly. Remove from pan. Cool on wire rack before frosting.

3. To prepare frosting: Beat together powdered sugar, softened butter, and maple flavoring by hand or mixer. Stir milk in gradually until you reach a medium-thin, spreadable consistency. Spread over top of each nut roll. Sprinkle with chopped nuts.

4. Makes 6 loaves, approximately 12 slices per loaf.

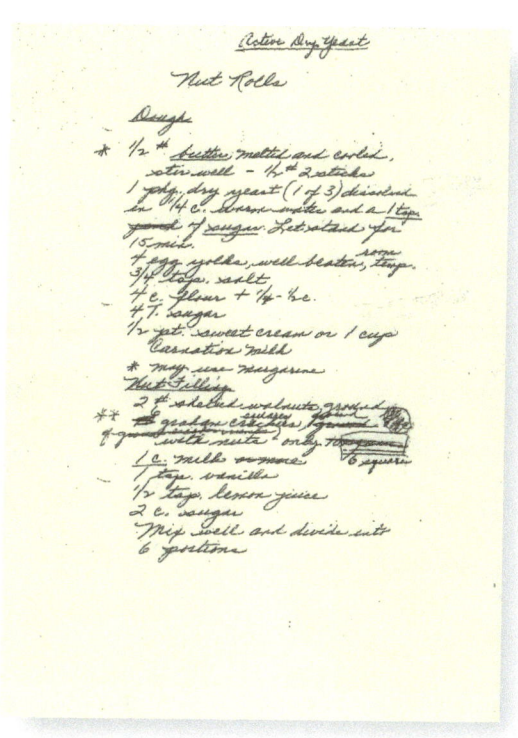

CAKES AND PIES IN HARVEST-GOLD LIGHT

RECIPES
Italian Love Cake • Maple Pecan Chiffon Cake •
Swiss Chocolate Squares • Old Fashioned Raisin Pie •
Pistachio Cheesecake

In the *new* upstairs, as we called everything that year of 1976, my mother imagined gathering the great cooks of her time with us in one big open space. The spindles on the half-wall of the kitchen opened their arms to everyone she had loved. But with Raffaela and Stella both deceased, she and her cooking life began to be molded by external forces. As she set about planning for a kitchen speckled with light everywhere, contractors, designs, and her dreams further cemented her American ways. With laser-like focus, she created a triangulated workspace of color-coordinated harvest-gold sink, refrigerator, and stove, nailing the design like a gymnast sticks her routine.

    That kitchen above ground on Lincoln Street belonged to my mother's model home, complemented by the coral-orange and seafoam-green colors that lifted the living room to new heights. In the dining room with matching décor, the unspoken tagline *don't go in there* floated somewhere above the threshold. She also took hold of the concept of a mudroom, except my mother's room was not for mud—it was for receiving guests through the garage because they hadn't graduated to the main front door. The mudroom also held a second freezer full of vegetables boxed, blackberries and strawberries picked, food we couldn't consume in one year, let alone five.

    Whenever she did cook upstairs for the length and breadth of the holiday season, she always threatened, "I'm going to hang a *Kitchen Closed* sign over the doorway." Though its design allowed for passage through, her kitchen was a sacred altar. No procession occurred without explicit permission.

The kitchen upstairs could also boast of something the basement one could not: The presence of cakes. Here where she could keep an eye on the timer and the cake's rise, where the new oven was more predictable, she mixed them, baked them, welcomed them like time-honored guests. Peaches and cream cake, tomato soup cake, special Italian cake...but none compared to the fanciful birthday cakes in my memories.

For my son's first birthday, my parents flew from Ohio to Oregon. Inside my mother's suitcase, a *Baker's Coconut Animal Cut-Out Cakes* booklet rested beneath tissue paper leafed over her clothing. After twenty or so years on the shelf, this reference material had been summoned to help her practice the same magic on her grandchildren that I remembered from my own youth.

The cover featured a boxy cake shaped as a prancing lion, strutting with licorice legs and sporting a mane made from coconut dyed burnt sienna. Inside the booklet, a white hobby horse cake was flaked with coconut, Life Savers pushed into the frosting to resemble spots. The Noah's Ark of my childhood didn't originate from any Bible; instead its animals marched birthday by birthday, cake by cake, straight out of that book.

In 1959, companies eagerly sold homemakers on the idea anyone could wow their family and friends and sculpt animal figures and other forms from two sheet pans of baked batter—if they knew how to cut the cake. One equal square of cake might hold the beginnings of the horse rocker, legs, and head. Another triangle might become the body. My mother would move her pantry supplies—or the entire household, kids included—down the street, if it meant her table sat level to the millimeter so she could fashion cakes and casseroles, pizzas and pies, into accurate portions.

Soon enough, though, we tired of animals, and a new cake began to define our birthdays: the chiffon. Developed in 1927 by Harry Baker, the chiffon cake recipe was kept secret until he sold it to General Mills. The company introduced the cake to the world in 1948 with the headline: "The first really new cake in 100 years!" In my mother's recipe books, the number of chiffon cakes rivaled the number of her children and grandchildren. Orange, lemon, maple pecan, pineapple, even a pumpkin chiffon pie. When I complained, "I don't want one of those for my birthday," my mother looked up through her reading glasses, her nostrils in a slight flare. "Why not? You like my chiffons, and you love pineapples." Her kind voice did not pose this as a question, but a conviction.

When we demanded more, she pushed to reach new heights. Pineapple Carrot Cake, Peanut Butter Cake, and so many attempts at variations of zucchini cakes, they needed their own cookbook. But it was Swiss Chocolate Squares, Ho Ho Cake, and Italian Love Cake that topped the list of most requested family favorites.

When grandchildren finally arrived, my mother returned to her shaped-cake roots. In Oregon for Davis' birthday, she had made the Spot the Fox Terrier cake from the *Baker's* book and let her grandson finger-fork frosting into his mouth, smear the paste of sugar across his high-chair tray, and rub it into her sleeves. Her first four grandchildren, all born within a twenty-eight-month span, went on to become the recipients of fire engine cakes, dinosaurs, a backhoe; cakes shaped like the Scooby Doo mystery van, Pokémon, and Bob and Larry from *Veggie Tales*; a basketball court, a baseball diamond, and a bowling alley lane complete with ten pins. During Davis's early teen years, she aimed high and baked a round, golf ball–shaped cake. The dimples on the white ball, made with a simple butter knife, demonstrated her clear command of icing techniques. She staked an outright claim on my jealously and on her grandson's stomach and heart.

The upstairs kitchen in my youth was also a postscript to my day. I could easily slip the last of my worries into questions about clearing the table or washing or drying the dishes. After dinner, with siblings out of sight, I stood at my mother's side to talk about things that didn't come up at the table. She and I were about the same height for a while, until her spine began to cave. We cleaned the dishes in tandem with matching harvest-gold dish cloths and towels. I was a one-on-one kind of a person, more like my dad. She was warm and friendly, opinionated, and an animated conversationalist. If she asked the right questions, I'd bare my soul.

"I don't understand boys," I told her one evening, after sharing the tragic news of my high school breakup. She didn't have much advice, other than "Someday, you'll find the right person." We cleaned up after dinner through other breakups and challenges too: a setback in college when I wanted to change my computer science major; the time I informed her the new guy in my life, Devin, was divorced; and later, the day we rubbed bowls dry after he died. She was there to help cleanse my soul and wipe away the thoughts that clogged my mind.

To this day, I lather and rinse the dishes meticulously out of respect for her and our after-dinner dissections of life. Gratitude has also seeped in. When Mark cleans up after dinner, there I am, wiping away the trickles along the counter and down the cabinets. In the two of us, I see echoes of my parents standing side by side, sharing in the details of their day or a meal. It is a blessed intimate portrait of a marriage, of commitment to a cause. A kitchen cleaned—and closed.

My mother mapped the layout of our large family home not only to restrict us kids from ruining her pies and cakes, but to suppress the advances of our untidy lives into her territory. Her own space, she kept hidden away, much like the revelations about her history that remained hidden in the closet of her heart. Whenever she was losing a battle in life, the baseboards, laundry, and other objects of her scrubbing and scorn took the brunt in her attempt to win the war on messes. When that didn't work, she mixed and melded instead.

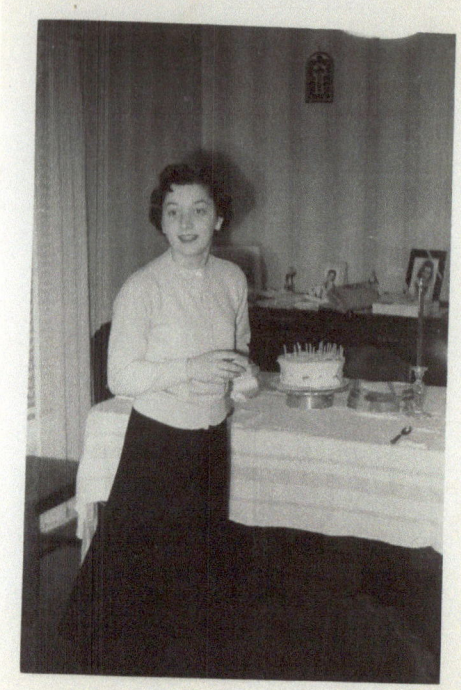
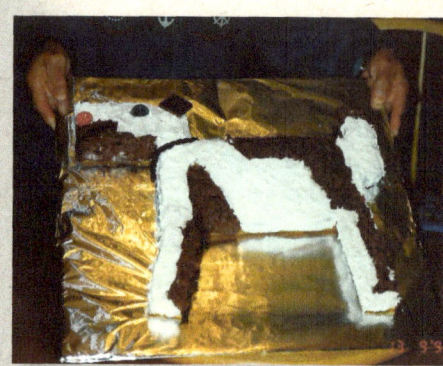

FROM TOPLEFT Jean Giuliani, birthday cake, 1940s; "Spot" – Davis Wick's birthday cake, 1997; Stella Januzzi's birthday, with grandchildren. 1970s

ITALIAN LOVE CAKE

Italian Love Cake, with its similarities to the limoncello cake found on Italian American restaurant menus, has nothing to do with love, and everything to do with calories. It is comfort food on a hot or cold day, and a balm to heal all aches. When my first husband died, I asked my mother for this recipe so I could wallow in something sweet and comforting. Food was an escape, as was the kitchen. Perhaps then, this cake had everything to do with love.

CAKE
- 1 (15.25-ounce) package lemon cake mix
- 2 pounds ricotta cheese
- 4 large eggs
- ¾ cup sugar
- 1 teaspoon vanilla extract

TOPPING
- 1 (3.4-ounce) box instant vanilla pudding
- 8 ounces Cool Whip, thawed
- 1 cup milk

1. For the cake: Grease and flour 9-x-13-inch metal or glass pan. Preheat oven to 350° if using a metal pan, or 325° for a glass pan. Prepare cake mix according to package directions and pour into prepared pan.

2. In a large bowl, mix ricotta cheese, eggs, sugar, and vanilla by hand; do not use beaters. Distribute evenly over prepared cake batter.

3. Bake for 40–45 minutes. Or until toothpick can be removed cleanly. Remove from oven and let cool.

4. For the topping: Combine all topping ingredients and layer over cooled cake. Refrigerate until set, at least 2 hours, or overnight.

5. Makes 20–24 squares

MAPLE PECAN CHIFFON CAKE

This cake recipe was part of a steady rotation of chiffon cakes in our house. Pumpkin chiffon arrived on occasion for Thanksgiving, while lemon and orange showed up during the spring and summer seasons. This one satisfies a sweet tooth, and given my love of maple frosting, if I had a favorite among the chiffon cakes my mother made for my birthdays, this might have been it. My mother believed it was important to use Soft Silk cake flour for chiffon cakes.

CAKE
- 2 ¼ cups sifted cake flour (Soft Silk) or all-purpose flour
- ¾ cup sugar
- ¾ cup brown sugar, packed
- 1 teaspoon salt
- ½ cup vegetable oil
- 5 egg yolks
- ¾ cup cold water
- 2 teaspoons maple extract
- 1 cup egg whites (from 7 or 8 eggs)
- ½ teaspoon cream of tartar
- 1 cup finely chopped pecans

ICING
- ½ cup powdered sugar
- 1 tablespoon milk
- ½ teaspoon maple flavoring (or any other intriguing flavor)

1. For the cake: Preheat oven to 325°. In a medium bowl, sift together flour, sugar, brown sugar, and salt. Make a well in flour mixture. Add oil, egg yolks, water, and maple flavoring. Beat with wooden spoon until smooth.

2. Combine egg whites and cream of tartar in a large mixing bowl. Using a hand mixer, beat until egg whites form very stiff peaks. Pour egg yolk mixture gradually into, beaten egg whites, gently folding in with rubber scraper just until blended. Gently fold in pecans.

3. Pour into ungreased tube pan. Bake at 325° for 55 minutes, then increase the oven temp to 350° and bake for another 10–15 minutes, until light brown on top. Invert cake, still in pan, onto funnel. Let hang until cool. Unmold then plate.

4. For the icing: Mix powdered sugar and milk to form a glaze. Add maple extract and drizzle over top and along ridges of the cake.

5. Makes 10–12 servings

SWISS CHOCOLATE SQUARES

This recipe was one of the most requested cakes for birthdays and other special occasions in my house growing up. However, not every wish of ours was my mother's command. There were times we were relegated to chiffon cakes instead.

CAKE
- 2 cups flour
- 2 cups sugar
- 1 cup water
- ½ cup butter
- 1½ ounces (1½ squares) unsweetened chocolate
- 2 eggs
- ½ cup sour cream
- 1 teaspoon baking soda
- ½ teaspoon salt

MILK CHOCOLATE FROSTING
- ½ cup butter
- 6 tablespoons milk
- 1 ½ ounces (1 ½ squares) unsweetened chocolate
- 4 ½ cups powdered sugar
- 1 teaspoon vanilla extract
- ½ cup chopped nuts (optional)

1. For the cake: Preheat oven to 375°. Grease a jelly roll pan.

2. In a large bowl, combine flour and sugar. Set aside. In a medium saucepan, combine water, butter, and chocolate. Slowly bring ingredients to a boil, then remove from heat. Add chocolate mixture to sugar and flour and stir. Add eggs, sour cream, baking soda, and salt. Mix well. Pour into greased jelly roll pan and bake for 20–25 minutes.

3. For the frosting: In a large saucepan, combine butter, milk, and chocolate. Bring to a boil slowly and continue boiling for 1 minute. Reduce heat to medium and stir in powdered sugar. Remove from heat and beat with wooden spoon until smooth. Stir in vanilla.

4. Frost cake while still slightly warm, but not too hot to ensure frosting does not run. Sprinkle with nuts. Cut into squares when cooled.

5. Makes 16–20 servings

OLD FASHIONED RAISIN PIE

My mother cooked this traditional pie for my father, since his mother had excelled at baking too and passed this recipe to her. He was also a fan of her pecan pie, but she set her sights on perfecting this raisin pie especially for him. In her archives, she kept a second and third raisin pie recipe, one of which was from Uncle Don, no relation but the husband of her dearest friend, our "Aunt" Mary Jane. She would have treasured the recipe after a visit with Don and Mary Jane, who had moved to DC where Don worked in the Library of Congress. But given that he was a librarian, his recipe was succinct, and my mother, no doubt, moved on from his shortened version quickly to create her own. I prefer a balsamic or fig vinegar in this dish for an added tang of flavor.

2 cups raisins

2 cups water

½ cup packed brown sugar

2 tablespoons cornstarch

½ teaspoon ground cinnamon

¼ teaspoon salt

1 tablespoon vinegar, white or balsamic

1 tablespoon butter or margarine

2 (9-inch) pie crusts

1. Preheat oven to 425°, or to 400° if using glass pie pan.

2. In a small saucepan, combine raisins and water. Bring to a boil, then continue cooking for 5 minutes. In a separate bowl, blend brown sugar, cornstarch, cinnamon, and salt. Add to raisins and cook over medium heat, stirring, until dissolved. Remove from stove and add vinegar and butter. Cool slightly.

3. Gently press one pie crust into 9-inch pie pan. Spread raising filling into bottom crust and cover with top crust. Crimp or flute the edges. Pierce pie with a fork or cut slits in the middle to allow steam to escape and for a crispier crust.

4. Bake for 30 minutes until golden brown, checking at 25-minute mark to ensure even cooking. Let cool completely. Serve with ice cream or homemade whipped cream.

5. Makes 6–8 servings

PISTACHIO CHEESECAKE

Until my father developed heart problems, he celebrated the evening's end with a bowl of ice cream. Pistachio was his favorite flavor, a preference inherited from his parents and the tastes of their native Calabria. My mother's binders contained eight varieties of cheesecake, so this is one she might have pursued when pistachios were available. I use ricotta in this recipe to add a creamy, nutty note, something warm and *meravigliosa*, like the fond memories I have of my father, eating ice cream while punching in numbers on the adding machine after a long day at the shoe store. His numbers didn't always add up, but this recipe will. It's best if the ingredients are brought to room temperature before you begin. You can buy store-bought pistachio paste in a jar, or make your own by grinding pistachios into a paste with a bit of water.

CRUST
- Scant ½ cup graham cracker cookie crumbs
- ¼ cup chopped pistachios
- 2 tablespoons sugar
- 2 tablespoons melted butter

FILLING
- 3 large eggs
- ¾ cup sugar
- 14 ounces ricotta cheese
- ¼ cup Greek yogurt
- ½ cup pistachio paste
- 1 teaspoon vanilla extract
- 1 teaspoon almond extract
- 1 teaspoon lemon zest
- 1 teaspoon salt

FOR TOPPING
- powdered sugar
- lemon zest
- crushed pistachios

1. For the crust: Preheat oven to 350°. Grease 8-inch springform pan with a cold dab of butter. In a medium mixing bowl, blend crust ingredients into a smooth paste. Press into the bottom of prepared springform pan. Bake for about 10 minutes, until the top begins to brown (this will happen quickly). Let cool while blending filling.

2. For the filling: In a large bowl, combine eggs and sugar. Fold in ricotta cheese and yogurt. Using a hand mixer, beat until blended. Add remaining ingredients.

3. Reduce oven temperature to 325°. Pour filling into crust in springform pan. Bake for 1 hour. Let cool in pan. Remove from mold. Dust with powdered sugar, lemon zest, and crushed pistachios.

4. Makes 8–10 servings

FROM THE GARDEN WITH LOVE

~~~~~~

RECIPES

Basic Tomato Sauce • Pizza Dough • Zucchini Squares •
Zucchini Casserole with Cottage Cheese and Monterey Jack Cheese •
Eggplant Parmesan • Marinated Eggplant • Stuffed Cabbage

~~~~~~

Many refer to it as passata—that pulp of tomatoes pressed through pillowcases and strained into old bottles or jars for eventual use in pasta sauces. *Passata*, an Italian word, indicated something had been passed. Like turning the soil to burrow in tomato plants, turning vines into tomatoes, tomatoes into sauce. That sauce would be passed into meals, and those meals into near-religious experiences.

We called the results of that summer-long process "Mom's sauce," but it began near winter's end—with Dad.

Every March, he stopped in at Willow's Hardware to buy twine and stakes and rent a tiller for the garden. "Damn, more snow," he said, and shoveled the accumulating flakes to wait for the spring thaw. He'd be ready when the right weather arrived.

After seeding, digging, staking and growth, the garden came to us. No matter how crammed our calendars were, no one was ever too busy for my father to ask, "Can you kids water the garden while I'm gone?" Our excuses ran as long as the freeway behind our house, for miles in both directions. But if we wanted to eat, we did the job. All summer, the basement held the burgeoning stores of plum and beefsteak tomatoes. Tomatoes piled up two by two on Formica counters. The rounded fruit spilled out onto the shelves of the second refrigerator, and years later snuck its way into every bag we lugged back to our own homes as adults. By August, it was time to hang onto to those tomatoes for good.

In my mother's recipes, I never found instructions for the work of my father's tanned hands as he clutched each tomato, squeezed it slightly to ensure ripeness, placed it in an old bushel basket, and ported the filled baskets inside, where they were stored in the basement until it was time. There were no directions either, for the second, fairer set of hands wearing a silver wedding ring, fingernails rounded to a point, that joined together with the first hands as they cut tomatoes into quarters. But I didn't need instructions—I could still hear the sound of chunks of tomatoes plopping into a colander, which filtered juice to save for later. Juice with the terroir of grass, sand, and the stand of pines that kept out the diesel fumes from the interstate a hundred yards behind and below the house. Terrain of city water from the sprinkler and the rain my dad swore off—until he needed it, and then he prayed.

Jars of coarsely cut tomatoes were sealed in the large enamel stock pot. When my mother had need of ritual, she would twist her red rubber jar opener around the seal to pop one open and inhale the fertile scent. Like virgin olive oil from the first press, but better. From her cupboards, she'd retrieve the tomato press, wrap her fingers around its handle, and crank out her tomato puree, or passata. No pillowcases were involved—she wouldn't have wasted such fine linens as those from her mother's carriage overseas. Instead, she pushed the flesh of dozens of tomatoes through a strainer that resembled a rotary food mill. The aluminum steel of the strainer scraped along its base. My mother's arms, hardly thickening with age, spasmed with muscle as the rotor spun around. The tomatoes weren't pressed into a paste so much as into a dreamy puree, deeply flavored without the use of anything artificial. Its sugary scent was a call to home. The heaviness of the labor, the dampness, the complaints of kids who had to water the lawn and garden, were all lifted by the tomatoes' striving to reach for the greatest heights in flavor. Freed of this weightiness, the puree could float on air.

My mother added to her sauce what she deemed important, or what was available from the garden that day, week, or year. Her sauce was more special than anyone else's, because in her recipe she recommended "2 quarts of canned tomatoes—I can my own."

There were pleas to commercially jar the sauce and call it *Mom's Sauce*, but it wasn't going to happen. They would have had to bottle up the soil and the breeze, the terroir of wood stakes and bristling twine, of Dad's sweat on his white safari hat, and all that grumbling we did when asked to water the tomato plants. "Oh, we don't want to do *all* that work," they said, as if their performance in the kitchen and garden up until that moment had been easy.

※

Whenever the lone rotary-dial phone clinging to a half-wall between the tight kitchen and the newly added family room rang out on a Friday afternoon, one of us ran to answer knowing who was on the line. "Hello?"

"Hallo," my father said, in the strange dialect that mimicked his Italian father's. Phoning from the shoe store, he asked, "How was school? (*Good.*) What kind of grades did you get today? (*Good.*) What's goin' on with you kids? (*Nothing.*)" And then: "Are we having Mom's pizza, or am I picking it up? And what kind of pop am I supposed to bring home from the store?" (We weren't *soda* people.)

If "Mom's sauce" meant love and the bounty of the garden, "Mom's pizza" was a metonym for Friday night, when the family shoe store stayed open later than its usual weekday shutdown at five o'clock. Weary, my dad would reconcile the cash register with the day's sales, jump into the Suburban, and head for home. We often didn't see him until seven or eight o'clock, unless we had a softball game and his brother agreed to cover for him, or business died down before the closing bell.

Was it pickup or homemade? He waited on the line. Would our dinner be made by the Italians at Yala's Pizzaria down the street from the store, or by Mom pulling at her own dough—and hair—that night? Our tired dad always rooted for homemade for the sake of cost and comfort, and because it meant one less stop on his way home. We did too. Chants of "c'mon, Mom, make your pizza tonight," reverberated throughout our neighborhood kick-the-can games, though her pizza wasn't something we shared with others. It could only be stretched so thin.

Finally, Mom pulled her hands out of the sink or the refrigerator, or stepped away from the stove, and signaled toward the phone with a rolling pin between her hands. "She's making homemade tonight, see you soon, bye."

Her early pizzas were pressed into circles. But in later iterations, she stretched the dough into a rectangular pan. It took a pizza the length of a football field to satisfy our family, and the square slices ensured as much pizza equality as possible in a family of seven. Once the crust was safely snuggled against the angled sides of the scratched cookie sheets, she spooned fresh, homemade tomato sauce over the pressed dough. Her artistry in dusting the cream-and-red canvas with gratings of Romano cheese was incomparable. She scattered just enough for the granules to bubble and crust over to perfection in the oven, then topped the pizza with slices of the tooth-pulling kind of pepperoni, which dotted the pizza like cherries on a sundae's mountaintop. Strips of mozzarella were secondary—more expensive. Our taste buds preferred the zing from more pepperoni and Romano cheese. Sometimes, she added a snip of homegrown basil or oregano leaves. The surface gleamed after a final drizzling of olive oil.

With due respect to other combinations of pizza toppings—like fig and prosciutto, which I'd break down doors for—I craved that simplicity. The Romano cheese tingled in my mouth, made me salivate. Mom was the crust-eater. She didn't waste her work. The rest of us fought over what was left behind, scrapes of burnt cheese or that last slice of pepperoni that, after caving upward from the heat, had slipped away quietly from the rest of the party.

That end-of-week ritual offered us the freedom to be a family at a time when we desperately wanted to scatter. What we could not forsake was pizza night: Dad's time away from the harried busyness of the store, and Mom's strong-armed efforts in the kitchen to create a centerpiece that would ground us—as opposed to being grounded—around a table set for seven where she cut the pizza into eighths.

※

Beyond tomatoes, my father had additional obsessions with sustenance and growth. His favorites—other than his children—included the family heirloom of eggplant. A well-known species in most southern Italian regions, my father's pear-shaped eggplant was cut and marinated for jarring, or sliced and frozen in little white boxes, which would be used near-exclusively for eggplant parmesan. His passion for his parents' people also extended to a coveted fig tree. Each spring, he carried forth a scarlet wooden pot where the fig tree, a grafted branch handed down from his father, had wintered beneath a burlap blanket. I never knew how much he missed his dad until I missed my own, recalling how the fig tree grew as my father's strength waned. The tree never gave us more than a few dozen figs a year. But we welcomed them plain or smothered in mascarpone cheese and showered with powdered sugar. Each of them was treated like a prodigal child. *Come noi che ritornavamo a casa.* Like us, they were returning home.

But the one obsession he could not, would not, forsake was that of zucchini. In late summer, in the middle of peeling another of the dark green cylindrical vegetables that were her nemesis, my mother would look over at my father from her stead at the sink. "Ette, why did you plant so much zucchini this year?" She bemoaned the crop that grew in near-legendary quantities in every Italian American's garden, including ours. The bumper yields haunted kitchens across the entire Lake Erie region of Ohio.

The first description of a vegetable with the name *zucchini* occurred in a book published in Milan in 1901. Early descriptions added the names of cities to "zucchini" to categorize it and give it regional flair, and the first record of zucchini in the United States dates to the early 1920s, coinciding with the great migration of Italians from southern Italy. My father didn't know or care about any of this, and yet zucchini's journey followed the same path that his father and his uncles had taken. He grew zucchini as naturally as he grew his thick black hair.

For my young, married father, the garden was not only a source of food on the table, but also of nourishment for his solitude. He worked that loamy soil of northern Ohio, happy to have an abundance of something other than kids—something green that wasn't money. Just enough weak-kneed northern sun penetrated the air in June and slanted its warmth just so along his ten rows of beefsteak and Italian plum tomatoes and the mounds he built for zucchini plants. Straight lines he understood. The wavy paths of his children and wife, he did not.

Dad didn't think ahead or worry about how my mother would have to shed hundreds of zucchini of their skins, grate them, and let them dry out on paper plates. Pancakes? We thrilled at the mention of them for dinner. But when plates of fir green–speckled floured stacks showed up on the table—without syrup, only sour cream—shouts of *"you want us to eat that?"* greeted the chef. *Cucinala come vuoi, sempre cucuzza è!* Cook it how you want, it's still squash.

It was my mother who formed Zucchini Squares out of zucchini logs and baked Zucchini Casserole with Cottage Cheese and Monterey Jack Cheese. Even cake was not immune to the charms of this pepo. Zucchini Bread with Pineapple was met with cheers. Chocolate Zucchini Cake was nonnegotiable. Zucchini with sausages, peppers, potatoes, and onions sizzling in a skillet was part of the family's *cucina povera*—Italian peasant cooking. She expertly flayed a zucchini like a fisherman did a trout and hid its flesh in the nooks and crannies of every meal.

Later, my father's playground for his plants took the shape of a rectangular wrinkle of dirt in the northwest corner of our lot. Tomatoes were staked on the western end to ensure they received the maximum amount of exposure to the sun. Next came the peppers and beans. Finally, the bushy tentacles of zucchini inched outside the short, wire fence and slowly reached toward their last call from the kitchen and my mother.

After the kids had left the family home, my dad continued to push his zucchini plants into the stubborn ground. It was Mom who finally stopped.

She ignored whatever he brought into her kitchen, having lost the desire not only to scold him about the squash but to do anything with the plentifulness—tomatoes included. Her forgetting and her absent-minded absence in the kitchen convinced him to bring the growing and the harvest to a halt.

We all knew by then the vegetables were a metaphor for my father's commitment to their marriage, to keeping their time together from going fallow after those fifty summers of love.

CLOCKWISE FROM TOP LEFT Enrico Januzzi's garden, 1970s; Paul, Laura, Annette Januzzi, with zucchini; A bumper crop of tomatoes and eggplant; Ettore and Jean Januzzi with Davis Wick, fig tree in background, 1990s; Ettore Januzzi's garden, 1980s.

BASIC TOMATO SAUCE

My mother spooned this sauce over her famed raviolis, used it for spaghetti night, or layered it across her homemade pizzas. On our way out for a night with friends, we'd serve ourselves, lathering the warming sauce over a toasted slice of Italian bread as we slipped through the kitchen. That one slice of bread would be make this recipe with tomatoes from the store, my mother proudly documented on her handwritten recipe, "I can my own."

3 tablespoons olive oil

1 medium onion, chopped

2 cloves garlic, minced

12 ounces tomato paste

12 ounces water

2 quarts canned tomatoes or 2 (32-ounce) canned whole peeled tomatoes

1 ½ tablespoons fresh or ½ teaspoon dried oregano

1 tablespoon fresh or 1 teaspoon dried basil

1 tablespoon sugar

1 ½ teaspoons salt

⅛ teaspoon ground black pepper

1. In a large pot or Dutch oven, heat olive oil over medium heat, add onion and garlic, and sauté until tender. Add tomato paste and water, stir, and reduce heat to low.

2. Press tomatoes through a rotary mill to puree, or puree in a blender. Strain through a sieve to eliminate any seeds. Add tomato puree to the pot and mix well. Add oregano, basil, sugar, salt, and pepper and stir until blended. Bring to a slow boil, then lower heat and simmer for about 2 hours. Serve over a large bowl of pasta of your choice. Or cool and freeze until use.

VARIATIONS

- For a thinner sauce, eliminate the tomato paste. Simmer until sauce thickens slightly.
- Sauté mushrooms, zucchini cubes, peppers, or any other veggies of choice and add to sauce right before serving.
- Brown ground meat such as beef, pork, turkey, or bulk sausage. Drain and season as desired. Add to sauce and cook until heated through to flavor the sauce.
- Add hot pepper flakes for a bit of heat. Or get creative with additional herbs or spices to change things up, such as a bit of chili crisp or fennel pollen.
- Add a splash of whatever red wine you have opened to the pot, as well as a pinch each of cayenne pepper and cinnamon.
- While tomatoes are cooking, toss in a rind from a chunk of Parmesan or Romano cheese to thicken the sauce.

3. Makes 2 quarts.

PIZZA DOUGH

Fridays when I was a child were pizza day, times two. For hot lunch at school, we might order pizza—more rubbery bread than anything else—topped with a cheese that sprang back after you bit into it. "Are you kids buying today?" our parents asked, and left a quarter on the counter for each "yes." We had been educated in the ways of hard, mocking Italian cheeses, so school cheese was not a dairy product our taste buds welcomed readily. But we ate it to appease the pizza gods that might take our side later if we failed tests, got in trouble around the house, or yelled at my mother. She'd yell back, "Wait 'til your father gets home!" While normally, this was a threat, on Fridays, "wait 'til your father gets home" took on the flavor of homemade pizza, of gardens and ancestors and time slowed down.

When stopping for aperitivi in Sulmona years later, we decided the Romans had a leg up on Napoletana pizza, because they make a *pinsa* dough that's infinitely tastier and lighter and contains less gluten. However, Mom's is still the best.

- 1 ¼ cups warm water, divided
- 1 teaspoon sugar
- 1 (¼ ounce) package dry yeast
- 3 cups flour
- 1 teaspoon salt
- 2 tablespoons olive oil

1. Preheat oven to 450°.
2. Mix together ¼ cup warm water, sugar, and yeast and set aside while mixing other ingredients.
3. In a large bowfl, mix flour and salt. Add yeast mixture, oil, and remaining 1 cup warm water. Mix slowly until well blended. Cover and let dough rise in a warm place for 2–2 ½ hours. When ready to use, divide dough in half and stretch each piece into a 12-inch round or 7 x 12 greased baking pan. Top as desired and bake 8–10 minutes.
4. Makes two 12-inch rounds

ZUCCHINI SQUARES

When these zucchini squares first appeared on our table, naturally, we revolted. By the end of dinner, we begged for more. They also make for a great after-school snack or appetizer.

- 3 cups unpeeled, shredded zucchini
- 4 large eggs, slightly beaten
- ½ cup olive oil
- 1 cup Bisquick mix
- ½ cup Parmesan cheese
- ½ cup grated or finely chopped onion
- ¼ cup chopped fresh parsley
- ¼ teaspoon garlic powder
- ¼ teaspoon salt or ½ teaspoon seasoned salt
- dash of ground black pepper
- 1 clove garlic, minced (optional)
- 8 slices bacon, cooked and crumbled (optional)

1. Preheat oven to 325°.
2. Set shredded zucchini on a layer of paper towels to drain. In a large bowl, combine beaten eggs, olive oil, Bisquick, Parmesan, onion, parsley, garlic powder, salt, and pepper. Toss in minced garlic and bacon if including. Fold zucchini in to blend well. Pour mixture into a greased 9-x-13-inch pan.
3. Bake for 30 minutes, or until squares are set and slightly browned on top. Start checking at 25 minutes.
4. Makes 24 2-inch squares

ZUCCHINI CASSEROLE WITH COTTAGE CHEESE AND MONTEREY JACK CHEESE

Cottage cheese was a staple in our home. Given the complex carbohydrates we consumed, this dish was our version of macaroni and cheese, though we all disdained cottage cheese as a rule—all except Mom, that is. During the height of my mother's dieting phase, if she could have consumed cottage cheese morning, noon, and night, she would have. In this recipe, the cheese is intertwined with our family vegetable. The Monterey Jack cheese and dill give this dish a savory lift.

---

3 pounds zucchini

dash of salt

1 cup low-fat cottage cheese

1 cup shredded Monterey Jack cheese

2 eggs, slightly beaten

1 teaspoon dill weed or seed

1 cup breadcrumbs

2 tablespoons melted butter

1 tablespoon Parmesan cheese

1. Preheat oven to 350°. Spray 9" x 13" casserole dish with oil or grease with butter.

2. Cut zucchini into cubes, leaving skin on. Bring a large pot of water to boil with dash of salt and cook zucchini cubes until tender, yet crisp. Drain and cool slightly. In a large bowl, mix zucchini, cottage cheese, Monterey Jack cheese, eggs, and dill.

3. Combine breadcrumbs and melted butter. Pour zucchini mixture into prepared casserole dish and sprinkle with buttered breadcrumbs, *or* sprinkle ½ cup buttered breadcrumbs on bottom of dish, then pour in zucchini mixture and sprinkle remaining ½ cup on top.

4. Bake for 15 minutes. Sprinkle Parmesan cheese over top. Bake for an additional 15 minutes.

5. Makes 12–15 servings

EGGPLANT PARMESAN

Throughout my mother's recipe collection, she attempted to add back in Italian words of her ancestors that had gone missing from her vocabulary. This recipe, handed down from my grandmother, Stella, for example, she names *melanzana parmigiana casseurola*. If she never conquered the language she lost, she achieved the essence of those words in her every dish she made. While she carried two recipes for eggplant parmesan in her collection, this one has stood the test of time for its simplicity.

---

2 large eggplants
dash of salt
1–2 tablespoons olive oil, more if needed
1 cup flour
1 egg, beaten
¾ cup Italian-style breadcrumbs
2 (14.5 ounces) cans tomato sauce
½–¾ cup Parmesan cheese

1. Peel skin from eggplant. Slice each eggplant crosswise into rounds about ½ inch thick. Place on a large plate covered with paper towels and sprinkle with salt. Set aside for 1 hour. Drain well.

2. Heat oil in large skillet over medium high heat. Place flour in shallow bowl or on wax paper. Working in batches, dip each eggplant round in flour and fry in olive oil until slightly browned. Add additional oil for frying if needed. Drain on fresh paper towel. In a small bowl, mix beaten egg and breadcrumbs to make a creamy spread. Add water or additional breadcrumbs as needed to reach a creamy texture.

3. Preheat oven to 350°. Spread a layer of tomato sauce on bottom of a 7-x-12-inch baking dish. Place one layer of eggplant across the bottom. Spread a layer of breadcrumb mixture over slices. Add another layer of sauce and sprinkle with Parmesan cheese. Continue layering until eggplant and crumb mixture have all been used. Spread a final generous layer of sauce over top, and top with Parmesan cheese.

4. Cover and bake for 45 minutes. Uncover. Set oven to broil and continue baking for 5 more minutes to brown the cheese. Cool slightly before cutting and serving.

5. Variation: To bread eggplant slices rather than layering with breadcrumbs, after draining eggplant, dip each slice in flour, then beaten egg, then breadcrumbs. Layer in baking dish with sauce and cheese, then bake for 30 minutes.

6. Makes 8–10 servings

MARINATED EGGPLANT

Several marinated eggplants recipes were discovered within a pile of others belonging to Stella and Raffaela, except these were in my mother's handwriting. They would have been versions of marinating or pickling passed down from one of my grandmothers. "Canning" vegetables was a way of life in the Old World. During a recent visit to Calabria, my cousin Concetta pickled or preserved green tomatoes, cippolini (onions), and eggplant, and labeled them all to sell at San Donato di Ninea's autumn festival. Though my grandmothers' recipes usually lacked specific measurements, my mother took copious notes from her mentors. Like converting cabbage into sauerkraut, the eggplant in marinade was a way to hold it up well to serve as a topping for crostini, a condiment on sandwiches, or as side dish in winter months. Before serving, I like to sprinkle fresh grated lemon or orange zest over the eggplant and bring out the mint flavor.

---

1 large eggplant
salt, as needed
1 clove garlic, sliced
¼ small onion, sliced
1 cup olive oil
¼ cup white vinegar
1 teaspoon chopped fresh basil
1 teaspoon chopped fresh oregano
1 teaspoon chopped fresh mint
½ teaspoon orange zest

1. Peel skin from eggplant. Slice the eggplant crosswise into rounds around ¼ inch thick. Place on a large plate covered with paper towels and sprinkle with salt. Set aside for 2 hours. Drain well.

2. Layer in sterilized one-quart jar, starting with eggplant, onion, garlic. Repeat twice. In a small bowl, combine olive oil, vinegar, basil, oregano, mint, and orange zest. Whisk to blend. Pour mixture over eggplant in jar. Tightly close lid and shake. Refrigerate for two days, shaking occasionally.

3. Serve as is or chopped alongside fresh bread, on top of crostini, or as addition to chilled pasta salads.

4. Makes approximately ½-quart marinated eggplant.

STUFFED CABBAGE

For many years, I didn't think cabbage was closely related to Italian food. But now, I see it the same way as the countless unrelated "aunts" and "uncles" in our lives—necessary to our survival. The ancient Romans considered cabbage to have medicinal properties, including relief from gout, headaches, and food poisoning. Many sailors pickled cabbage for long voyages to prevent scurvy. Thankfully, we no longer concern ourselves with scurvy. We can enjoy the stuffed version of this useful vegetable instead.

While my mom experimented in the kitchen, my father's repertoire grew too. He began to grow fresh greens for salads (we always ate ours at the end of the meal, and were not excused until we'd done so), as well as heads of cabbage. It was his way of extending his time spent in the garden. And ours at the table.

- 1 medium cabbage
- 1 medium onion, chopped
- 1 celery rib, finely chopped
- 1 clove garlic, minced
- ¼ cup olive oil or 4 tablespoons butter
- 1 ¼–1 ½ pounds ground turkey, pork, and/or beef
- ½ cup rice, parboiled for 10 minutes and drained
- 1 large egg, beaten
- 1 teaspoon salt
- ¼–½ teaspoon ground black pepper
- ½ teaspoon paprika
- 2 (12-ounce) cans condensed tomato soup (do not add liquid)
- ½ cup sour cream
- Lemon juice, for serving (optional)

Preheat oven to 300°.

1. Bring a large pot of water to boil. Add cabbage and cook until wilted. Reserve 2 cups cabbage cooking liquid and set aside. Using fork and knife, leaves off cabbage and discard core. Set leaves aside to drain while preparing filling.

2. In small sauté pan over medium heat, cook onion, celery, and garlic in oil or butter until onion is translucent. Transfer to large bowl and combine with ground meat, rice, egg, salt, pepper, and paprika. Place about ¼ cup mixture on each cabbage leaf and roll, keeping hard vein on the outside. Tuck ends in. Repeat with remaining filling. Use extra or small cabbage leaves to line bottom of a large roasting pan. Arrange cabbage rolls on top.

3. Combine reserved cabbage liquid, condensed tomato soup, and sour cream. Pour over top of rolls. Bake for about 2 hours, checking for doneness starting at around 90 minutes. Do not allow to burn. When they come out of the oven, I squeeze a bit of lemon over rolls to brighten up the dish.

4. Makes 10–12 servings

SUPPERS OF SUBSTANCE

RECIPES
Braciola • Chicken Piccata • Chicken Paprikas with Dumplings • Chicken Cacciatore • Veal Scallopini with Mushrooms and Peppers • Zucchini and Italian Sausage Skillet Supper • Vegetable Lasagna (Lasagna Primavera) • Rice Croquettes (Arancini)

After breakfast most Monday mornings, our grade school band of five tumbled down Ridgeland Drive, headed for the bus stop at the edge of a busy Route 58. My father departed for the shoe store with lunch and thermos in hand (or sometimes, having forgotten both). My mother disappeared down below and began her day in silence.

In the basement, she laid out the week's laundry on the floor across layers of day-old *Lorain Journal* or *Amherst News-Times* papers. The fluorescent-lit room had all the appearance of a crime scene, jeans spun out from their piles with legs splayed at impossible angles. Undershirts and underwear—all white—awaited a scrubbing on her wooden washboard. Before she knew it, time had slipped by. Preparations for supper needed to begin.

As a kid, I never imagined how much work—and bravery—was necessary for any mother or caregiver to develop a supper plan seven days a week, but plan and execute my mother did. Did she look forward to Mondays, when she could get rid of the rest of us in the house? I'm sure of it. Laundry started, beds made, her mind was free to roam and her hands easily formed meatloaf. She cherished the predictability, too, of the dependable washer cycle or the timer that rang when the chicken was baked, so unlike the unpredictable moods of five kids and their demands.

For any parent, whether working away from or in the house, the romanticized notion of a leisurely meal never was and never will be a reality. Not for Italian women, like my cousin, Concetta, and her mother preparing a birthday feast for her 20-plus guests, nor for Italian American women either. However, in our home in the seventies, Americanism seeped in. Conveniences peddled to the American woman were hard to pass up. Who could forget the Hamilton Beach 14-speed blender, the magnetic GE combination can opener and knife sharpener we cut our fingers on, or the wood-grain Crock Pot? Or who wanted to forget Birds Eye frozen fish fingers?

The convenience of other cultures' fare trickled into our home too, like tacos, enchiladas, and chow mein dinners, though my mother had already been borrowing recipes from other ethnicities for years. While some might call preparing food from other cultures appropriation, my mother would insist it was more appreciation. Raised in the light of the ethnic mosaic of Lorain, her friends were Polish, Greek, Czech, and Puerto Rican. She and my father had experienced xenophobia through decades where they appeared to be on the wrong side of a world war or to bear the "wrong" color skin. Was it okay for some Americans to borrow from the Italians their music, food, and traditions, while others bristled at the mere presence of Italians taking up space? On this point, my parents struggled. But my mom offered to her world what the world offered to her. Chicken paprikas from Hungarian friends; nut rolls inspired by Slovakian kolache; Lipton onion soup mix added to her potato planks or hamburgers. She envisioned herself as sophisticated, as worldly, as American-chill as Cool Whip on angel food cake. While she served us those burgers, she craved McDonald's, which had come to Amherst as the seventies ended. Late Friday nights, Mom would raise her finger in the air as if to stop all time, and ask whoever was home to listen, "Hey, you know what I could go for?" We all knew—a Big Mac.

American corporations and capitalism had left women like my mother in the middle, juggling too many duties to be any one thing; she must be all of them at once. Mid-week, she often turned to what she knew. With a penchant for orderliness, she would return to her natural inclination to cook something Italian, like a piccata, a scallopine, or plain old spaghetti and meatballs, which was never plain to us. Coming home from a late night of after-school sports, the smell of tomatoes simmering on the stove, a tinge of beef in the air as it tumbled in the sauce, immediately put us at ease.

My mother had a prescribed process regarding meals for each day of the week. With that, her experiments, her trial and errors, happened outside the realm of family dinner making use of the household's five untrained palates.

On Sunday evenings, she sat down at the oval kitchen table with her trademark high-pitched sigh. "Has anyone seen my glasses?" The pink, octagonal glasses soon positioned atop the bridge of her nose, she picked up the *Cleveland Plain Dealer* and clipped recipes from the magazine section. The snipping was a familiar and soothing sound. Stacked beside those sheets, a few other newspapers—the *Elyria Chronicle*, the *Lorain Journal*, the *Amherst News-Times*, and *La Gazzetta Italiana*—awaited her discovery and delight. By night's end, she had also pried open her three-hole-punched binders and sweat over how her cooking might load our bellies throughout the week or wow her party or card club guests.

On Mondays, she mulled over her selections. Tuesdays, she made her list, checked it three times, and aligned it and her coupons by grocery aisle. On Wednesday mornings she grocery shopped, sometimes with my dad on his designated day off from the store. If it was summer and you were smart, you found something else to do—an outrageous offer to clean the baseboards, anything to be out of sight. Back from the store, she began testing dishes on anyone who randomly mamboed through the kitchen to lament about summer reading, complain about a sister who had borrowed clothes and not given them back, or yell about a brother who pushed around the little ones.

On occasion, her results yielded a dish that didn't live up to its intriguing name and wound up in the garbage instead. From the kitchen, we heard, "Oh, nuts," or "damn." The fate of a dish was made known in the sound of recipe pages being ripped to shreds, notebook pages snatched from the coils or rewritten. Amounts or finicky temperatures were reworked based on how the upstairs or downstairs oven was working. Some outcomes yielded tears saltier than her mistakes when we didn't approve.

And if she didn't appreciate our response to her hard work, she would make her disapproval known: "Go to H-E-double toothpicks."

On Thursdays, when she hosted guests for pinochle club or Magic Chef night, my mother secreted away the books and shoeboxes bloated with recipes and tossed the newspapers into a cardboard carton in the garage in an early attempt to recycle. The house, the kitchen, revealed themselves to be in perfect order as three women gathered around the gray card table whose legs poked into the green carpet in the living room and left tracks in a way we were never permitted to do. As my godmother, Sarah Magazine, my Aunt Mary Jane, and other guests waited to play pinochle, avoiding any mention of the booby prize, they were anxious for my mom to serve up dessert. Who was naïve enough to cook dinner among four such fabulous cooks, three of them Italian? Like any good chef, they all liked their own way best.

※

Those gustatory experiments never ended—especially on us. From the now-familiar-to-me Cincinnati Chili to anything containing Miracle Whip, she tested a wide array of recipes on her unsuspecting children before serving them in high fashion to guests or friends. Throughout decades as wife and mother, she patted eggplant, whirred strawberries, or whisked sugar and egg into pastry with the express intent to serve delectable creations to her pinochle card club, her former coworkers from Magic Chef, and the parish priests when she hosted them for dinner in our home. Her children were simply the discriminating targets of her trials.

As a young Italian American, she had already navigated the rollicking seas between her roots in the Adriatic coast, the south of Italy, and small-town Ohio; between two languages; and between two cultures, the one behind, and the one ahead. Once installed in our family home, she embarked upon another journey. This time, she would traverse between two factions to please—her guests and her kids. As she subjected herself to the opinions of her kids with less-developed palates than her own, to our estimations of how things should be—*not enough salt, too many nuts*—she imparted upon us some wisdom about effort, planning, plating, servitude. "Would you kids just stop?" she would say. "I'm trying to get something right."

FROM TOP LEFT Devin Wick and Jean Januzzi, Oceanside, Oregon, 1996; Ettore and Enrico Januzzi hunting, 1962; Annette and Davis Wick, making a supper of sustenance, 2024

BRACIOLA

Groans in the household rose to the ceiling if *meatloaf* was announced for dinner, but for some odd reason, when my mother turned to another roll of beef, braciola, which she called Meat Loaf Braciola in her binders, praise erupted instead. Perhaps the cut of steak, the extra crunch of parsley, or the addition of bacon gave us reason to cheer. Leftovers were always welcome the next day in our lunch boxes while my classmates ate their bologna sandwiches. Braciola can be made using a standard meatloaf recipe or round steak. This recipe uses round steak. You also can choose to make a large braciola loaf, or four to six smaller "beef birds" if you purchase pre-sliced packaged round steak.

- 1 pound round steak
- ½ teaspoon salt
- ¼ teaspoon ground black pepper
- 1 egg
- ¼ cup seasoned breadcrumbs
- 2 tablespoons grated Parmesan cheese
- 1 small onion, chopped
- 1 garlic clove, minced
- 1 tablespoon thinly sliced fresh basil
- 1 tablespoon chopped fresh parsley
- 1 cup shredded Italian blend cheese (Parmesan, mozzarella, Romano, Asiago), plus 2 tablespoons
- 2 strips bacon (optional), cooked and diced
- 1 hard-boiled egg, chopped
- 1 tablespoon olive oil
- 3 cups tomato sauce

1. Preheat oven to 350° for meatloaf. For beef birds, you will not need the oven.

2. For best outcome, pound round steak to less than ¼ inch thick. Season each side with salt and pepper.

3. Beat egg in medium bowl. In a smaller bowl, mix breadcrumbs, grated Parmesan, onion, garlic, basil, and parsley. Add to beaten egg and mix again. You may need to add water to make the mixture easier to spread. Place steak on wax paper. Beginning in the middle, spread breadcrumb mixture across steak, leaving a 1-inch border around edge. Sprinkle about 1 tablespoon shredded cheese across the top. If adding bacon, scatter bacon over breadcrumb mixture. Add chopped egg and 1 cup shredded cheese down the center. Moisten hands and, with the help of wax paper, roll steak to enclose filling until ends meet. Use toothpicks to secure.

4. For beef birds, heat oil in Dutch oven over medium heat. Brown beef birds for 3–4 minutes per side. Add tomato sauce to pot and continue to simmer for 15 minutes, until beef is cooked through.

5. For braciola, place braciola seam-side down on foil-lined roasting pan or oiled glass pan. Bake for 45–50 minutes, then pour tomato sauce over the top and bake 10–15 minutes more. Sprinkle with additional cheese and serve.

6. Makes 1 large braciola or 4–6 smaller birds

CHICKEN PICCATA

This is a mouth-watering recipe not only due to the lemon it contains, but also the garlic, which was more a specialty in our household. Perhaps my mother didn't care to have five hungry kids, as she put it, "always breathing down my back while waiting for dinner" with hints of garlic on their tongues, but regardless, this recipe was the first-place winner among two other chicken piccata contestants. Her suggestions at the top said, "use this recipe," and given her collection of cookbooks, that means this version won out over many from church collections and other Italian-inspired volumes.

- ¼ cup flour
- ½ teaspoon salt
- ¼ teaspoon ground black pepper
- 1 ½ pounds chicken cutlets, sliced or pounded thin
- 3–4 tablespoons olive oil
- 1 cup fresh sliced mushrooms
- 1–2 cloves garlic, minced
- ½ cup chicken broth
- ¼ cup dry white wine
- 2 tablespoons freshly squeezed lemon juice
- ½ teaspoon thinly sliced fresh sweet basil (optional)
- 2 tablespoons capers
- 2 tablespoons minced fresh parsley

1. In a shallow bowl, combine flour, salt, and pepper. Dredge chicken cutlets in flour mixture and set aside, reserving the remaining flour. In a large sauté pan, heat 1 tablespoon olive oil over medium heat. Working in batches, add chicken and brown on first side, then add ½ tablespoon more oil, flip, and brown on the other side. Remove to paper towel–lined plate. Repeat with remaining chicken, adding ½ tablespoon more oil with each batch. Keep chicken warm beneath foil.

2. In sauté pan, heat 1 tablespoon olive oil and add mushrooms and garlic. Cook until mushrooms are cooked through, 5–8 minutes. Add remainder of the flour mixture. Add wine, broth, lemon juice, and basil, if using, and cook until slightly thick. Add capers. Return cutlets to the pan and cook until heated through. Sprinkle with parsley and serve cutlets with sauce drizzled over.

3. Makes 5–6 servings

CHICKEN PAPRIKAS AND DUMPLINGS

One of the benefits of living in the diverse ethnic community of Lorain was the proximity to new flavors, and Hungarian dishes in particular influenced our family palate. We all saw chicken paprikas (my mother's spelling) as another version of gnocchi and sopped up its tangy sauce with Italian bread leftover from breakfast. The inclusion of evaporated milk gives the dumplings an added creaminess. My mother's recommendations, such as "do not use boiling method to cook chicken," demonstrate her clear desire to get this one right, and not let her Hungarian friends know otherwise.

CHICKEN

- ¼ cup vegetable shortening, or 2 tablespoons butter combined with 2 tablespoons olive oil
- 4–5 pounds bone-in chicken, cut into pieces, or 6 breast halves
- 3 medium onions, chopped
- 1 tablespoon paprika
- 1 teaspoon salt
- ½ teaspoon ground black pepper
- 1 ½ cups chicken broth
- 8 ounces sour cream
- 1 tablespoon cornstarch

DUMPLINGS

- 2 large eggs, well-beaten
- ⅓ cup evaporated milk
- 2 ½ cups flour
- ½ teaspoon salt
- ¼ teaspoon ground black pepper

1. For the chicken: In a Dutch oven, heat 1–2 tablespoons shortening over medium heat. Brown chicken pieces on all sides, adding as little additional shortening as possible as you continue to keep chicken from sticking to pan or burning. Add onion and sauté until soft. Add paprika, salt, pepper, and broth. Simmer 35–40 minutes until the chicken is tender.

2. Combine sour cream and cornstarch and add to chicken. Mix well and heat thoroughly, but do not boil. For the dumplings: In a small bowl, combine beaten eggs and evaporated milk. In a separate bowl, combine dry ingredients, then blend into egg-milk mixture. On a floured cutting board, roll dough out into two thin ropes, each about 1 inch thick. With a knife, cut off small pieces about of dough 1–2 inches in length, and place on wax paper–lined cookie sheet. Repeat with remaining dough.

3. Bring a large pot of salted water to boil. Drop dumplings in and cook until they have risen to the surface, then cook for an additional 2–3 minutes. Drain and add to the chicken. If dumplings absorb most of the gravy in the paprikas, add additional broth mixed with cornstarch until sauce reaches your desired texture.

4. Makes 8–10 servings.

CHICKEN CACCIATORE

In Italian, *cacciatore* translates to "hunter." This nourishing dish certainly filled the bellies of hunters in our family, as my father, brother, and grandfather often disappeared over Thanksgiving break to hunt rabbits and squirrels. Thankfully, neither animal appeared in our cacciatore dish, though the rabbits' tails appeared later in our junk drawers as good luck charms.

2 tablespoons flour

1 teaspoon Italian seasoning

½ teaspoon salt

¼ teaspoon ground black pepper

4 boneless, skinless chicken breast halves (about 1 pound)

2 tablespoons vegetable oil or olive oil

2 cups sliced fresh mushrooms

1 green bell pepper, diced

1 small onion, thinly sliced

3 cups tomato sauce

1 cup shredded provolone cheese

8 ounces fettuccine

1. In a plastic bag, combine flour, Italian seasoning, salt, and pepper. Add chicken to the bag and shake to coat with mixture. In large skillet, heat oil over medium-high heat. Add floured chicken and brown on all sides. Remove chicken to paper towel–lined plate. Lower heat to medium, add mushrooms, peppers, and onions to skillet, and cook until tender, about 10 minutes.

2. Stir in tomato sauce and return chicken to skillet. Cover and simmer 15 minutes or until chicken is fully cooked. Meanwhile, cook fettucine as directed. Top each chicken breast with ¼ cup of cheese and serve over hot pasta.

3. Makes 3–4 servings

VEAL SCALLOPINI WITH MUSHROOMS AND PEPPERS

It's no secret veal is a popular meat in Italian American cooking. Someone once asked if my mother used veal in her meatballs. Our basic spaghetti-and-meatballs meals contained no such thing: Veal was reserved for other occasions. My mother served this dish often when she wanted to keep something on stove while shuttling around five kids, or when she wanted to impress priests and other guests easily and quickly. The addition of nutmeg for sweetness was too tempting for even the men of the cloth to refuse.

- 2–3 tablespoons butter
- ½ pound mushrooms, sliced
- 1 green bell pepper, cut into strips
- 2 cloves garlic, minced
- 1 pound veal cutlets, sliced thin and cut into 1-inch pieces, or left whole and pounded thin
- 1 tablespoon flour
- salt and ground black pepper
- ⅛ teaspoon nutmeg
- 1 small onion, sliced
- ½ cup dry white wine
- ½ cup tomato sauce

1. In a large skillet, melt 1 tablespoon butter over medium heat. Add mushrooms and peppers and sauté until soft. Remove to a small bowl and set aside. In the same pan, add additional butter and sauté minced garlic until lightly browned. Add veal and sauté, turning to brown both sides. Sprinkle veal with flour, salt, pepper, and nutmeg. Add onions, wine, and tomato sauce. Cover and cook, stirring occasionally, about 20 minutes or until veal is tender. When veal is tender, return mushrooms and pepper to skillet and cook 5–7 minutes. Add a more wine or water if sauce is too thick.

2. Makes 4–6 servings

ZUCCHINI AND ITALIAN SAUSAGE SKILLET SUPPER

As proof that my mother improvised, this dish was often accompanied by diced potatoes as well, which I've included in this version of the recipe. The skillet supper was another variation on "breakfast for dinner," which often included pancakes or sausage and eggs. I love the surprising addition of mint here to keep the taste buds on alert.

- 2 tablespoons olive oil
- 1 medium onion, chopped
- 1 clove garlic, minced
- 3 small (6-inch) zucchini, diced
- 1 medium green bell peppers, chopped
- 1 yellow bell pepper, chopped
- 3 medium tomatoes, peeled and chopped
- 3 sprigs parsley, chopped
- 2 mint leaves, chopped
- Salt and ground black pepper to taste
- 1 pound mild or hot Italian sausage (about four large sausages), fully-cooked
- ½ cup potatoes, diced and cooked
- 3 large eggs, well-beaten
- 2 tablespoons Romano cheese

1. In a large skillet, heat oil over medium heat. Sauté onion and garlic until garlic is fragrant. Add zucchini, green pepper, yellow pepper, tomatoes, parsley, and mint. Cover and cook, stirring occasionally, for 30 minutes. Cut cooked sausage into ½-inch-thick pieces. Spread sausage and potatoes over top of vegetables.

2. In a small bowl, mix beaten eggs and cheese. Pour over sausage and vegetables. Cover and cook until eggs are cooked through. Blend all together and serve.

3. Makes 4–6 servings

VEGETABLE LASAGNA (*Lasagna Primavera*)

My mother's vegetable lasagna recipe was widely known among most of my friends, who loved the deviation away from traditional lasagna. However, its legendary status was established by my first husband, Devin, who requested it more than any other recipe in my mother's arsenal. On the recipe, she wrote, "a favorite with my family, especiallymy son-in-law." She prepared this lasagna long after his death, pouring her love for him and our ache over his loss into each casserole dish.

LASAGNA
- 12 lasagna noodles
- 10 ounces frozen chopped spinach or broccoli
- 1 medium carrot, grated
- 1 large onion, chopped
- 2 cloves garlic, minced
- ½ teaspoon dried basil
- 4 tablespoons butter or margarine
- ½–1 teaspoon salt
- ⅛ teaspoon ground black pepper
- 1 pound ricottta cheese
- 1 egg
- 1 tablespoon sugar
- dash of ground cinnamon

SAUCE
- 5 tablespoons flour
- ¼ teaspoon nutmeg
- 4 tablespoons butter
- 4 cups milk or heavy cream, heated
- 1 cup grated Romano or Parmesan cheese, divided
- 4 teaspoons chicken bouillon
- ½ teaspoon salt
- dash of ground black pepper

1. Preheat oven to 350°.
2. Cook lasagna noodles as directed, then drain, transfer to a bowl of cold water, and set aside. Drain spinach or broccoli well on a paper towel–lined plate. In a medium sauté pan, cook spinach, carrot, onion, garlic, and basil in butter until onion softens. Add salt and pepper. Set aside.
3. In a small bowl, combine ricotta cheese with egg, sugar, and cinnamon. Set aside.
4. For the sauce: In a small bowl, combine flour and nutmeg. In a medium saucepan, melt butter. Gradually stir flour mixture into butter. Slowly add hot milk and stir until liquid slightly thickens. Add ½ cup grated cheese and chicken bouillon. Season with salt and pepper. Mix half of the sauce into the vegetable mixture.
5. Drain lasagna noodles well. Grease a 9-x-13-inch baking dish. Spread a small amount of cheese sauce across bottom. Top with a layer of noodles, a layer of ricotta cheese mixture, and a layer of vegetable-sauce mixture. Repeat layering, ending with noodles. Pour remaining sauce over all and sprinkle with remaining ½ cup grated cheese.
6. Cover and bake for 45 minutes. Uncover. Cook 2–3 minutes more to crisp the cheese.
7. Makes 10–12 servings

RICE CROQUETTES (ARANCINI)

This recipe was dated 8/30/63, and my mother recorded it had been passed down by "Mother Januzzi"—Stella. It's a quintessential Italian nonna recipe, with instructions like "a little less if you wish," "add some garlic powder," and a tip to heat the oil "just like for donuts." Today, rise croquettes [sic], also known as *arancini* (Sicilian origin) or *suppli* (Roman origin), are part of a lively street food scene and appear on many Italian restaurant menus. Along the streets of Tropea in Reggio Calabria, when sunbathers tire of the heat, they climb up one of two long stairways back into town for a quick arancino. We found arancini made with potato dough, but most are made with fresh rice or day-old risotto, which is often my preference. Either way, they are simply rice balls originally designed to carry typical southern Italian meat-filled arancini or these vegetable ones over a long distance. They can be consumed warm or cold.

- ¾ cup Romano cheese
- 1 garlic clove, minced, or ½ teaspoon garlic powder
- 1 teaspoon minced onion, or ½ teaspoon onion powder
- 2 tablespoons minced fresh parsley
- 1 tablespoon minced fresh sweet basil
- 1 teaspoon celery salt
- 4 cups milk
- 1 cup raw rice (regular, not minute rice; I use carnaroli or arborio rice)
- 1 teaspoon salt
- 2 eggs
- ¼ pound pancetta, chopped and cooked (optional)

FOR BREADING
- 1 egg, beaten
- 2 tablespoons milk
- 2 cups fine breadcrumbs
- Vegetable oil, for frying

1. In a small bowl, stir together Romano cheese, garlic, onion, parsley, basil, and celery salt. Set aside.

2. In a medium saucepan over medium-low heat, combine milk, rice, and salt and cook, stirring constantly, until rice is soft and all milk is absorbed, about 20 minutes. Remove from heat. Add eggs one at a time, beating with a wooden spoon quickly, or egg will cook before mixed through. Remove from heat. Add cheese-and-herb mixture. Cool and refrigerate overnight.

3. Cook pancetta in skillet. Remove and drain on paper towel-lined plate. Add to rice mixture. Roll mixture into 1 ½-inch balls, or size of your choice. For the breading, in a small bowl, combine beaten egg and milk. Place breadcrumbs in another small bowl. Dip each arancini in beaten egg, then coat in breadcrumbs. Let stand while preparing oil.

4. Fill a Dutch oven or heavy frying pan with about 2 inches of oil. Bring oil to medium heat. Add arancini to hot oil and cook until browned on all sides.

5. Drain on paper towels. Serve alone or with a tomato sauce.

6. Makes approximately 40 arancini

BLISSFUL WEDDING SOUP

RECIPES

Meatballs for Wedding Soup and Sauce •
Cheese Croutons (*Crostini di Formaggio*) •
Chicken Broth (*Brodo di Pollo*) and Wedding Soup

During holidays in my mother's kitchen, everything would be set up just right. *Tutto a posto.* Five dozen quarter-sized, cooked-but-still-frozen meatballs exhaled their juices as they thawed in a metallic bowl. Atop that bowl, another—the ceramic dough-mixing bowl—stood on alert, filled with parsley-flecked cheese squares the size of croutons, *crostini di formaggio*, which tumbled over one another like newborn pups. Also at the ready? An enamel stock pot filled with my mother's broth, either recently made or coaxed from a Thanksgiving turkey that had likely been stuffed with a chestnut dressing.

Like us kids, those disparate ingredients would soon be unified in the traditional soup my mother served at holiday meals.

But while she changed in the bedroom from her floral pink morning duster into her cooking clothes—maybe a satiny sweatsuit from the '70s—one kid or another would sneak down the sherbet-green-carpeted stairs to the kitchen, lift the plastic wrap off the ceramic bowl—a crinkling gave you away—and pluck a cheese square from inside. As a sacrifice to the soup gods, the square—like a communion wafer, but better—was silently swallowed whole. Such was our devotion to my mother's wedding soup.

The phrase "wedding soup" originated from *minestra maritata* (married soup), a reference to the way the flavors of greens and meat were married with one another. The name had nothing to do with wedding vows. Another variation of the soup containing more meats was popularized in Spain long before pasta or minestrone shapes were accessible or affordable.

In our family, "wedding soup" meant risking entry into the kitchen we were often barred from on other occasions. It was our chance to exalt, once and for all, my mother's prowess in her place. The soup wasn't so much a recipe, though Mom credits her mother for one, as an inventory of ingredients highlighting the tastes of a distant home across the seas. The list of components begins with meatballs similar to those that accompanied spaghetti nights, from a recipe Mom developed over the years.

I can still summon the image of her approaching this blessed creation: She takes off her silver wedding band—the only time she's not bonded to the cause of matrimony—and next her birthstone ring, the one with two garnets and three diamonds that sparkled as bright as her wedding ring. She dips her three middle fingers on her right hand into a measuring cup filled with water, then pats the inside of her left hand with those same digits. Scooping a blob of ground meat mixture into her hands, both palms roll the mush around until the ball's surface is extra smooth. The resulting meatball is released onto a foil-lined pan alongside others of exactly equal quarter-sized proportions.

For non-Italian family and friends, it's important to dispel the myth that wedding soup was served at weddings. It wasn't. My parents' total wedding reception bill for the Italian Mutual Hall amounted to $466 in 1961, including bar costs, and there was no mention of hot liquids on the menu. My mom would have been petrified to slurp soup during her own wedding dinner for fear of spilling, or watching as broth dribbled from the mouths of her guests. When my son made plans for his marriage ceremony, he sent me a text: "Will we have wedding soup at the reception?" I thought about it. I'd have to grocery shop in a city I didn't know and cook in a kitchen not my own. With the wedding taking place in Utah, where altitude affected all kinds of baking, the time zone changes also impacted my mood. I'd have to produce for numbers I couldn't predict. In the end, I'd essentially have to be my mother. Instead, I wrote back, "Davis, the soup is named for how it comes together," not for the function at which it was served.

BLISSFUL WEDDING SOUP

Before completely divulging my mother's culinary secrets, I must dispense with one of my own: When given the chance to order *minestra maritata* on a menu, I vacillate. First I think, the restaurant most likely won't serve it with crostini di formaggio, the cheese squares that traditionally accompanied Rafaella's and my mother's recipe. Every holiday my mother baked several pans of cheese squares, made from eggs, a zesty Romano cheese, and a dash of baking soda to help them rise, with herbs like parsley included to offer a hope of spring in the bowl and a little extra crunch on the tongue. For us, wedding soup without those croutons wasn't wedding soup at all. But then, I'll order the soup anyhow and say, "It's not as good as Mom's." The smug satisfaction and comfort gained from this knowledge is worth every ounce of indecision, every penny spent, and every spoonful of soup consumed that I didn't like. Each time, it's a chance to award the gold medal to the one I loved.

In addition to the cheese squares, one other ingredient made my mother's soup unique. She cut French toast, sometimes tinged with cinnamon, into small cubes and added them to the mix, giving a sweet, continental flair to the soup in her ceramic tureen. It was an odd and surprising supplement to the dish, like breakfast for dinner. I could find no reference for its addition, until I learned the Abruzzese occasionally add a pinch of cinnamon to the soup. No one ever complained about the unusual ingredient—though they might complain when my mother folded in strands of escarole or endive in a nod to her mother or an attempt to eliminating waste, adding a bitterness to the soup and to our objections.

How was it served?

My parent's wedding gifts had included 1940s Ohio-inspired Franciscan Apple ceramicware with accompanying gravy, salad, and vegetable bowls (as if she needed an excuse to serve us anything leafy and green), and little soup bowls. Her collection, which also included a set of Amish Butterprint mixing and serving bowls and a milk-glass bowl, was displayed at every banquet table set for visitors and guests during extended celebrations in our home, though the bowls never toiled more than at Christmastime, when my mother attempted to instill a bit of propriety in her kids.

We were also fancy enough to be reared by someone who had purchased a white *zuppiera*—a tureen made from ironstone, a type of earthenware made of clay and feldspar. Why would you not buy a special repository for your celebrated wedding soup? The tureen was perhaps dearer to her than her first grandchild. The lipped octagonal opening required precise ladling of broth, and our bowls had to be ceremonially positioned just so at our places, as if placed by a waiter at a five-star restaurant.

When demanded to line up, we fell into a column. My mother ladled the wedding soup from the tureen into her apple-patterned oatmeal bowls and handed them off to a procession of children, directed to march like the *Sound of Music* kids. After slurping the last drops from our bowls, we marched to the kitchen and immediately rinsed each dish. "You've got to scrape off all the cheese," my mother said. It was essential that we leave no particle of meatball as a pockmark on the bowls—or her reputation.

For the entire week following Christmas, I would reheat any remaining broth and soup fixings for lunch—or breakfast. Nowadays, after the guests are gone and kitchen clean, my heart falls when I discover the soup fixings bowl nearly empty. Seated alone on my kitchen stool, I'll sop up the last squidgy cheese square or French toast crumb, confident in the knowledge that the flavors of my *minestrone maritata* had blended brilliantly, uniting mother and me one more time.

CLOCKWISE FROM TOP Annette Januzzi and Jean Januzzi, forefront, at holiday dinner meal, 1975; Ettore Januzzi serving soup, with Annette and Devin Wick, 1970s; Wedding soup ingredients.

MEATBALLS FOR WEDDING SOUP AND SAUCE

My mother left in my care a confounding variety of meatball recipes. One recipe made 240 regular-sized meatballs, which she and her mother had used when cooking Italian dinners at church. Another recipe was delivered to me over the phone, but she varied the measurements, perhaps to keep her secrets close to her heart. She wrote on one such recipe, "what I've developed over the years." The first recipe below is for the meatballs she used in wedding soup, and came from her mother Raffaela. The recipe that follows is the standard meatball recipe she used to accompany pasta dishes. In addition to the larger size, the second recipe also differs in that it includes Parmesan cheese, which wasn't needed for the wedding soup meatballs, as they would be accompanied by Romano cheese squares in the soup. Here's a tip: Occasionally, I'll add a little Romano to the mixture anyhow.

MEATBALLS FOR WEDDING SOUP

- 1 ½ pounds ground meat (a mix of ground turkey and lean ground pork)
- ¼ cup Italian breadcrumbs
- ¼ cup water
- 1 egg
- 1 garlic clove, minced
- 1 ¼ teaspoons salt
- dash of ground black pepper
- 1–2 tablespoons olive oil

1. In a large stainless-steel bowl, combine all ingredients except the oil by hand until blended well. Shape meat mixture into 1-inch balls.
2. In a large sauté pan, heat oil over medium-high heat. Brown meatballs a dozen or so at a time, then remove to paper towel–lined plate to drain. Drop into simmering soup until cooked through, about 30 minutes.
3. Variation: To bake meatballs instead of frying, preheat oven to 350°. Line a cookie sheet with aluminum foil and spray foil with cooking spray. Place meatballs on cookie sheet and bake for 10 minutes, then turn and place back in oven for 10 minutes more. Drop into simmering soup until cooked thoroughly, 30 minutes. May freeze for two weeks until ready for use.
4. Makes approximately 80 bite-sized meatballs

MOM'S MEATBALLS FOR SAUCE

- 1 pound ground meat (a mix of ground beef and lean ground pork, or ground turkey)
- ½ cup Italian breadcrumbs
- ¼ cup grated Parmesan cheese
- 1 egg
- ½ cup water
- 1 garlic clove, minced
- 1 teaspoon salt
- dash of ground black pepper

1. Follow directions above to mix and shape meatballs, but shape into 1 ½-inch balls. Fry meatballs in oil or bake in oven according to directions above, then drop into simmering sauce until cooked through, about 30 minutes.
2. Makes 24 meatballs

CHEESE CROUTONS (*Crostini di Formaggio*)

Every holiday, my mother baked more pans of these cheese squares than was required for wedding soup. Not all the squares made their way into the pot or bowls. My mother knew her kids would unwrap the container where the croutons awaited on Christmas Day and sneak a few squares to satisfy our hunger. I still do, and my kids do, too. Back then, our mouths watered over the blend of Romano cheese, parsley, and salt. For us, only wedding soup with the croutons was *real* wedding soup. Our family recipe had been handed down by Raffaela, and perhaps my mother conjured her mother when she had need in making these. Her recipe collection also included a separate version shared by another Abruzzese woman, Lillian di Donato, a neighbor who translated the letters my mother received from cousins in Italy. In recent years, I've made the crostini and cut them into larger squares for appetizers that also disappear before guests arrive.

---

6 eggs

½ cup or less chopped fresh parsley

2 ½ cups grated Romano cheese

2 tablespoons flour

¼ teaspoons baking powder

dash of ground black pepper

1. Preheat oven to 350°. Grease and flour a 7-x-12-inch oblong pan.
2. In a medium bowl, whisk eggs, then add parsley. In a larger bowl, blend Romano cheese, flour, baking powder, and black pepper with a fork. Stir egg mixture into cheese-and-flour mixture until all ingredients are wet. Pour into prepared pan and bake for 20–25 minutes. Cool in the pan, then cut into ½-inch squares. May freeze for two weeks until ready for use.
3. Makes approximately 120 croutons

CHICKEN BROTH (*Brodo di Pollo*)

Some kids were weaned on Campbell's. We lived for the version of chicken broth that tasted most like chicken. Giblets were a key ingredient, as well as the surprise tomato, which jumped out at me later when I read my mother's recipe to make for myself. I hadn't known of her secret ingredient. Nowadays, when I make my own broth after Thanksgiving using smoked turkey, I can say this hews closest to my mother's recipe. She suggested to "use the broth for wedding soup"—as if there were a choice.

- 1 (4–5-pound) stewing chicken, cut into pieces
- chicken giblets (gizzards, heart, liver, and neck)
- 1 tablespoon salt, plus more to taste
- 2 stalks celery, cut into chunks
- 2 medium carrots, cut into chunks
- 1 large tomato, rinsed and quartered (optional)

1. Rinse chicken pieces and giblets thoroughly in cold water. Place in large stock pot and fill with cold water to cover. Add salt and bring all ingredients to a boil. As the water boils, skim the foam with a small coffee strainer or other skimming device for 20 minutes. Reduce heat to medium-low and add vegetables. Cook, maintaining heat at medium-low and adding more water as needed, for 1 ½–2 hours or until carrots are tender. Salt to taste.

2. Once you're satisfied with the flavor, remove chicken, giblets, celery, carrots, onions and remains of tomato. Discard onions and giblets. Strip chicken meat from the bones and chop into pieces to save for use later in soups or other recipes. Cut celery and carrots into pieces and reserve for later use as well.

3. Strain broth into 1-quart mason jars and refrigerate for 24 hours. Skim off fat that has risen to the top of the jar before using.

4. Makes 4–5 quarts broth

WEDDING SOUP

Christmas and other holiday mornings, we were greeted by freshly brewed coffee and the sight of meatballs and cheese squares thawing in my mother's ceramic cream bowl. I rarely recall my mother making French toast. Instead, she purchased it frozen. I have occasionally bought the cinnamon French toast, which adds a hint of delight to the soup. Spinach and parsley are added at the end before serving to give this soup its bright appearance in the Franciscan ceramicware bowls.

- **120 meatballs, using recipe p168**
- **120 cheese croutons, using recipe above**
- **4-6 slices cubed French toast, prepared or frozen and thawed**
- **½ cup chopped fresh spinach**
- **¼ cup chopped fresh parsley**
- **10-12 cups chicken broth, using recipe above**

1. If frozen, thaw meatballs and cheese squares. In Dutch oven, bring broth to boil over medium heat. When ready to serve guests, add a serving size of 3-4 meatballs, 4-5 cheese croutons, 2-3 cubes French toast. Top with a few pinches of spinach and parsley in each bowl.
2. Makes 20–24 servings, depending on bowl size.

CHESTNUT DRESSING

As was typical in the seventies and eighties, my mother stuffed her turkeys at Thanksgiving. This gave the cooked turkey more flavor for later, when the bones, with strands of turkey still clinging, would magically become broth. Now, most cooks caution against placing the dressing in the turkey and instead bake the mixture separate from the roasting turkey.

Scores of chestnuts appear at late-autumn festivals across Italy, including in Abruzzo and Calabria. In Ohio, however, chestnuts appear only at seasonal market stands, or are imported directly from Italy and sold at Italian grocers. Whenever you're lucky enough to discover them, perhaps during a holiday stroll of a historic town, grab them while they're hot. Or carry them home to cook later in a dish like this. You can use any type of bread cubes here, but I like using day-old homemade cornbread with a savory seasoning to give this dish a lift.

- 1 cup chestnuts, prepared as below, chopped
- 1 cup butter
- 2 cups diced celery
- ¾ cup chopped onions
- 3–4 ounces canned mushrooms, or 4 ounces fresh, chopped
- ½ teaspoon chopped fresh parsley
- ½ teaspoon chopped fresh sweet basil
- 2 eggs, beaten
- ½ cup Romano cheese
- 1 teaspoon salt
- 24 ounces unseasoned bread cubes or 4 cups cubed day-old bread
- 3 cups chicken, turkey or vegetable broth
- ¼ cup cooking sherry

1. Cut two slits in the shape of a cross on flat side of each chestnut. Place chestnuts in salted water and bring to a boil, then reduce heat and simmer for 20–25 minutes. Outer shells should begin to curl up when cooked. Remove chestnuts from water one at a time and, using a knife, release outer shells and inner skins. Set nuts aside to cool and chop.

2. Preheat oven to 375°.

3. In a medium sauté pan, melt butter over medium heat. Add celery, onions, fresh mushrooms (if using), parsley, and basil and cook until soft. Cool completely.

4. In a large bowl, combine chestnuts and vegetables with eggs, cheese, and salt. Stir in broth. Add bread cubes and cooking sherry and toss to mix. Bake for 20–30 minutes, or until crisp and browned on top.

5. Makes 10–12 side servings

SOUPS FOR SALVATION

RECIPES

Escarole and Orzo Soup with Turkey Parmesan Meatballs •
Cheese Tortellini Soup with Cannellini, Kielbasa, and Kale •
Cioppino • Caramelized Onion and Portobello Mushroom
Soup with Goat Cheese Croutons • Minestrone

While wedding soup ruled our branch of the family tree, it was nearly never let out of the house to share. Others wouldn't understand—or perhaps my mother just wanted to keep some traditions to herself. Other soups, though, she shared generously. The local Catholic churches played an outsized role in our childhood and the formation of our values, or so my mother would have loved to believe. That notion propelled her. In exchange for her kids' salvation, and her husband's too, she extended her service to God beyond the pews and directed that generosity through her pots.

Both my parents grew up attending St. Peter's Church in Lorain, the church of my father's baptism and their wedding vows. Later in life, in Amherst at St. Joseph's Catholic Church, the sermons of an aging Father Kreps caused my father to catch a few winks in the pews. Oftentimes, the priest's voice rose an octave as if on purpose to wake Dad. Or my mom leaned over and motioned with her elbow for one of us to "wake your father up."

On Ridgeland Drive, our neighbors next door, Aunt Kay and Uncle Jim Kelly (not blood relatives), often hosted an older, diminutive visiting priest to St. Joe's, Father Metzger. Kay and Jim were older than my parents (though Kay was probably around fifty, in my kid's mind, they were at least sixty and Father Metzger was practically ancient). Aunt Kay, a busty, opinionated woman with a coif of white curly hair, would chastise my mother, tired of our incessant trespassing through her lawn: "Jean, I'm telling you, you have to keep those kids busy." "Oh Kay," my mother laughed graciously, "You're too much," as if she hadn't already tried with some measure of success. If Kay didn't take credit for telling my mother how to get us to behave, she should have. If she didn't recognize herself as my mother's first food critic, she should have done that too.

My mother's role models were gone. Rafaella had died in 1964, Stella ten years later, both while we lived on Ridgeland Drive. In their absence, Aunt Kay became like family, pushing my mother to go beyond our lot lines and beyond her own imagination in the kitchen too. Kay and Uncle Jim bore no children except for Gigi, a black poodle who was the pride of Aunt Kay and a nuisance to Uncle Jim. So they treated us like their kids, yelling at us, giving us presents, and breaking bread—or cookies—together over a meal. "Jean, no doubt this is the best pot yet," Kay would say, wiping her jowled cheeks with a napkin to remove the last vestiges of the garden from her visage. My mother invited Jim and Kay to dinner often, and as a result her culinary reputation in the parish developed a small buzz.

Several years later we moved closer to St. Joseph's, if only to appease my mother in moving closer to God. "What'cha making, Mom?" a roamer through the kitchen might ask. If she answered, "Dinner for the priests," you didn't want to be the person still holding a pot lid from spooning out sauce or with your nose poked into the oven, because her next question would be, "Can one of you take this to the priests' home?" When it was my turn, I walked or biked begrudgingly, taking up as much time as possible, dreading the encounter with nemeses like Father Kreps. A quick press of the doorbell, and I tripped stepping backward down the steps to wait. Father's towering figure ghosted the doorway. "Come in, come in." When I refused—contact with the priest might infect me with a holiness we all tried to slough off—he shrugged. "Bless you and your mother," I heard as I scurried away.

Enter Father Weber, a young priest assigned as associate pastor to St. Joseph's. Handsome with a pudgy face and curly reddish hair, Irish-funny in his delivery of jokes at all hours, and a lover of all things Cleveland, including the losing sports teams, he noodled his way into my mother's heart. How? By complimenting her cooking, of course, and preaching the gospel of my mother's culinary talents. Irish with the nose of a Roman, he could catch the scent of oregano and basil from blocks away. He found reasons to stop by and say hello: to pray for a distant cousin who had died, or to talk about CCD classes, which my mother taught. "Say, Jean, what're you cookin' today," he'd ask, his voice bubbling and his mouth already watering with enthusiasm, ready to offer praise at a moment's notice if he were offered a seat at the table. Father Weber was eventually transferred (though he returned to attend to my brother's wedding and Mom and Dad's funerals), but my mother kept cooking for the Church. The way to salvation marched straight through the kitchen in our home.

While other parishes turned to fish fries as money-making ventures during Lent, St. Joseph's hosted soup suppers. The events involved little setup and plenty of donations, many of which came from my mother. For these suppers, she prepared her wildly acclaimed soups such as Cheese Tortellini Soup with Cannellini, Keilbasa, and Kale, rich with ricotta-stuffed tortellini bobbing like little earlobes in the pot. That soup was legendary among ravenous elderly church patrons, who lined up beside her pot with Styrofoam bowls for my mom to spoon it into. Her repertoire of soups was beefed up through her commitment to these outings. Mom's archives contain a lengthy list of intriguing soup recipes for the culinary archaeologist: Squash and Sweet Potato, Caramelized Onion and Portobello, Curried Cream of Eggplant, and fourteen others, including a Lettuce Soup and the Creamy Zucchini Soup my siblings and I dreaded.

My father obliged Mom, carrying the steaming pots behind her. All that toiling to muddle vegetables into minestrone, she viewed as reparations on our behalf. The more I followed my mother's instructions and evaluated her choices for serving a population that may or may not have been welcoming to the idea of culinary or other sort of advancements, the more I realized she too was working out changes in her life and ours. My dad bragged that the last remnants of her tortellini soup were demolished before the others. This proclamation suited my mother, who was already held in high regard on par with the priests by the parish community, a distinction we mocked mainly because we were insanely jealous. My mother had come *thisclose* to achieving gastronomic perfection, but she was seeking a different sort of deliverance.

After I moved away, Mom and I exchanged recipes over the phone. "*Ribollita*?" I asked about a recipe found in an old cookbook. "Reboiled soup," she said, as if I should have learned this in some Italian class, even though her own mother forbade the language in their home. "My mother made it all the time." As Americans' tastes for Italian food shifted during the late 1990s and ribollita made it into the mainstream, she returned to more original Italian creations like Escarole and Orzo Soup with Turkey Parmesan Meatballs, surely at my father's behest.

Some soups never made it the priests, and those were our holy ones. Wedding soup. My mother's tangy chicken brodo, which caused my tongue to curl, having started in the winter months as basting liquid for turkey or chicken roasts. She added *pastini,* tiny diamond-shaped *paste, stelline,* or the small tubes of *ditalini,* shapes ending in *-ini* meant for the *bambini* we were. Thanks to her ancestors' vicinity near the pope and her own proximity to the stove, she had turned her *italianità* into a holiness, and saved us all.

FROM TOP Jean Januzzi's soup tureen; Annette Januzzi Wick's chestnut stuffing; Annette Wick with Marisa Sanelli at Agriturismo Pietrantica before soup is served, 2024.

ESCAROLE AND ORZO SOUP WITH TURKEY PARMESAN MEATBALLS

In my mother's middle years, she busied herself trying out new recipes. When she later returned to attempt this traditional soup once more, she couldn't locate the other half of the original recipe. But I can confirm that this approximation closely resembles her original one. The turkey meatballs here show her growing appreciation for a healthier diet. Despite her perfectionist ways, Mom was always interested in testing variations and changing things up.

¾ pound ground turkey

½ cup breadcrumbs

1/3 cup Parmesan cheese

1 egg

dash of salt

dash of ground black pepper

¼ cup water or milk

2–3 cups chicken broth

3 carrots, peeled and chopped

½–¾ cup chopped escarole, cut into bite-sized pieces, rinsed, and pat

½ cup orzo

1. In a medium metal mixing bowl, combine turkey, breadcrumbs, Parmesan cheese, egg, salt, and pepper. Add water or milk and mix to moisten. Roll into bite-sized meatballs. Place on wax paper–lined cookie sheet and place in freezer.

2. In a Dutch oven, heat chicken broth to a boil. Add carrots and orzo. Reduce heat to medium and simmer uncovered for 8 minutes. Add turkey meatballs and simmer for 10 minutes. Stir in chopped escarole and simmer until meatballs, orzo, and escarole are tender, 5 minutes longer. Season soup to taste with salt and pepper. This can be made ahead and refrigerated or frozen; rewarm over medium heat and add more broth.

3. Makes 4–6 servings

CHEESE TORTELLINI SOUP WITH CANNELLINI, KIELBASA, AND KALE

Parishioners at my parents' church lined up for this soup, and we did too. It's clear my mother was in her experimental phase, post-children, when she created this recipe, as she shockingly used kielbasa instead of Italian sausage, as well as Asiago cheese, which had become widely available to her after we moved out. If you'd like to make this soup a day ahead, follow the directions up through adding the fennel, then cool slightly, cover, and refrigerate. The next day, bring to simmer before adding the tortellini.

- 2 tablespoons olive oil or vegetable oil spray
- 12 ounces fully-cooked smoked kielbasa sausage, thinly sliced
- 1 medium onion, chopped
- 1 fennel bulb, cut into 3/4-inch squares
- 4 cloves garlic, minced
- 1 ½ tablespoons chopped fresh thyme
- ½ teaspoon crushed red pepper
- 10 cups low-sodium chicken broth
- 4 cups chopped kale or escarole
- 15 ounces cannellini beans, rinsed and drained
- 2 dozen small, homemade cheese tortellini, or 1 (9-ounce) package
- 1 cup grated or shredded Asiago cheese (or Parmesan)

1. Heat oil in a large pot or Dutch oven over medium-high heat (or spray pot with cooking spray). Add kielbasa, onion, fennel, garlic, thyme, and crushed red pepper and sauté until vegetables are soft and kielbasa is browned on all sides, about 12 minutes.

2. Add broth and bring to a boil. Stir in kale and cannellini beans, then reduce heat to low and simmer until kale is wilted and fennel is cooked through, about 4 minutes. Add tortellini and simmer until pasta is just tender but firm to bite, about 5 minutes.

3. Ladle into bowls and sprinkle with cheese.

4. Makes 10–12 servings

CIOPPINO

My mother and I swapped recipes for cioppino through the years, and in her boxes of recipes, I located one based on a recipe from a San Francisco travel advertisement. If my dreams always looked toward to the Pacific Northwest, my mother's had reached for the sunnier climate of California, ever since a road trip she took there in 1957 as a single woman. This soup filled her imagination and belly when travel couldn't fill her itinerary for life.

Given my propensity for Oregon seafood, I'll make this during my trips to the Oregon coast with locally sourced bay shrimp, oysters, and rockfish, along with the addition of a few threads of saffron added at the counsel of a fishmonger based in a little seafood shack called Barnacle Bill's. Though prices have skyrocketed for Dungeness crab based on the challenge of fishing sustainably, it's always included in any version of cioppino I cook, even if there are only a few shreds added as garnish.

- ¼ cup vegetable oil
- 2 medium onions, chopped
- 3 cloves garlic, minced
- 2 tablespoons sugar
- ½ teaspoon salt
- ½ teaspoon ground black pepper
- ½ teaspoon dried basil (or ½ tablespoon fresh)
- ½ teaspoon dried thyme (or ½ tablespoon fresh)
- ½ teaspoon paprika
- 1 (14.5-ounce can) diced tomatoes
- 2 (8-ounce) bottles clam juice
- 1 (8-ounce) can tomato sauce
- ¼ cup lemon juice
- ½ pound shrimp (preferably small bay shrimp)
- ½ pound scallops (preferable small bay scallops)
- ½ pound firm white fish, cut into chunks
- ¼ pound Dungeness or other crabmeat
- 4-6 saffron threads (optional)

1. Heat oil in a Dutch oven over medium heat. Add onions and garlic and sauté until soft, about 5 minutes. Stir in sugar, salt, pepper, dried basil, and dried thyme. (If using fresh herbs, wait to add them later, before the crab). Add paprika, tomatoes, clam juice, tomato sauce, and lemon juice. Bring to a boil, then reduce heat and simmer for 30 minutes. Add shrimp, scallops, and fish and simmer for 5 minutes or until cooked through. Sprinkle shreds of Dungeness crab atop each serving. Place a saffron thread atop the crab.
2. Makes 4–6 servings

CARAMELIZED ONION AND PORTOBELLO MUSHROOM SOUP WITH GOAT CHEESE CROUTONS

Mushrooms were always part of our family's repertoire, unsurprisingly given their influence in the regions of both Abruzzo and Calabria. The variety known as "common mushrooms" are white and immature, while an immature brown mushroom would be called an Italian brown mushroom or a cremini. The larger portobello is known for its maturity. Given our family's focus on finances, my mother steered toward more common varieties or those available at Italian grocery marts. While we used standard-issue button mushrooms in some recipes, the portobello mushroom turned into a prized favorite as it became more widely available.

- 3 tablespoons butter, divided
- 2 large onions, halved and thinly sliced (about 5 cups)
- 4 sprigs fresh thyme
- 1 ½ pounds portobello mushrooms, stemmed, caps halved and cut crosswise into ¼-inch-thick strips
- 3 tablespoons Cognac or brandy
- 3 cloves garlic, minced
- 8 cups vegetable or chicken broth
- 1 cup dry white wine
- Salt and ground black pepper to taste

GOAT CHEESE CROUTONS

- 18 (1-inch-thick) slices French baguette, toasted or 2 cups cubed day-old bread
- 8 ounces goat cheese, softened to room temperature

1. In a large stock pot, melt 1 tablespoon butter over medium-high heat. Add onions and thyme. Cook, stirring, for about 8 minutes until slightly softened. Reduce heat to low and cook, stirring occasionally, until onions are caramelized, 20 minutes. Transfer to a medium bowl.

2. In the same pot, melt remaining 2 tablespoons butter over medium-high heat. Add mushrooms and sauté until soft, about 12 minutes. Add cognac and garlic and stir for 20 seconds. Stir in onion mixture, broth, and wine. Bring to a boil, then reduce heat to low and simmer until onions are very tender, about 45 minutes. Discard thyme sprigs. Season with salt and pepper. (The soup can be made 1 day ahead and refrigerated; reheat before adding croutons and serving).

3. For croutons: Preheat broiler. Spread goat cheese on baguette slices or slather across bread cubes. Place bread on cookie sheet and set under broiler. Broil until cheese begins to brown in spots. Sprinkle croutons over bowls of soup., or serve slices alongside soup.

4. Makes 8–10 servings

MINESTRONE

Any recipe that would use up large quantities of what my father grew in the garden was a welcome addition to our household menus. For this soup, we used peas or green beans, both garden products, interchangeably. The peas add a liveliness to the minestrone, while the beans give this dish some heft. The mention of frozen vegetables refers to the white, waxy paperboard boxes that dominated the family freezer.

2 cups peeled, cubed potatoes
¼ cup olive oil
1 cup chopped onion
1 cup chopped leeks
¼ cup minced fresh Italian parsley
2 cups diced carrots
1 cup diced celery
1 cup fresh or frozen green peas or chopped green beans
2–3 cups chicken broth
2 cups fresh or canned diced tomatoes
½ teaspoon salt
¼ teaspoon ground black pepper
1 cup cubed zucchini
2 cups cannellini beans
2 tablespoons chopped fresh basil
¼ cup grated Romano cheese

1. In a medium saucepan, cook potatoes in boiling water until soft. Drain and set aside. In a large stock pot, heat oil over medium-high heat. Add onions, leeks, and parsley and sauté for 5 minutes. Add additional oil if necessary, then add carrots, celery, and peas and sauté until soft.
2. Add broth, tomatoes, salt, and pepper. Bring to a boil, then lower heat and simmer for about 20 minutes. Add zucchini and cook 5–10 minutes longer.
3. Add cannellini beans and cooked potatoes. Cook for 5 minutes. Top with fresh basil and remove from heat. Serve with cheese.
4. Makes 4–6 servings

EASTER DAY TRIUMPHS

RECIPES

Hot Cross Buns • Leg of Lamb, Italian Style • Lamb Kabobs (Arrosticini) • Classic Tiramisu

My mother's crusty Hot Cross Buns and Casatella, a soft, Italian Easter bread, were both untouchable until after the sins of those seated in the church's sixth row of east-side pews were forgiven. Easter Sunday morning also included a visit to Calvary Cemetery to commune with our forebears. Our friends and lovers found it an odd tradition, this parade through the graveyard to honor our lineage. Having often visited the granite stones of my brother David, our grandparents, godparents, and one set of great-grandparents, we followed an invisible trail of tears.

Spiritual and ancestral obligations checked off, there was another detour to the Easter Basket for family photos. Lorain's Lakeview Park staff maintained, with ample care, a 20-foot-high painted concrete basket filled with nine multicolored eggs. We wore frilly dresses in pastel colors to match the concrete eggs, white tights and the rims of our white patent shoes soiled after tramping through the cemetery. Our stomachs were near cramping from hunger, but the kickoff to the Easter meal had yet to be revealed.

As we returned home from these forays, colorful woven Easter baskets, filled with parental devotion, teased us away from temptation. Our assigned baskets were stuffed with jellybeans counted out in equal numbers and marshmallow chicks whose sugar had hardened overnight, all lorded over by one frightening hollow chocolate bunny.

"God, Mom, when we can eat?" I can still hear my brother's voice now.

"Don't use the name of the Lord in vain," she said, while running around cutting, thawing, rinsing, baking, cooking, and placing scraps of paper with recipe names in serving bowls. The hot cross buns would have to wait a little longer while Dad—who the cursing usually came from—was prepping the antipasti tray.

With hands still sun-kissed in wintertime, he stood calmly in our sunny yellow kitchen, opened his palm, and said, "Hand me the *finocch*," like Prometheus, prepping the fennel to deliver fire to mortals.

He obsessed over everything Italian, including the nutty, piquant cheeses that made every mouth in our family salivate. In seventh grade, I finally figured out that other families in Amherst didn't shop at the Italian grocery Gust Gallucci's in Cleveland, the way mine did after many Italian shops in Lorain had closed and the items weren't available locally. Dad made weekly trips there for *alimenti* and returned with the coveted finocch.

In our home, there were no charcuterie boards. We had one tray for relishes and one for antipasti with meats and cheeses. The electric can opener buzzed at Dad's fingertips. Out of the can came mounds of American black olives pouted onto the star-shaped glass platter. Those olives joined the Italian ones bougt at Gallucci's, bathed in a brine of Calabrian peppers. Once the remaining items, which included gherkin pickles I begged for, were arranged, Dad stepped in, cut the *finocchio*—fennel—and added the curved cups to the plate.

As a child, I had little appreciation for fennel's mythical history; I just loved its punch on my tongue. But the best fennel in the world, considered the gold standard by some, was raised only a two-hour drive from the Iannuzzi family's hometown of San Donato di Ninea. Preferred over other varieties for its stronger fragrance, longer-lasting flavor, and less-stringy stalk, it grew in Isola di Capo Rizzuto, at the bottom of the boot's heel.

Our ancestors come to us through muscle memory. During the holidays of my youth, I had sat rapt, motionless at the dinner table, listening as my grandparents and parents dropped the final vowel in their Italian words: *Pass the capicol. Hand me the prosciutt. And don't forget the finocch.*

Later, when I hosted holidays for our multi-branched families, fennel was always present on a large wooden board where we blended the relish trays with the antipasti ones. Invariably one kid or another who wasn't Januzzi-related would ask, "What's that?" "Italian celery," I'd answer, "or finocch," using language as a muscle too. Bulbs of fennel found their way back into my hands, stubby like my father's, waking up a yearning for him that has never disappeared.

With souls saved, Easter baskets opened, and the holiday meal in the works, finally, our incisors could dive into mom's hot cross buns, with cross-shaped lines piped perfectly straight and raisins numbered in proper proportion in each bite. If those buns represented Jesus's death, my mother's baking resurrected her children, who were nourished by her sweet and chewy Casatella bread or Cuzuppe di Pasqua (Calabria). Her version resembled challah. The loaf, with lemon juice added for proofing and tightening the gluten bonds, was braided and sometimes formed into a ring, then topped with hard-boiled eggs dyed in pastel colors.

A year after my mother died, I went crazy in search of the Easter bread recipe, but found only a cryptic record in my father's handwriting, "Easter Bread," acting as a bookmark for my mom's forgetfulness. I swam through stacks of recipes stored in three children's shoeboxes (the shoe store never left our blood). The third box opened to a library's worth of pamphlets peddled to the American consumer, like *Fish Facts* or *The Mazola Salad Bowl*. Finally, staring down at an open page of the Culinary Arts Institute of Chicago Cooking Magic series' *The Italian Cookbook*, I saw *Pane di Pasqua all'Uovo* (Easter bread), with "*all 'Uovo*" crossed out.

My mother's variations on the recipe—detailed in her tight handwriting—climbed up and down the margins. "Bake 350°, 1 hr. Frost and use sprinkles." A curved arrow at the bottom pointed to three words in her handwriting. "Punch down good."

One Easter in the late 2000s, on one of the last holidays when two parents, five adult children, their spouses and grandchildren, and a new dog, Enzo, were all present, we were blown away by a popup snowstorm. The traditions of Easter kept us warm. With our outsized appetites for holding on to memory, we munched on antipasti, guzzled down wedding soup, and surrendered to my mother's ravioli submerged in sauce. There was sliced ham afloat in pineapple-ring juices, or a crisp leg of lamb. For dessert, we'd have tiramisu or a chocolate marble cheesecake. As my father bit into a piece, swirled smears of brown and cream framed his grinning mouth, delighted to be surrounded by these confections and connections. Proof my mother had expertly executed her variation on *punch down good.*

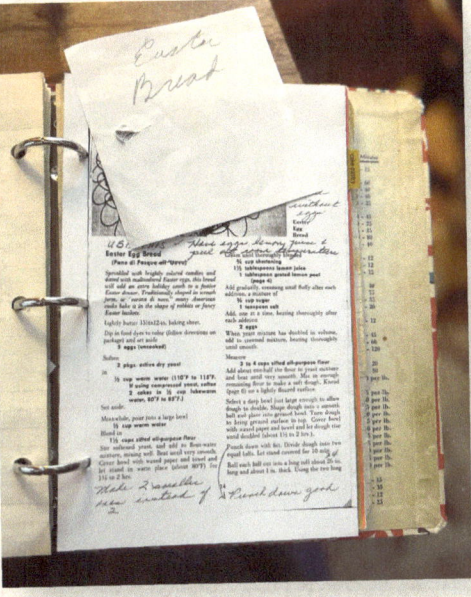

CLOCKWISE FROM TOP LEFT Ettore Januzzi, enjoying pastry and nut roll. Easter, 2008; Jean Januzzi's pane di Pasqua, 1980s; Jean Januzzi's binder with missing Easter bread recipe; Paul, Jeanne, Laura, Beth, Annette Januzzi. Easter at the Lorain Easter Basket, 1973; Ettore and Jean Januzzi with Davis Wick, making the relish tray, 2000.

HOT CROSS BUNS

The origins of hot cross buns are difficult to trace, but thanks to their obvious reference to the Christian tradition of venerating Jesus crucified on the cross, hot cross buns are no stranger to any Catholic household at Eastertime. Similar Italian recipes will call for chocolate instead of raisins or citron instead of candied orange peel. Yet candied oranges are a traditional delicacy of southern Italian regions like Calabria, given their climate, and personally I prefer the orange peel.

At Easter, we swallowed handfuls of jellybeans or Reese's cups, then tore into a plate of these hot cross buns, shoveling the entire bun in our mouths when possible. The raisins and candied orange peel add a necessary touch of sweetness—something we, as kids, definitely did not contribute to the overall feeling of the moment!

---

3 medium eggs, divided

2 (¼ ounce) packages active dry yeast

½ cup sugar

¾ teaspoon salt

½ teaspoon ground cinnamon

¼ teaspoon ground nutmeg

4 cups flour, divided

1 ¼ cups milk

2 tablespoons butter

1 ¼ cup raisins (preferably golden)

¼ cup diced candied orange peel or citron

½ teaspoon lemon zest

ICING
1 cup powdered sugar

1–1 ½ tablespoons orange juice, lemon juice or milk

1. In a small bowl, beat 2 eggs. Set aside. In a large mixing bowl, combine yeast, sugar, salt, spices, and 1 ½ cups flour. Set aside. In a small saucepan, combine milk and butter and heat to 130° (do not scald). Add to the flour mixture. Beat for 2 minutes with a hand blender or electric mixer at medium speed. Add beaten eggs and ½ cup more flour and beat for another 2 minutes on high speed.

2. Gradually stir in remaining 2 cups flour, raisins, orange peel or citron, and lemon zest. Turn dough onto lightly floured board and knead lightly for approximately 5 minutes. Grease a clean bowl with shortening or oil. Place dough in bowl and cover. Let rise in warm place for 1 hour until doubled.

3. Punch down dough. Divide into 18 equal parts. Shape each piece into a ball and place in greased or lined muffin pans. Let rise again until doubled, 45–60 minutes.

4. Preheat oven to 400°. Beat remaining egg and brush tops of buns with egg glaze. Bake for 10–12 minutes until golden. Cool on rack.

5. For icing, combine powdered sugar and juice. Drizzle icing over each bun in shape of a cross.

6. Makes 18 buns

LEG OF LAMB, ITALIAN STYLE

If we were *something* Italian, or Italian *something*, this dish proves as much. We never ate lamb unless it was Italian style. Lamb always appeared in spring, as la Pasqua was a traditional time to begin thinking about lamb and spending time outdoors.

- ⅓ cup lemon juice
- ¼ cup olive oil
- 1 tablespoon dried oregano
- 2 teaspoons chopped anchovies
- 1 teaspoon dry mustard
- ½ teaspoon garlic powder
- 1 teaspoon salt
- 5–6 pounds leg of lamb
- ½ cup cold water
- ¼ cup flour

1. Combine lemon juice, oil, oregano, anchovies, dry mustard, garlic powder, and salt to make a marinade. Place lamb in a plastic bag, add marinade, close, and set in a dry bowl. Marinate for two hours at room temperature or overnight in the refrigerator, occasionally squeezing meat and plastic to distribute the marinade.

2. Preheat oven to 325°. Place lamb fat side up in shallow roasting pan, reserving marinade. Roast for 3–3½ hours, basting with marinade occasionally, until lamb registers 175°–180° on meat thermometer.

3. Combine reserved marinade and pan juices in a saucepan and add enough water to make 2¼ cups. Combine ½ cup cold water and flour and stir into saucepan. Cook over medium heat until bubbly. Serve alongside roast.

LAMB KABOBS (*Arrosticini*)

During our first night in Abruzzo, we found a nearby trattoria, Gran Torre. *La cena* later consisted of tooth-sinking *arrosticini fatti di mano*, mutton skewers made by hand. The meat melted in my mouth. As if to say welcome home, the *cameriere* brought forth plates of *chittara carbonara* and *trofie di speck, gorgonzola, e noci* too.

We found the same on our hike along the Campo Imperatore in the Gran Sasso of Abruzzo's Apennine Mountains, where *spiedini* (skewers) or *arrosticini* (roast) of *agnello* (lamb) are cooked over an open coal fire and consumed within full view of pastures and hiking trails. In Abruzzo, the spiedini are made using small squares of mutton. At home, I use a stew meat cut of lamb. Following our climb, we discovered *pecorino spalmabile* in the nearby *ristoro*. This spreadable pecorino was lathered on bread toasted over the same hot coals used to roast arrosticini or spiedini and *carciofo* (artichokes).

In Abruzzo, they use a large *cubo* to slice the lamb into kabob-sized portions and skewer, before cooking spiedini, usually lamb or mutton. If a cubo or the view overlooking rugged cliffs are not available, this recipe's directions will have to suffice. When cutting lamb into bize-sized pieces, you can do same with the peppers, and use grape tomatoes and pearl onions sparingly.

LAMB
- 2 pounds boned lamb
- ½ cup red wine vinegar
- ½ cup water
- ¼ cup olive oil
- 1 small onion, finely grated
- 1 clove garlic, minced
- 1 tablespoon salt
- 1 teaspoon chopped fresh oregano leaves
- ½ teaspoon ground black pepper
- ¼ teaspoon ground allspice

SKEWERS
- 2 firm medium tomatoes, quartered
- 2 small onions, quartered
- 1–2 green bell peppers, cut into 1-inch squares
- 10 mushroom caps

1. Cut lamb into 1-inch cubes (or your preferred size for kabobs) and place in glass casserole dish. In a stainless-steel mixing bowl, combine all remaining ingredients to make a marinade. Pour marinade over the lamb and marinate overnight, stirring occasionally.

2. Set grill to high heat. Thread lamb and vegetables onto skewers, alternating between lamb and veggies. Place skewers on grate and grill, rotating one-quarter turn every 2 minutes or so, until all sides are browned. Cooking time will vary by size. Remove and serve.

3. Makes approximately 10–12 skewers

CLASSIC TIRAMISU

Bowls were my mother's prized possessions. She marked Fourth of July with a Fire King bowl and used her upside-down triangular tulip bowls by Anchor Hocking for potato, macaroni, or three-bean *insalata* during summer cookouts. When distinguished guests visited for the holidays, we were granted the favor to savor the tiramisu being presented in a flared, frosted Libbey dessert bowl with golden foliage. Though her bowl collection seemed endless, there was never an overabundance of servingware on the table—just an overflowing fountain of love and goodness. Mom tested two versions of tiramisu, which translates to "pick me up," before settling on the one below. Her rejected recipe includes a note: "This caused a big mess." What you can play with is a variety of garnishes or additions such as a spring rhubarb compote or other fruit creations to serve alongside the dessert.

FILLING
- 6 egg yolks
- 1 ¼ cups sugar
- 1 ¼ cups (10 ounces) mascarpone cheese, room temperature
- ½ cup whipping cream
- 1 tablespoon powdered sugar
- ¼ teaspoon vanilla

BRANDIED ESPRESSO
- 1/3 cup hot water
- 2 teaspoons instant coffee or espresso granules
- 1 teaspoon brandy or other liqueur (I use Nocino for a smooth, nutty flavor)

TIRAMISU
- 2 (3-ounce) packages ladyfingers, cut in halves widthwise
- sweetened cocoa powder, for garnish
- chocolate curls, or milk chocolate bar, shaved, for garnish
- pistachios, chopped, for garnish

1. In a medium bowl, combine egg yolks and sugar. Using a hand mixer, whip until thick and lemon-colored, about 1 minute. Place mixture in a double boiler over boiling water, then reduce heat to low and cook 8–10 minutes, stirring constantly. Remove from heat. In a large bowl, beat mascarpone cheese well. Add egg mixture to mascarpone.

2. In a separate bowl, combine whipping cream, powdered sugar, and vanilla. Using a hand mixer, whip until stiff peaks form.

3. Fold whipped cream into egg-mascarpone mixture. Set aside.

4. For the brandied espresso: Combine hot water and instant coffee. Stir until coffee is dissolved, then stir in brandy.

5. Line bottom and sides of a 3-quart bowl or glass baking dish with ladyfingers. Brush with brandied espresso. Spoon half of mascarpone mixture into ladyfinger-lined bowl or dish. Repeat with another layer of ladyfinger halves, espresso, and mascarpone cream.

6. Garnish with sweetened cocoa and chocolate curls. Cover and refrigerate for several hours or overnight. Sprinkle with chopped pistachios.

7. Makes approximately 8-10 servings

CHRISTMAS MADE BY RAVIOLI PRESS

RECIPES
Breaded Calamari • Ravioli with Ricotta and Meat Fillings • Grandma DeLuca's Gnocchi

---

A week or two before Christmas, my mother hung up the kitchen phone in silence. Was she upset because Uncle Tony and his family wouldn't be joining us for Christmas Eve? The cousins were close in age to us, and we often took road trips to Canada and Cincinnati with them. Maybe they were going to *the other side of the family*? My parents each had only one sibling—an anomaly for Italians, perhaps explained by the brutal conditions in Italy their parents had fled. So when they visited *the other side of the family*, that left us with just us.

Did my mother ever ask herself, *if I changed the menu, might the relatives be more inclined to join?* Her menu for *vigilia di Natale* always celebrated the *Festa dei Sette Pesci*, or Feast of the Seven Fishes, an Italian American tradition celebrating the 4,700 miles of coastline immigrant families had left behind to consume the riches of whatever fish they could find stateside. Spoltore was in the province of Pescara, known in the 1000s as *Piscaria* ("abounding in fish"). Fish was in our blood.

The *festa* tradition included fried *baccalà*, smelts—small fish eaten whole, slimy heads and guts and all—and other fishes we didn't have words for. While in Italy on a boat trip, Mark and I ate at a waterside restaurant in Massa Lubrense where the *cameriere* asked if we were ready for our next course of *pesci*. "*Che tipo?*" I asked. "*Pesce è pesce.*" However, given the lack of access to the seas in Ohio, *Pesce non è pesce ovunque*. Fish is not the same everywhere.

Seven fish courses—the same number of courses as we had family members—was a difficult task for my mother to achieve on her own. My parents already had plenty of elf work to perform that night: watching *The Bells of St. Mary's*, setting out a plate of cookies for Santa, making sure we went to bed.

The vigilia di Natale would begin with Sea-Sau brand shrimp cocktail, frozen and packaged in small, fluted glasses. Once thawed, the little shrimp and sauce would find a home in a milky white bowl, cold to the touch, and await their place at the table. These were followed by breaded calamari as the *primo pesce*. Despite the common misconception, calamari is not octopus. The word *calamari* means "squid" in plural form. You'd never eat just one.

Calamari made its way onto our plates in a variety of ways: with tentacles and tubes floating in marinara; lightly breaded and fried, sometimes basking in a delightful lemony sauce to mask its rubbery texture; or in a simple preparation of oil with red and green peppers, garlic, and salt.

Next came the harsher sounding *baccalà*. While baccalà and *merluzzo* (cod) are similar in the water, at the table there are some key differences. Cod is used for *stoccafisso*, air-dried stockfish preserved without salt. Baccalà is salt-cured, and in our family's kitchen, the little fishes, already prepped by the fishmonger, lay in a bed of oil or were fried in breadcrumbs, like sun worshippers lined up on the *spiaggia*.

As the courses continued, my mother would produce a lavishly garnished broiled orange roughy with orange slices on top, or a flounder primavera. Our festa rotation also included fried smelts, heads and all, now a delicacy on some menus. While no self-respecting northern Ohio cook would get by without a nod to local perch and walleye, native to Lake Erie, perch existed mainly to use the last crumbs of Shake-n-Bake coating during Lenten Fridays. And other people ate walleye. Not to say, today, I don't crave its flaky texture and sweet taste. Thus, neither appeared to grace the Christmas Eve table.

My mother might have fallen short of the Feast of Seven Fishes by a dish or three. Perhaps Uncle Tony and his family didn't come by on Christmas Eve because she served fish, or maybe they simply had other obligations.

I watched as my mother, her rounded cheeks sunken in, let the phone fall back onto its hook. Her expertise was clearly designed for an audience more appreciative than her children.

Competition was fierce with the *other side* in Italian American families as coveted holidays were alternated, split, or shared. Certainly, the food served and the prowess of the cook played a role in deciding where to eat.

How did Uncle Tony answer for his family, on the rare occasion they declined my mother's invitation? In a nod to *The Godfather*, I'd like to think my uncle said, "Jean, I'll take your cookies, but I'll leave the baccalà."

The following morning, my parents were tasked with getting Santa's visit right. But once the commotion around gifts settled, another commotion began as they set out to make the ravioli—and everyone else in the house—boil.

First, my mother would set aside two Amish Butterprint bowls, one gooseberry pink and the other teal blue, for "red" meat ravioli and "blue" cheese ravioli. One stainless-steel stock pot simmered on the upstairs kitchen stove with sauce pressed from tomatoes from the garden. She and my father would bring two other pots of water to near-boiling on the basement Magic Chef stove, lined with tin foil to protect the burners. Potholders crocheted with yellow and white yarn in the shape of a star or woven from colorful bands were at the ready. My father turned on the humidifier to soak up moisture as the pots raged, anger boiled, and sweat poured out over what could go wrong. Busily, my mother would count meat and cheese ravioli she had made in the weeks before and frozen. If we were lucky, they came up even enough to split between the number of guests.

At the basement stove, my mother gently laid the ravioli in the pots and used slotted, stainless-steel spoons to calm the pasta in its agitated waves of boiling water, along with the household's nerves. In the double basin, harvest-gold porcelain sink upstairs, an oversize metal strainer sat to the right on a rubber dish drain.

Next, my father donned a red-and-blue apron, tying it over his white shirt and cinching the pockets, barely, around his proud Italian waist, forcing my mother to search for another apron to cover up her classical cream shirt and black skirt or pants.

We'd all listen for my mother to shout, "Ette!" and for my father to say, "you kids better get down here and help your mother." He carried the pots upstairs and poured the floppy, cooked ravioli from stock pot into strainer while my mother yelled from below, "Don't pour them out so fast, they might break!" One of us kids ladled sauce into the bottom of the pink bowl, then carefully layered pillows of pasta one atop another. *Sauce, ravioli, repeat,* and the same in the blue bowl too. Most likely, after a few rounds we threw the rest in and let them drown in the red sea so no would notice they weren't neatly layered.

After the sacred bowls were served to family, relatives, stragglers, neighbors, priests, and boyfriends still in good graces, we were charged with clearing the bowls and rinsing them before the sauce congealed or the cheese curdled into a paste on dinnerware called into service only twice a year.

Then came the midnight fight over leftovers—with my father hollering out from his den, "You kids get in here and clean up your mess."

CLOCKWISE FROM TOP LEFT Ettore and Jean's First Christmas, 1961; Uncle Tony DeLuca, playing Santa, 1966; Fresh off a trip from Abruzzo, Annette Januzzi Wick making ravioli again, 2022.

BREADED CALAMARI

When teaching young tongues to appreciate the cultural touchstones of her family, my mother turned to a standard. Breaded calamari became our first introduction to the magical world of sea creatures dined on during the holidays, and later at Italian American restaurants and fresh from the sea in Italy. She was sly in coaxing us into culinary comforts. In winter, I like to serve this with tomato sauce. When spring arrives, I add fresh pesto into an aioli to compliment the calamari.

½ pound fresh or 1 (8-ounce) package frozen calamari

1 ½ cups breadcrumbs

3 cloves garlic, chopped

2 tablespoons grated Romano cheese

1 tablespoon fresh parsley

1 teaspoon salt

½ teaspoon ground black pepper

½–¾ cup olive oil

Basic Tomato Sauce (included in this book), for serving

1. Preheat oven to 350°.
2. Rinse calamari and drain. Mix breadcrumbs, garlic, Romano cheese, parsley, salt, and pepper in plastic bag and shake to blend. Pour ½ cup olive oil into a shallow bowl. Dip each piece of calamari in olive oil, then place in bag, shake, and transfer calamari to lightly-oiled cookie sheet. Repeat, adding more oil to bowl if needed, until all calamari have been breaded.
3. Bake 15 minutes. Serve with warm tomato sauce.
4. Makes 4–6 servings

RAVIOLI WITH RICOTTA AND MEAT FILLINGS

I once wrote a recipe poem called "How to Make Ravioli—and Everyone Else in the House—Boil." Timing was of utmost importance with this dish, only because of my mother's perfection. Tensions in our house rose as the temperature of the cooking water in the pots on the basement stove rose. The faces of all who helped turned tomato red. You were better off not helping at all.

My mother used this pasta dough recipe frequently, having inherited it from her mother, Raffaela. Over time, flour quality and egg sizes have changed, and my family has adjusted the recipe accordingly. Just as the regions of Italy all have their own proprietary names for similar-style foods, family pasta dough recipes too have been altered and changed so that no two are exactly alike. Some say to include salt, some say none. Some use water, others do not. When pressed for time, I use Marcella Hazan's quick fix of 2 eggs and 1 cup flour to make an easy pasta dough. What matters most is that the dough produced the right amount of protective coating for the ravioli. For the ricotta filling, my mother's traditional recipe detoured from the typical savory mix by blending in sugar and cinnamon. This small deviation was influenced by her Abruzzese roots. When pressed by her pushy kids to explore variations on fillings, she developed chicken ravioli and spinach ravioli options.

PASTA DOUGH
- 2 ¼ cups flour
- ½ teaspoon salt
- 4 medium eggs
- 1 ½ teaspoons water
- Cheese, Meat, or Chicken Ravioli Filling (recipes follow)
- 1 tablespoon olive oil

1. In a large bowl, combine flour and salt. Form a well and break eggs into well. Whisk eggs, then add water and continue mixing to gradually combine wet ingredients into flour. Place dough on a floured board and knead. Knead and rest several times until dough comes together smoothly. When rounded, a simple finger press into the dough should not stick. Allow dough to rest in the refrigerator for 15 minutes, if possible, for gluten bonds to form. Split dough into quarters. Using one quarter, flatten until ½ inch thick. Using a pasta roller, roll dough into flat sheets until reaching the 3rd to final setting on pasta machine.

2. My mother added, "I use my spaghetti machine to roll out flat pieces to fit over my Ravioli Chef (form). This makes perforated squares." Lay one sheet of dough flat across the bottom form. Spoon 1 teaspoon filling into indentations. Lay second sheet of dough across filling. Press second form into both layers. If you don't have a ravioli press form, roll out dough layers as quickly as possible to approximate

measurements of the form (12 ½ inches x 5 ½ inches). On bottom layer, fill into 10 even spaces, place second layer over top. Use a round or square fluted-edged cutter, and cut into similar sizes as form. Press edges together with fork. Another option is to use a round or square fluted-edged cutter to cut out single pieces, fill, fold over, and press together with fork.

3. You can cook the ravioli immediately, or place them on wax paper–lined cookie sheets to freeze. Once frozen, transfer to plastic Ziplock bags and store in the freezer until ready to use.

4. To cook ravioli, bring a pot of salted water to boil and add oil. Add ravioli and reduce heat to medium. Boil for 5 minutes for freshly made ravioli or 10 minutes for frozen, until they rise to the surface and filling is cooked through.

5. Serve with tomato sauce and a sprinkle of grated cheese.

6. Makes approximately 40 raviolis.

RICOTTA RAVIOLI FILLING

2 pounds ricotta cheese

1 large egg

¼ cup grated Parmesan cheese

3 tablespoons sugar

dash of ground cinnamon

1 cup cooked spinach, chopped (optional)

1. In a medium bowl, mix all ingredients until well-blended. Use to fill ravioli.

MEAT RAVIOLI FILLING

1 ½ pounds ground beef, pork, and/or turkey (I use turkey and pork, uncooked)

¾ cup seasoned breadcrumbs

1 teaspoon salt

⅛ teaspoon ground black pepper

¼ cup water

1 large egg

1. In a medium bowl, mix all ingredients until well-blended. Use to fill ravioli.

CHICKEN RAVIOLI FILLING

2 cups cooked shredded chicken

1 cup cooked chopped spinach

½ cup breadcrumbs

½ cup grated Romano cheese

1 clove garlic, minced

1 tablespoon minced fresh parsley

2 fresh basil leaves, minced

2 eggs

2 tablespoons vegetable oil

1. In a medium bowl, mix all ingredients until well-blended. Use to fill ravioli.

GRANDMA DELUCA'S GNOCCHI

While my cousin Michael Ann recalled that Aunt Mary, her father's cousin, used to proffer bowls of steaming, creamy gnocchi, this dish was known as mine. If my mother made gnocchi, other siblings would jokingly say, "of course you made it for her. She's your favorite." If gnocchi are on the menu, I never refuse due to its reminder of that special bond my mother and I shared. Her ricer takes up residence next to my frittata pan patiently awaiting use.

6 medium Idaho potatoes
2 large or 3 small eggs
2 ½–3 cups flour

1. Peel and cut up potatoes. Bring a pot of salted water to boil and add potatoes, then lower heat to a simmer, cover, and cook until tender, 20 minutes.

2. Mash with a masher, preferably a ricer. Allow to cool completely.

3. In large bowl, beat eggs. Mix potatoes with eggs, then gradually mix in flour until dough reaches a soft rolling consistency. Roll into a long ¾-inch-diameter rope. Cut rope into pieces about 1¼ inches long. With index finger, make an indentation in each piece while rolling at the same time, or press tines of a fork into each piece.

4. Cook gnocchi immediately, or place on a wax paper–lined pan and freeze. Once frozen, transfer to Ziplock bags and store in the freezer until ready to use.

5. To cook, bring a pot of salted water to boil and add gnocchi. Cook for 3–5 minutes. They will float to surface when cooked. Serve with tomato sauce or your preferred sauce.

6. Makes approximately 12 servings

CARRYING ABRUZZO AND CALABRIA HOME

RECIPES

Lentil Soup (*Zuppa di Lenticchie*) • Gnocchetti Stew (*Stufato con Gnochetti*)
• Chestnut Puree (*Purea di Castagne*) • Pizzelle •
Viola's Crostata • Celli Ripieni • Fried Dough (*Crespelle*)

I was saddened to come home from Abruzzo not only because of severing the familial connection but the region's staples weren't necessarily within my reach in Cincinnati. A few months later, in my hometown, I attended the CincItalia festival. What do they sell? Arrosticini. How had I missed that all these years of my attendance?

What else did I do? I adopted a sheep from La Porta dei Parchi, an *agriturismo* in the province of L'Aquila, to ensure access to some of the best cheeses in the world. In my first box, I was gifted *caciocavallo* (which translates to "horse," for the two spheres of cheese tied together during the aging and hung over a stick, resembling a horse's saddle), *pecorino con zaffarano* (Pecorino with saffron), *pecorino on ginepro* (with juniper), *ricotta affumicata* (smoked ricotta), many *marmellate* (jams) and *mieli* (honeys), and a canister of olive oil.

Weeks after my return, I perfected the *zuppa di lenticchie* (lentil soup) that we had cooked in the kitchen at Rifugio della Rocca with proprietor Susanna Silvati in Calaccio. I used the famed lentils from Santo Stefano di Sessanio, where a purplish hue tinted the fields. I chased after the recipes for the *gnochetti* and the *stufato* (stew) made with a soffritto base that we had been served by Marisa Sanelli at Agriturismo Pietra Antica after our Grand Maiella hikes. But there were still a few other items left to replicate and conquer in my Abruzzo repertoire.

On Abruzzo's Costa dei Trabocchi, a bike trail along the Adriatic, the bike shop proprietor spoke no English. He'd wished us *buona fortuna* as we rode off on a forty-kilometer trek.

After a stop for a long lunch at one of the trabocchi, little fishing huts that hung over the waterline, we still had twenty kilometers to go. Dusk hurried along. We mistakenly exited the bike path. An argument ensued, as happened whenever we were lost in a new land. *Cento è cento* came to mind again. Finally, the light of Vasto shined down on us. Our albergo was in the historical center, 450 feet above sea level—up a steep incline. We huffed with our e-bikes the final one hundred yards, while two carabinieri easily pedaled past.

The next morning, the previous day's exertion kickstarted a hunger in me. On the host's terrace, a platter of pastries came into view, filled with cookies that had been formed in a waffle iron. *Ferratelle*. Mom's pizzelle.

Pizzelle played a large role in our Abruzzese platters of *dolci*. My mother gifted me a pizzelle maker for my first wedding, and the cookies have been part of my rotation ever since for Christmas, birthdays, graduations. For Mom's birthday in her care home and for the gatherings we held after she died. And for my son's wedding a month before we left for Abruzzo, when he married his college sweetheart, I had shined up the stainless-steel cover of the pizzelle press, wrapped it in bubble wrap, and warily shipped it west with tracking information.

Back at the residenza, I bit into the ferratelle and could hardly chew through tears.

I recalled how on early mornings and late nights throughout my childhood, my mother took up her post in the basement. She heaved her ceramic bowl onto the counter to mix the pizzelle's sticky egg-based dough. Once the cast-iron press was heated and any remaining oil had burned off, she slid the dough off her fingers onto the press and closed it shut. After a minute of wiping away a bead of sweat, she flipped the press over the stovetop burner for the time it took to say a Hail Mary, according to the legend of the *nonne*. Next, she gently forked beneath the tendrils of a fragile pizzelle edge and lifted it to a cooling rack.

Despite the way the land, the *terra*, fed into our gustatory lust in Abruzzo, when I took a bite, I said, "it's not as good as Mom's." What I really meant was, "It's not Mom."

Another forty-kilometer bike ride loomed ahead to return to Ortona, this time, downhill. One last pastry patiently waited on my plate. As I bit into a shortbread-like crust with raw sugar sprinkled on top, my senses filled with a magical familiarity of the Concord grapes my grandparents grew and made wine from. A chocolatey, berry-flavored jam coated my tongue. The combination embodied the frugality of my ancestors and the extravagance of my ability to go abroad. I experienced the relief one feels when closing in on a quest.

I called the host to our table and asked about the cookies. He called them *celli ripieni*, or *uccelli ripieni*, stuffed birds. Small rectangles of dough were stuffed with jam, then folded and the edges pressed together. The ends were crimped, and the points were pinched together to resemble a beak.

Those cookies haunted me like a cartoon bubble hanging over my head.

Around Christmastime, I reached out to my cousin Viola in Abruzzo looking for advice about the celli ripieni. She referred me to an Italian recipe. Conversion calculator in hand, I tossed some salt over my shoulders. The best cooks knew to try and taste and try again. I stuffed every bit of Italianness I could into those little cookies.

The celli accompanied me wherever I went. To a Hannukah celebration (they were *kind* of blue inside), to the Irish in-laws, onto my cookie platter at Christmas, to a New Year's Day dinner. I ate them until my supply ran out. I ate them on Mom's birthday, falling one day after the Feast of the Epiphany. I might have been the only one who ate them with such ravishing desire, as I alone knew the heartache and joy that had led me to their discovery.

The olive oil canister from Abruzzo's La Porta dei Parchi remained in the dark recesses of my pantry, only a cup or so left. I resolved not to deplete those stores until my return to Italy.

My stock from Calabria differed slightly from what I'd brought back from Abruzzo. Olive oil from two estates: Barone Macri and Constantino, where we were schooled in the importance of D.O.P. designation, which requires products to be locally grown using traditional methods. During our visit to Agricola Constantino, Mark and I were both horrified to find that our olive oil palates could not always distinguish the pure oil from the one with seed oil additives. We also accepted that it would be plenty difficult for me to find olive oil from Abruzzo or Calabria in Cincinnati. Many farms and families in Calabria retained their stores for themselves. I joked that even my family hadn't given any away.

Back home, there were no fresh Calabrian chilis to cut into our pasta dishes. Instead, jars of 'nduja and *marmellata di cipollo di Tropea* (red onion jam of Tropea) became ingredients in my five-pepper chili, although I wasn't able to trace the Tropea onion crèma we enjoyed at a vineyard one night. We packed 'nduja in jars and into a vacuum-sealed package that we had yet to open weeks after arriving at home. The 'nduja and a *confettura calabrese* with bergamot and pepperoncino were tossed into stews and spread onto crackers to cozy up with some Bianco Sardo cheese from our local shop.

We also brought home the cedron liqueur and cream of cedron liqueur that had accompanied our meals, as did the Greco Bianco passito, an elegant, sweet wine with aromas of peach and honey. Cedron and bergamot were not limited to the foods we ate in Calabria, but were also ingredients in a *crema unica al cedro* I purchased for my face, bergamot perfume, and a bergamot essential oil, not to be used in cooking, only in refreshing.

In Abruzzo at Tenuta del Priore, we had learned how to order their Vecchio Priore and Kerrias of Montepulciano d' Abruzzo via bank transfer, and we did the same with Barone di Macri wines. Barons were landed nobles of the lowest rank in the feudal system, and the Barone title brought to mind a 1931 letter my great-grandfather Vincenzo had written to his son Enrico. "A person comes from Tuscany and he bought the baron's mountain," he wrote. "His name is Amerino. The owner pays us L100 / month. He has a gun and is a serious person." At Barone di Macri, we bought the Terre di Gerace red, a youthful wine made from Nerello Calabrese and the fragrant Greco Nero; a young rosato and bianco of the same grape; and a magliocco dolce, an ancient Calabrese vine.

With Concetta and Stella Macrini on my mind, I made some crespelle and a crostata with a fig jam, and included chestnuts in the next time I baked my mother's pecan nut cups. The result was reminiscent of the bocconotti filled with nuts known innately to the San Donatese. Chestnut stuffing had already been on my menus at times, but now I would try the chestnut puree, possibly serve it on a silver platter as Grandma Stella recommended.

Mostly, what I carried home was a lesson in language—how it hurts, how it heals. In Italy, I would see *peperoncino* on a menu and finally recognize its spelling with one "p". Often, when speaking of my mother in her care home,

I'd forgotten the simple *casa di cura*. Reading it in Italian on the sign of a *casa di cura* made it real. For once, the focus wasn't always on the mouth, but on the mother tongue.

Toward the end of our trip, somewhere along the streets of Diamonte, I turned to Mark to say something—and forgot my English words. My thoughts had become Italian, in the dialect of those I loved. For a middle child whose mother always said, "you feel things too deeply," this new ache felt innately Italian.

My parents mourned what they hadn't been able to share with their children, but they didn't have the language—or the time. For them, food became secondary to who was doing the feeding, who was being fed. To assuage my ache for more wouldn't come only in edible form, but by digging into this insistence for connection, and honoring the swirling winds around Spoltore and San Donato di Ninea that had beckoned me there.

CLOCKWISE FROM TOP LEFT Italian scooter draped with Tropea red onions, Calabria, 2024; Calabrian chili peppers hanging outside of Concetta Macrini's home, 2024; Mark Manley and Rifugio della Rocca proprietor Susanna Silvati, Calaccio, 2022; Annette Januzzi Wick with pizzelle, Vasto, 2022; Annette Januzzi Wick and Concetta Macrini; A traditional Turdiddru Santunatisi

LENTIL SOUP (ZUPPA DI LENTICCHIE)

In the hills of Abruzzo, Italy, the town of Santo Stefano di Sessanio celebrates its crop of small brown lentils. During our recent stay, Susanna, the host of nearby Rifugio della Rocca offered us a robust soup yielded from these tiny delights. Yearning to replicate the earthy, newly harvested taste and the Abruzzese experience, I created this version with the packages carted home in my suitcase. Following our Abruzzese outings, I learned to eat more beans, *lenticchie*, *fagioli*, *cici*, because they are as ancient as the *Iliad*.

~~~~~~

1 cup small, brown Santo Stefano di Sessanio lentils (or small French lentils)

⅔ of a sweet Italian pepper, diced (see note)

1–2 cloves garlic, whole

2 tablespoons tomato paste

1–2 teaspoons olive oil

2 teaspoons salt

1 bay leaf

4 ½ cups water

1. In a large Dutch oven, combine all ingredients and bring a boil. Lower the heat to medium-low and cook for 30 minutes or until the lentils are of desired consistency. Remove garlic cloves before serving.

2. Note: Sweet, mild Italian peppers are called *friggitello* or *friarelli peppers*. They're also known as Golden Greek peppers. In the US, we might know them as "pepperoncini," but they are not the same as Italian peperoncini, which are hot Italian chili peppers.

3. Makes 4–6 servings.

GNOCCHETTI STEW (*Stufato con Gnocchetti*)

Following a strenuous hike into the Grand Maiella to the San Bartolomeo Ermitagio, we headed toward Decontra, Abruzzo. There, we were welcomed to the Agriturismo Pietra Antica by Marisa Sanelli. Marisa's guests included groups from Germany and Belgium along with us, and she asked each of us to perform a song from our home country. We sang James Taylor's "Sweet Caroline" well enough for her to prepare us a hearty hunters' stew made with a *soffritto* base. This is my version. I use smaller *gnocchetti* to make it easy to slurp up all the ingredients in one spoonful.

---

1 pound boneless chicken breasts
1–2 tablespoons olive oil
3 carrots, diced
3 celery stalks, diced
½ medium onion, diced
½ teaspoon dried basil
½ teaspoon dried thyme
½ teaspoon dried oregano
1 (8 ounces) can ceci beans (chickpeas), drained
1 (4 ounces) can tomato paste
1 pound ricotta gnocchetti (recipe follows), cooked and drained

1. Place chicken in a medium stock pot and add enough cold water or stock to cover. Bring to a boil, then reduce the heat and simmer for 10 minutes. Remove chicken and cool. Shred by using two forks to pull apart.

2. Heat oil in Dutch oven over medium heat. Reduce heat to medium-low, add carrots, celery, and onion, and sauté until onion is translucent. Add herbs, then stir in ceci beans and tomato paste until blended. Add chicken and bring back to a boil, then reduce heat and simmer for 30 minutes. I like a thickness to my stews and soups, but if you prefer, you can add water for a thinner texture. Add cooked gnocchetti and serve with a grated pecorino or other sheep's milk cheese.

3. Makes 3–4 servings

RICOTTA GNOCCHETTI

2 cups ricotta cheese
2 medium eggs
1 cup grated Parmesan cheese
pinch of salt
2 ¼ cups flour

1. Drain ricotta by spooning it onto paper towel–lined plate. In a large bowl, mix drained ricotta and eggs until creamy. Add Parmesan cheese and salt, then blend in flour, a few handfuls at a time, until mixture is compact, but soft enough to roll. On a floured pastry board knead dough to form a loaf. Cut off pieces and roll each into a log as thick as a finger. Cut each log into 1-inch pieces, lightly dusting with flour as needed to keep from sticking. You can cook gnocchetti immediately, or place on a floured cookie sheet and freeze until ready to cook.

2. To cook, bring a pot of water to boil and add gnocchetti. Cook for 3 minutes, or until they float.

3. Makes 40–45 gnocchetti.

CHESTNUT PUREE (PUREA DI CASTAGNE)

Chestnuts are prevalent throughout Italy. Chestnut flour is often used for "bread of the poor." And the nuts have long been an understated but valuable resource for many. The Genoese once pleaded with landowners to plant four trees per year: chestnut, olive, fig, and mulberry. I'd like to do the same.

Chestnut trees have a silvery, shiny bark, and their nuts fall onto the ground—or are beaten with sticks, such as bamboo, to knock them off—still sheathed in a spiky coat. By the time they reach the grocer, the husks have been removed. Those who harvest these in the wild, as my cousins do, must take care to remove the prickly shell before collecting them together.

This recipe was discovered in my mother's archives, written in the distinct handwriting of my grandmother Stella Januzzi.

~~~~~~

2 pounds chestnuts
¼ cup butter, melted
¼–½ cup whipping cream
salt to taste

1. Bring two large pots of salted water to a boil. Make two slits on the side of each chestnut in an X shape. Add chestnuts to first pot of water and boil for 10 minutes.

2. Remove one nut at a time, leaving the rest in the pot, and remove its shell and skin. This is easier while the nuts are still warm. Place shelled nuts into second pot of boiling water, then reduce heat and simmer until tender, about 15 minutes.

3. Pour chestnuts and cooking water in to jars or a large bowl, cover, and refrigerate until cooled. Drain nuts and puree in a food processor. Place nut puree in top of double boiler over hot water. Add melted butter and whisk in enough cream to reach the consistency of whipped potatoes. Add salt to taste. Heap high on a silver dish and garnish with herbs.

4. Makes 6-8 side servings.

PIZZELLE

The magic behind homemade pizzelle wasn't just in the diamond or floral patterns on the press, or how no spoonful landed on the iron the same, and therefore no cookie rolled off looking the same. To reproduce the crispness and flavor of my mother's pizzelle, you would need to incorporate not only the smears of oil left on the iron, but also the years of elbow grease poured into each pizzelle. This is the recipe she made with her electric Vitantonio press, the same one I use in my kitchen. She followed a slightly different recipe for her old-fashioned Vitantonio three-part cast iron press. There's also a circular press which might produce a more perfectly rounded cookie. Who needs perfection in the shape when the taste is all that matters?

- 6 medium eggs, room temperature
- 1 ½ cups sugar
- 1 cup butter or margarine, melted and cooled
- 2 tablespoons vanilla or anise extract
- 1 ¾ cups flour
- 4 teaspoons baking powder

1. In a large bowl, whisk eggs. Add sugar gradually and whisk until smooth. Stir in cooled butter and extract. In a separate bowl, mix flour and baking powder, then add to egg mixture and stir to mix. The dough will be sticky. Allow dough time to rest, especially if the butter has not cooled completely.

2. Heat pizzelle maker to appropriate setting. Drop dough by small tablespoons on pizzelle iron and close for ten seconds or less. Each press will vary. Remove pizzelle to wire rack to cool. Experiment with timing, which may vary based on age of press. Pizzelle should come out without hints of browning.

3. Makes 80 cookies.

VARIATIONS:

- Chocolate Pizzelle: Add ½ cup cocoa powder, ½ cup sugar, and ½ teaspoon more baking powder to flour mixture before combining with egg-butter mixture.
- Lemon-Anise Pizzelle: Use 1 tablespoon anise extract and grated rind of 1 lemon. For a deeper flavor, add 1 teaspoon ground fennel seeds (not powdered fennel) or fennel pollen.
- My mother also jotted down: "May use ¼ teaspoon cinnamon, 1 teaspoon vanilla, and 1 teaspoon lemon extract.".

The tips in my mother's recipe are their own study in perfection:

- Place small tablespoon full in center of each pattern.
- First ones may not do well.
- Hold handles together while baking.
- Light will go on and off during baking, indicating thermostat automatically keeping grids at baking temperature.
- Never use water on pizzelle maker. Brush grids with steel brush before storing. Use damp cloth on chrome.

VIOLA'S CROSTATA

One of the secrets to baking Italian specialties is contained in this recipe. *Lievito* can refer to either baking powder or dry yeast. When a *bustina di lievito per dolci* is called for, Italians do not use a bread yeast. They use a *pane degli angeli*, an Italian rising agent made with vanilla and baking powder, perfect for baking. You can find these packets through online sources, or any Italian cousin.

Upon my return to the states from Abruzzo, I comforted myself with baking every kind of crostata di frutta, like the one made by Marta at Il Marchese del Grillo in Sulmona. Hers was filled with *marmellata di uva* (grape jam), also known as *scrucchiata*, a seasonal rustic jam made during the fall harvest from the pulp and skins of Montepulciano grapes.

This recipe is from my second cousin Viola Giuliani (on the Scurti family side, not the Giuliani side), who I discovered after a long search for relatives across social media. Her great-grandmother Concetta, was my grandmother Rafaella's sister. The recipe, written in Italian and translated and refined by me, was accompanied by this note: "Do it and let me know you will surely like it. I make one a week. –Viola."

---

1 egg
3 egg yolks
1 cup melted butter
2 tablespoons milk
¾ cup sugar
zest of one lemon
1 (16-gram) package bustina di lievito per dolci (for cakes)
4 cups flour
6-8 ounces jam of choice (I use marmellata d'uva)

1. In a small bowl, blend together egg, egg yolks, butter, milk, sugar, lemon zest, milk, and lievito. Place flour in a large bowl and make a well in the center. Pour egg mixture into well and fold in flour to mix all ingredients together. Knead dough until thoroughly blended. Split dough into two portions, wrap individually in parchment paper, and allow to rest for 30 minutes in the refrigerator. (Dough may be refrigerated for up to 3 days at this point.)

2. Preheat oven to 350°. Let dough return to room temperature.

3. Working with one dough ball at a time, divide in half again and press one half into bottom and up sides of a 10-inch round crostata pan or other shallow round pan. Spread half of jam over the dough. Roll out other half of dough, cut into strips, and crisscross in basketweave fashion over jam. Or crumble dough between hands and sprinkle over top for a crumble topping, or use a cookie cutter in a star or flower shape to press out several cutouts and place over top. If making two, repeat with second dough ball and remaining jam.

4. Bake 10–15 minutes, until bottom is lightly brown.

5. Makes 12 slices or 20 squares

CELLI RIPIENI (OR CELLI PIENI)

The sweet pastry of celli, with their light, nutty cocoa filling, have become a standard in my house since their appearance at breakfast one more morning at our *loggio*, following a lengthy bike ride and an interrupted night of rest in the town of Vasto. *Celli ripieni* roughly translates to "little stuffed birds," and these are also often referred to as *celli pieni* or *colli pieni*. When I presented these at wine tasting events, they were decadent enough for all to enjoy with a lovely pairing of wine. A cousin in Spoltore, Viola, gladly shared this recipe, which I adapted for US equivalents.

DOUGH
- 2 medium eggs
- ¾ cup plus 3 tablespoons sugar, plus more for sprinkling
- zest of 1 lemon
- 1 (16-gram) package bustina di lievito per dolci (for cakes)
- 4 ¼ cups plus 1 tablespoon flour
- ½ cup dry white wine, more as needed
- ¼ cup plus 1 tablespoon olive oil, more as needed

FILLING
- 1 cup grape marmellata or jam (see note)
- ¼ cup grated dark chocolate
- 1 tablespoon cocoa powder
- zest of 1 orange
- pinch of ground cinnamon
- ½ teaspoon Nocino or other walnut liqueur

1. In a small bowl, beat eggs, sugar, and lemon zest. Add lievito. Place flour in a large bowl and make a well in the center. Pour wine and oil into well and blend into flour with a fork. Fold in egg mixture. Continue to add more oil and wine as needed to bring dough together. Cover dough in plastic wrap and place in the refrigerator to rest for several hours.

2. To make jam filling, combine all ingredients and stir until smooth.

3. Preheat oven to 350°. Roll out a portion of dough on floured surface to ⅛ inch thick. Use a 2 ¾-inch round biscuit cutter to cut circles. Spoon ½ teaspoon jam filling into each circle. Fold dough over to enclose filling like a ravioli and create a semicircle shape. Pinch the ends into little beaks. Sprinkle with granulated or raw sugar. Repeat with remaining dough and filling.

4. Place celli on a parchment-lined baking sheet and bake for 15–18 minutes. Remove from oven when edges appear lightly browned. Before serving, use a sifter, sieve, or small shaker to apply powdered sugar for a festive touch.

5. Makes 36 cookies.

Note: I use a homemade concord grape marmellata inspired by the crostatas and celli served to us during our trip to Abruzzo. Another option is Tartilicious Grape Jam from the Local Kitchen blog, which was inspired by a recipe from Sherri Brooks Vinton's *Put 'em Up*.

FRIED DOUGH (CRESPELLE)

In Italy, every region, province, town, and family make its own version of crespelle, sometimes also called *grispelli* or *zeppole*. *Crespelle* is a generic name that seems to be used for a variety of fried doughs. Some resemble crêpes; others are made with a potato dough, covered in honey, or stuffed with anchovies or 'nduja. This recipe was given to me by Concetta Macrini and demonstrated just ten minutes before our departure from San Donato di Ninea. We had been drinking coffee and eating these crispy delights in the early mornings and late evenings. Now, it was time to carry them with me. The translated measurements are mine. This recipe calls for "oo" flour, used in pastries and pizza in Italy.

---

4 cups "00" flour

1 teaspoons yeast (not sweet)

1 teaspoons salt

½ cup warm water

olive oil for hands and cooking

Vegetable oil for cooking

1. In a large bowl combine flour, yeast, and salt and mix dry ingredients with a fork. Add warm (not hot) water and mix with fork or wooden tongs and spatula until dough is batter-like but not sticky. Cover and let rise 1 hour or more.

2. Fill a large pot or deep fryer with 2 inches oil, using equal parts olive oil and vegetable oil, and heat to 175°.

3. Shape pieces of dough into open rings about 3 inches in diameter, using thumb to poke a hole in the center. You can also use two teaspoons to scrape dough into balls for a fritter shape, or stretch pieces of dough into long, flattened strips. Whatever shape you choose, drop a few pieces of dough at a time into oil. If choosing open rings, use tongs to keep middle from collapsing. Cook for two minutes on each side until golden brown. Remove to rack to cool.

4. If you'd like, you can sprinkle with powdered sugar after they have slightly cooled for added sweetness.

5. Makes approximately 12 large crespelle

AFTERWORD

Today in Lorain, the loss of industry is palpable, but the desire for engagement hasn't changed. Here in this place where my great-grandparents and grandparents sowed their seeds, my parents found community in an enclave where Polish, Czech, Puerto Rican, and Italian immigrants lived together, and later with those who became their friends in Amherst.

Steering away from Lorain's lakeshore, in minutes, I could drive to my parents' childhood residences in Lorain, or to Calvary Cemetery. Inhaling, I could easily sniff out the corner of the former DeLuca's Bakery on 8th and Reid, where I can still see the specter of my mother waiting in line with five sets of grubby hands at her side. Jam made from wild black raspberries sourced in the woods behind our house awaited us at home, where it would be spread on DeLuca's toasted Italian bread. Across Broadway, the Black River flows now with tourism and heron rookeries.

I could also head straightaway to the homes of both sets of grandparents, which I could detect by the scents of fried crisp cannoli or vanilla cream puffs that linger in my mind. The aromas of a fig tree wrapped in burlap, Concord grape juices spilling off the vine, Uncle Tony's sharp cigarette smoke, both grandpas' cherry pipes. Uncle Albert's lake house, my mother's dream. The wisps of sweetness out of the Lorain Creamery doors on 17th Street. No matter the state of our relationships, weekly visits to these sacred places were a constant, and these memories remain imprinted on our skins and our tongues. Further up on the road, on

Broadway, the former Januzzi's Shoes building practically lights up in my mind. I see my grandfather remove a sticky brush from the shoe-glue jar, its chemicals piercing my nose. My car's engine purrs toward recollections of lunch with Dad at the now-defunct Burger Chef for flame-broiled burgers, away from the inquisitive eyes of my grandfather cobbling at his corner station, and of the employees who knew we were spoiled kids yet to learn the hard lessons.

Rolling slowly until I hit Sheffield, I can see my older sister and I working the shelves at one of the Januzzi shoe outlets. Behind that complex was the stretch of fields of the International Festival where I first discovered gyros. How my tongue desired the tang of a good red onion. I recalled asking my mother once, "Can we be Greek?" without realizing how close some of our DNA really was.

Circling out of Lorain and west on Route 2, I come to Amherst, where my family molded a new kind of Italian. An American one. Mostly, what they created was within themselves. The traumas they and their parents had withstood, the losses, the hopes that had died, the courage and love they discovered, all of these they endured by stuffing, rolling, and baking, strewing, staking, and planting in their safe spaces—the kitchen and the land.

In Amherst, a stop along the front lawn of our old house on Ridgeland reveals grass overshadowed by tentacles of thinning trees. That wouldn't do in my mother's imaginings, but maybe my father would have thrived below the canopy as his dad once did. Beneath whitened skies, our shouts of "Duck, Duck, Goose!" around the sycamore tree (whose seed pods we called monkeyballs) have been replaced by branches that crackle and sag. Cruising on over to Lincoln Street, a fence has been constructed around the house that was once ours. My parents never discussed that option to keep us close. Instead, food drew us in on the long line of yearning for home.

By the time I had left Amherst for college, the shoe store in Lorain had shut down. Malls were burgeoning. It was endtimes for the store and for our way of life. My parents held on to the lives they had formed at birth here, in a womb for immigrants to grow. Can we not make more room for those who want to come and try their hand at making life, in cities like Lorain that are trying to come back by way of water, industry, and food? Who among those people are making shoes or bread?. Who might bring the old ways, or something better? Who will remind us of the importance of coming together to giving back? Italian towns such as Badolato on their last breath have discovered new ways of welcoming immigrants, of portioning out parts of the city for foreigners, to allow for redevelopment. Can we do that too?

My parents continued their work with the church and with the Lorain Metropolitan Housing Authority. They spread their alms and kept up the traditions of the Spoltorese with their mutual aid clubs. The social contract of being an immigrant was not only about bootstraps for yourself; it had everything to do with bootstraps for the rest. That is why immigrants succeed.

During the pandemic, I volunteered for a food rescue outfit, La Soupe, founded by a local Cincinnati chef whose simple premise involved saving food squandered by grocery stores, restaurant kitchens, and farms; damaged through oxidation or packaging; or unwanted due to changing trends. Each drive to rescue food involved a risk to my health during those days, but fear of getting sick, getting lost, or finding myself in areas where others might not want to tread never crossed my mind. Fear of someone going hungry did. I could transport an entire grocery aisle inside my Venza and feed hundreds for lunch. I also transported both a heaviness and a sense of grace in me whenever recipients thanked me for the supplies, or for the simple act of kindness. Was I just a person who cared, in the days when it was hard to know who did or did not?

In the seventies, our parents hadn't lied when they claimed children around the world were starving. Many were—possibly even our relatives, then unknown overseas—we just didn't have access to their names or faces on the scale that we do now. Even in Italy, where the ground overflowed with a bounty of fruit and the sea tossed up its catch twice a day, in a country whose people are known for taking care of one another, there have always existed those who lacked access to leftovers.

Leftovers in English implies scraps or the bottom of the barrel; something for food pantries to serve. In Italian, though, the word for leftovers is *avanzi*, from *avanzare*—to push forward. To advance that day's meal to the next. To save or preserve for the future. The same root verb also forms the imperative *avanti*, meaning "onward" or "come in."

AFTERWORD

Each generation in my Italian and Italian American family moved onward: to liberate themselves from poverty, to ground themselves in richer soil, or to become *something Italian* from the starter yeast of what was formed before they were born. My insides contained whatever was left over from Vinzenzella, Raffaela, and Stella. From Annantonia, Carmela, and two Concettas. From Ettore, Enrico, Vincenzo, and Luigi, and the great grandfathers. From my dearest cousins in Spoltore and San Donato. And from whatever was planted in them, including the knowledge that a meal shared is a life reborn. No matter if it's conveyed across crates of comestibles yet to be consumed or transported over centuries through recipes and stories bound up in a book, or shared at a table where you are the foreign-born one.

It was this knowledge that drove my parents as they helmed our kitchen table and started their own provincial line, and it remains a core tenet of our Italian heritage: to be cared for by being fed.

ENDNOTES

1. Apicus, *Cookery and Dining in Imperial Rome*, ed. and trans. Joseph Dommers Vehling (Dover Cookbooks, General Publishing Company, 1977), 3.
2. Claudia Roden, *Claudia Roden's Mediterranean* (Ten Speed Press, 2021), 10.
3. Scurti-Giuliani-Januzzi Genealogy Report, Mirella Ammirati. 2021.
4. Sergio Natalia, "Abruzzissimo," *Terre in Viaggio* February 2023.
5. Michael L. Mullan. "The Civic Life of Abruzzo Transferred to Philadelphia: The Italian-American Voluntary Association, 1890–1924," *Italian Americana* 30, no. 1 (2012): 5–21.
6. Natalia, "Abruzzissimo".
7. "The Great Arrival," Library of Congress, Accessed April 1, 2024, https://www.loc.gov/classroom-materials/immigration/italian/the-great-arrival/.
8. "Clay," Ohio Department of Natural Resources, Accessed May 1, 2024, https://ohiodnr.gov/discover-and-learn/rock-minerals-fossils/common-rocks/clay
9. Eide Spendicato Iengo, "Dalle migrazione agli esparati, *Storia Urbana*" (Franco Angeli, 2002), 112. As quoted in Mullan, "Civic Life of Abruzzo."
10. Luigi Bisignani, ed., *San Donato di Ninea Notizie*, quoting Roberto Campolongo "Historical and Mineralogy Study: Above San Donato 1913", September 22, 2014, https://www.sandonatodininea-cs.it/2014/09/22/studio-storico-e-di-mineralogiasopra-san-donato-1913/.
11. "San Donato di Ninea: Amministratori che non vogliono l'affissione della targa conltro la n'dranghetta," Accessed January 2, 2025, https://cn24tv.it/news/34847/san-donato-di-ninea-amministratori-che-non-vogliono-l-affissione-della-targa-conltro-la-ndrangheta.html.
12. Angelo Pellegrini, *Immigrant's Return* (Macmillan, 1952), 11, 21.
13. Bob Cotleur, "It's Fitting Shoe Man Enrico Januzzi That His Sport's Hiking In the Woods," *Lorain Journal*, June 21, 1955.
14. "San Donato di Ninea," Accessed February 17, 2025, https://www.ilborghista.it/borgo-san-donato-di-ninea-cs-6866.
15. Edward Lear, *Journals of a Landscape Painter in Southern Calabria, &C, 1852* (Forgotten Books, 2018).
16. Caroline Golab, *Immigrant Destinations* (Temple University Press, 1977), 35, 58–59; Joseph Lopreato, *Italian Americans* (Random House, 1970), 93–95; Gabaccia, *Militants and Migrants*, (1970), 114–15.
17. Muriel Earley Sheppard, *Cloud by Day: The Story of Coal and Coke and People* (The University of North Carolina Press, 1947), 2.
18. Sheppard, *Cloud by Day*, 41.
19. "The Coal Strike of 1902," U.S. Department of Labor, Accessed March 10, 2024, https://www.dol.gov/general/aboutdol/history/coalstrike.
20. Draft and final copy of opening address to Oct. 3, 1902, Conference, TRP; Letter, Roosevelt to H. H. Woodward, Oct. 19. 1902, Roosevelt Letters, Vol. III, 356-57.
21. Sheppard, *Cloud by Day* 6.
22. "Centennial History of the Borough of Connellsville, Pennsylvania,

1806–1906," Accessed April 13, 2024, https://archive.org/stream/centennialhistoroomccl_0/centennialhistoroomccl_0_djvu.txt.

23 " Unidentified photographs of Italian residents," Accessed April 13, 2024, https://www.calascio.com/photo-gallery/unidentified-photos.

24 Francesco Filareto, *Fuga e ritorno di un popolo*, (Ferrari Editore, 2014).

25 Franc Sturino, *Forging the Chain: A Case Study of Italian Migration to North America, 1880–1930*, Il Circolo Calabrese, (Multicultural History Society of Ontario. Corporate, 1990), table.

26 G. Frederick Wright, ed., *A Standard History of Lorain County, Ohio*, (The Lewis Publishing Company, 1916).

27 Nicholas J. Zentos and Wendy Marley Zentos, *Ethnic Communities of Lorain County: History and Directory* (Zentos and Marley Zentos, 2009), 3.

28 Zentos, *Ethnic Communities*.

29 "Rules of the Workers' Society of Mutual Support of Spoltore, 1892," State Archives of Pescara, Box 2, Folder 42.

30 Sons of Italy by-laws, provided by Lorain Historical Society.

31 Discovery Day is Observed by Italians," *Lorain Morning Journal*, October 15, 1922.

32 Zentos, *Ethnic Communities*, 7, 52–53.

33 Zentos, *Ethnic Communities*, 7, 52–53.

34 "Liquor Violations," *Lorain Morning Journal*, April 22, 1970.

35 Thea Gallo Becker, *Images of America: Cleveland, 1796–1929*. (Arcadia, 2004), 84.

36 *Celebrations of Faith: A Century of Worship in Lorain County, Ohio*. (Lorain County Sacred Landmarks Initiative, 2020).

37 "Fireworks Shot Over City Park," *Lorain Morning Journal*, September 11, 1951.

38 Daniel Brady, Brady's Bunch (blog), August 27, 2015. https://danielebrady.blogspot.com/2015/08/. Repost of Bill Scrivo, *Lorain Journal*, August 15, 1976.

39 Lacis Museum of Lace and Textiles, 2016 exhibit, https://lacismuseum.org/exhibit/tatting/catalog.pdf

40 John Dickie, *Blood Brotherhoods: A History of Italy's Three Mafias* (PublicAffairs, 2014), 274.

41 Januzzi: Growing Up in Ethnic Lorain, *Lorain Morning Journal*, October 26, 1997.

42 Bob Cotleur, "It's Fitting Shoe Man Enrico Januzzi That His Sport's Hiking in the Woods," *Lorain Morning Journal*, June 21, 1955.

43 Dickie, *Blood Brotherhoods*, 274.

44 Author's personal collection.

45 Jack LaVriha, "Girls Taking Leap Year Seriously: Interest in Bachelor Series Shows," *Lorain Journal*, February 4, 1956, 13.

46 "Fort Knox History Timeline: U. S. Army, Accessed April 19, 2024, https://home.army.mil/knox/application/files/7016/0008/7184/Fort_Knox_Web_Timelinev2.pdf

47 "Shoe Store Owner Wrestles 'Gun' from 13-Year-Old Boy," *Lorain Journal*, March 22, 1974, 27.

48 "New Lorain Fountain to Be Ready Memorial Day," *Lorain Journal and Times-Herald*, May 16, 1936.

49 *Celebrations of Faith*, 9.

50 Pulse Lorain, Winter, 2011, https://www.pulselorainmag.com/featured/ethnic-lorain-county.

51 "Januzzi Shoe Store Experts Fit Customer Feet Properly," *Lorain Morning Journal*, August 23, 1965, 21.

ACKNOWLEDGEMENTS

To the Italians who endured centuries of dominance and overcame invaders of all kinds who wanted the land and its goods to claim as their own. To those who dared cross an ocean, and those who toiled on this side of the sea to dig in deep and plot out a better life. I have had that life.

To the Italians I have met along the way: my Italian language instructors, Michele Alonzo, whose passion inspired me long after his death; Gerardo Perrotta, who during our brief stint together always greeted me with a wide smile reminding me of my father; and Antonio Iemmola, for our long Zoom sessions and lessons that gave me the confidence to speak of my life in Italian, and for laughing with me along the way. Thank you for reminding me I am *una brava scrittrice. Saremo sempre amici.*

To my guides in Italy: Mirella Ammirati, for your patience as we worked across email and through a pandemic to find those missing pieces of my mother I desperately wanted to discover. Andrew John Miles and Katja Von Sweitzer, for showing me the other side of Abruzzo with love and wine and friendship—Palazzo San Benedetto awaits our return. And Marcello D'Aleo, Certified Meridianale Ricerche Genealogistica, and Brunella Brusco and Valeria Bisciglia of Le Vie della Perla, as well as Mario Aloe, and Ernesto Cucci, certified Italian mountain guide, who all returned to me the face and place of my father.

To the Facebook groups that formed long before this book was a dream of mine. Life in Abruzzo is a beautiful gathering of souls. When I am yearning for *compagni*, I need only visit the page to feel linked to the whole again. And the San Donato di Ninea community, where I keep the videos of the chestnut festival on repeat. Thank you for holding space until we met face to face.

To the restauranteurs of Greater Cincinnati, in particular, those in Over-the-Rhine, and the vendors of Findlay Market, who continue to cultivate our culinary communities. To Lauren and Chalice Hodge at Taste on Elm, who supported my first words and wine event.

To the not-blood families that have fed me, and to all the makeshift families I have fed. To those dinner guests who were lucky enough to find me in my "Italian years." To Daniel Tonozzi and Lily and Ugo Biondo, who greet me on the streets of Over-the-Rhine and force me to use the Italian language. And to the Italians and Italian Americans I meet every day in this city of German descendants who tell me of adventures with our culture and desires to immerse themselves in world we all dream of. May we never stop claiming it as our birthright too. To the writers in the Italian American community who have spurred me on through podcasts or messages: Adriana Trigiani, Jenn Martelli, Elisa Speranza. *Grazie mille per le tue gentili parole.*

To Uncle Tony, whose humor inspires me from the grave. To his family that dined with us always on Christmas Eve. Those nights are precious in my memory. Thank you to Michael Ann and Aunt Joan for sharing the photographs and helping me work out the relations. And Anthony for your kindness always to our family. To Uncle Albert, Paula Januzzi and Thomas Januzzi and other members, who helped draw the lines between figs and families and a shared history. I'm glad we've found a family root to hold on to. And the rest of our uncles and aunts, especially Comare Sarah and Compare Mike, for their everlasting friendship to my parents and guidance as my godparents. To cousins who are cousins—and those who are technically not. Mary Fran, for our long dinner in Pittsburgh and for giving me permission to honor these stories. Sue, for your laughs and guidance as my confirmation sponsor. Antonio Dottore, Luigina Dottore, and Viola Giuliani, in Spoltore. *Le Spoltorese sono forte e gentile.* Thank you. Bless you. Peace be with you. Without your embracing arms, Spoltore never would have felt like home. And to Vincenzo D'Annaballe for his steadfast promotion of Spoltore. Someday, Steubenville will reciprocate your devotion.

To the Iannuzzi cousins who awaited my arrival in San Donato, especially Concetta Macrini. My second-grade class once hosted an Italian student named Concetta. My parents thought she and I should be friends because her name was a family name of my great-grandmother and many aunts in the Italian Iannuzzi family. I'm glad to have finally found that friend in Concetta of San Donato. We will eat many chestnuts together. To Rico and Stella, offshoots of my grandparents, and to Vittorio for all your calls that guided me through Calabria, like having my dad on the other end of the line watching out for us.

To extended cousins near and far who guided me with photographs and tidbits of history. On the Januzzi side: Anita Dwyer, Lisa Marie Melby, and Anthony Gambatese; and on the Mazzà side, Toni White and Kathryn Shut.

A special shout out to the Old Photos of Lorain Facebook group for sharing the original photo of the Società Abruzzese, and to Peter Zelek, who dug through his archives. Without his copy, I never would have traced the provenance of the photo to Joseph Devito, who catalogued much of life in Lorain at the time, and his grandchildren, David DeVito and Sally DeVito Houk. And to Ericka McIntyre, the first editor to push me to envision my goal. To the University of Akron Press and Jon Miller, who showed belief in this project as a representation of northeastern Ohio. Without your prodding to gather more, much of this history would have been lost to time.

To the friends I've gathered along the way. From the time we were preschoolers growing up in Amherst, through my years at Akron (Jilly and Janice), into my married and motherhood years. Your enduring kindnesses shown to me along the way are proof that love doesn't always have to show up in food. Friendships too are the carriers of a certain kind of love.

To my countless writing groups and partners. The Cincinnati Library for holding all my holds. The Lorain Historical Society, Kaitlyn Donaldson, and Madison Maniaci, for researching my errant, incessant questions. The Lorain Public Library for being the first force in my early years before the Amherst Library and Cincinnati Public became my refuge in later times. Libraries are the inheritance we all deserve—spend your time there wisely. The *Lorain Journal* for your archives, and for documenting the lives of immigrants. Women Writing for (a) Change, where my first writings took root, and the regulars of Gugel Alley Writers, Rob, Chris, Kira, Cindy, Mark, Anjuli, Patty, Patricia, Nicole, Roger, Ann, Jim, at Roebling Books in Newport (and owner Richard Hunt), who inspired some of my later work. To all the poets and writers who have given me reason to keep the pen to page, but especially Eva Lewandowski, Dee Wiley, Ellen Austin Li, Claudia Reilly, and Elaine Olund, for creating that space that held our lives together through countless challenges and changes. To "my friend" Ron Ellis, for your shot of confidence. To Michael Dinallo, a brilliant musician, for our exchanges on "intentional art." To my colleague and esteemed poet, Pauletta Hansel, for showing me the way of the writer. And to my dear writing partner Tina Neyer, who has read these stories more times than I dare count. For all you have read about on paper, I owe you a grand feast in person. I can't wait for your work to be out in the world. To the readers of my Substack blogs. As the esteemed Ann Hagedorn once told me, "It's more important to have the best readers, than a bestseller." I've been lucky that way.

To my editor, Christine McKnight, an Italian American, for her brilliance in unscrambling the code of my DNA and my writing, helping me to sort facts and fantasies into truth. To Anna Perotti, also Italian, for her steadfast patience as I combed through photos to comb through memories. Deciding how to portray family in photos was maddening. She held me accountable, while also lifting the work higher than I could have imagined. To Romain Mayambi, whose work has been showcased in National Geographic, for humbly spending the afternoon in my home reminding me how beauty comes with laughter and tears.

To my Over-the-Rhine family who has showed up for countless meals, aperitivi hours, courtyard campfires, Opening Day parties, bourbon nights, and speakeasy evenings, the calories and the celebrations brought us together. The deep and abiding companionship and care we've developed for our special neighborhood and one another caused us stay.

To Judy and Don Wick, for the meals that were sacred because our time was too. Thank you for staying with Davis during my first trip to Italy. And to the rest of the Wicks for keeping me in your graces. For Aunt Lynne, who watches over me as I watch over her. May we break bread at Marion's one more time together. To Mark and Carol Manley, and the siblings and in-laws in Mark's family, for welcoming me, and welcoming Davis; for supporting my successes and helping to hide my failures too.

To my nephews who are part of the fab foursome, Zach, David and Drew, and to my four siblings who pushed my parents and each other so brilliantly to become something more Italian. To my brother Paul, my sister-in-law Kim, and my sister Jeanne, for baking, eating, and keeping the faith in our *Italianità*. To my sister Beth for her support when it was needed, and her husband, David, who motivates me to cook because he'll wash the dishes. To Laura: You are my touchstone. If Mom is on my shoulder when I cook, you are in my heart when I do the same. In a future space in time, we'll be together, eyes wide and laughing.

To my stepchildren and their partners and children: Cheryl and Chris, Shannon and Michael and Nora and Samuel, Kay and Casey, and anyone else waiting in the wings to join our fold, for the gift of expanding my repertoire to include the many and varied eating and migratory patterns in our own family. My mother's cookies still taste like home when made gluten-free, because they're made of stronger stuff than flour. And for moving to other coasts and forcing me to accept the fact that not all fish has to be Italian or from the Oregon coast in its origins to be good. *Pesce non è sempre pesce*. Fish is not the same everywhere. Finally, thank you for indulging my need to be Italian to feel at home in the world.

To my nieces and nephews, especially Gia and Sophia, may you have gratitude for and honor our heritage and your Italian names.

To Davis and Kyra: After experiencing Italy together, now you know there is nothing greater than to see with a new set of eyes and a new heart something you've always known in your blood. Kyra, best wishes for many luxurious Italian meals at your husband's hands, or mine. Davis, our meals together as young mother and young son will always be sacred to me. "You're a good cooker, mom," lives on in my head. I await some (half) Italian progeny. *Forza* and meatballs!

To Devin—for encouraging me to follow my mother, which also included following my stomach. For the many ways in which you gained my parents' love. I know your spirits are entwined together at some big old table in the sky, eating—what else—vegetable lasagna. And laughing. Yes, laughing.

To Mark, my greatest regret is that you never experienced my mother's cooking in full form, due to the slide of memory and time. And you didn't know my father in his wisdom of years. You did, however, witness my parents' radiance in Italy. No words can thank you for your ever-faithful guidance and love on this pilgrimage, and for understanding its importance. Even when you didn't understand, you managed to reap the sweet and savory rewards. There were days when I thought you were more Italian than I could ever be, especially when you drove through the straitjacket alleyways in Abruzzo and the morass of Rome. And that time in Calabria, with our car, and the *f— Fiat Pandas*. Whenever I yelled at you as we argued, you quietly listened. I knew who the Italian was, and I also knew who won. The two were not the same. As much as I have shared my Italy with my readers, our Italy is still ours—what we've explored, what we've yet to encounter, who we are without the rest of the world to intervene.

To Vincenzo Giuliani, Raffaela Scurti, and Luigi DeLuca. To Enrico Iannuzzi and Stella Mazzà. And to all the roots of those family trees, for forging ahead. *Finché c'è vita c'è speranza*. While there is life, there is hope. This book has been a gift to draw you into my dreams.

To Vinzenzella Jean Giuliani and Ettore Anselmo Iannuzzi, Nana and Papu, Mom and Dad. *You two*, standing over the sink, eating that last bite of supper off a plate or the final cookie crumbs. *Siamo sempre insieme a tavola. Vi voglio benissimo.*

ABOUT THE AUTHOR

Annette Januzzi Wick is a writer and author of I'LL BE IN THE CAR and I'LL HAVE SOME OF YOURS, a journey of caregiving and cookies. Her work has appeared in *Writer's Digest, Creative Nonfiction, Edible Ohio Valley, Belt Publishing, Italian Americana, MacQueens Quinterly, Soapbox Cincinnati, Cincinnati Magazine, Next Avenue, 3rd Act Magazine, Ovunque Siamo, Italy Segreta, Italian American* magazine, *La Gazzetta, NIAF Ambassador,* and *La Piccioletta Barca*. Her writings have also been anthologized in *A Song, Emerging Poems | Poems About Our Earth, Poetry for the Dementia Journey, Grief Becomes You,* and *Before the Diagnosis.*

She and her husband Mark live in an 1875 Italianate-style home in Cincinnati's Over-the-Rhine, where the original owners' ghosts occasionally haunt her and her ancestors continue to whisper in her ear. When she's not writing in Ohio, Annette can be found eating Dungeness crab in Oregon or moping around the house, eating *celli*, saying, *Mi manca l'italia.*

Ettore and Jean Januzzi, at a friend's wedding, 2000s.

www.ingramcontent.com/pod-product-compliance
Lightning Source LLC
Chambersburg PA
CBHW042053290426
44110CB00006B/163